8°°
495

Feeding
the
Soul

D0179434

Feeding the Soul

Daily Meditations for Recovering from Eating Disorders

Caroline Adams Miller

BANTAM BOOKS
NEW YORK • TORONTO • LONDON • SYDNEY • AUCKLAND

FEEDING THE SOUL

A Bantam Book / May 1991

All rights reserved.
Copyright © 1991 by Caroline Adams Miller.
No part of this book may be reproduced or transmitted
in any form or by any means, electronic or mechanical,
including photocopying, recording, or by any information
storage and retrieval system, without permission in writing from
the publisher.
For information address: Bantam Books.

Library of Congress Cataloging-in-Publication Data

Miller, Caroline Adams, 1961–
    Feeding the soul : daily meditations for recovering from eating
disorders / by Caroline Adams Miller.
        p.   cm.
    ISBN 0-553-35279-2
    1. Eating disorders—Patients—Prayer–books and devotions–
English. 2. Twelve–step programs—Religious aspects—
Meditations.
3. Devotional calendars.   I. Title.
BL624.5.M55   1991
362.2'5—dc20   90–47025
                                                                         CIP

Published simultaneously in the United States and Canada

Bantam Books are published by Bantam Books, a division of Bantam
Doubleday Dell Publishing Group, Inc. Its trademark, consisting of
the words "Bantam Books" and the portrayal of a rooster, is
Registered in U.S. Patent and Trademark Office and in other
countries. Marca Registrada. Bantam Books, 666 Fifth Avenue, New
York, New York 10103.

PRINTED IN THE UNITED STATES OF AMERICA

BME   0 9 8 7 6 5 4 3 2 1

To my parents
Bill and Millicent Adams
with love.

Acknowledgments

I'd like to acknowledge the following people with deep gratitude:

Judy Friedman, Debbie Martin, Elisabeth Talbot, Jackie Shuger and Joann Blackman for inspirational quotes and encouragement;

My agent, Vicky Bijur, and one of my editors, Michelle Rapkin, who dreamed up this book over lunch one day, and were ably assisted in its completion by my other editor, Maria Mack: and

My husband, Haywood, and my son, Haywood, IV, who provide me with endless joy, laughter and sustenance.

Feeding
the
Soul

We admitted we were powerless over food—that our lives had become unmanageable.
> —STEP ONE OF OVEREATERS ANONYMOUS

As we enter a new year many of us like to turn over a new leaf and start our lives afresh. For those of us who are recovering from an eating disorder it's a good time to recommit ourselves to abstinence from compulsive eating. And for people who haven't yet begun recovery but want to, this is an appropriate time to start.

Whether or not we are in a self-help group for compulsive eaters, the first step of Overeaters Anonymous is useful as a starting point for anyone who is addicted to food. Admitting powerlessness over anything is scary because we want to believe that self-control and willpower are the solution, particularly with our food problem. But deep down we know that controlled eating of our binge foods hasn't worked for us in the past.

If you still aren't sure about your powerlessness over food, ask yourself about the manageability of your life. Are you honest, happy and living the way you want to live, or does bingeing make this impossible? Do you spend too much time obsessing about food and its effects on you? You have the choice to stay stuck in a life where you repeatedly get in the way of your own happiness, or you have the ability to acknowledge powerlessness over behavior that brings you misery, and thus start on the road to a healthy life.

AFFIRMATION FOR THE DAY: I choose to live a manageable life today.

When old men gather, they say: "When I was a boy!" It really is the land of nowadays that we never discover.
—BOOTH TARKINGTON

A lot of older people I know like to reminisce about the past. They are fond of recalling the days when a bus ride was a nickel, movies were a quarter, television was unheard of and airplanes were new experiments. Gripped by nostalgia, they insist that life was wonderful when they were younger and that the present doesn't even begin to compare with what they once knew.

What's so interesting about people like this is that they often didn't enjoy the good old days when they were living them. Because they are chronically dissatisfied with their lives, the past assumes a joy that it may not have possessed and the future holds no promise. Life passes in a dull succession, and daily wonders go unnoticed and unappreciated.

Resolve today to discover "the land of nowadays," and to enjoy today while it's here. Don't set yourself up to be a reminiscing grandparent who is caught in a time warp and who can't enjoy the present or the future. If we can rejoice in each new day and resolve not to perpetually look back with nostalgia, we'll be able to fully appreciate the old Latin cry, "Carpe Diem!" or "Seize the Day!"

AFFIRMATION FOR THE DAY: I look forward to each new day that I am given the gift of life and abstinence.

I was gratified to be able to answer promptly, and I did. I said I didn't know.

—MARK TWAIN

There is really nothing more annoying than someone who pretends to know everything. Compulsive eaters frequently fall into this arrogant category; our low self-esteem causes us to cover up our insecurities with false bravado and the attitude that we don't need help or information from anyone.

Breaking down this wall around ourselves is hard, but it must be done for recovery to take place. We have to admit that we don't have all the answers, especially on the issue of our compulsive eating. After all, if we did, we'd have been happy, healthy and at a comfortable weight years ago.

Admitting you don't know everything takes courage, honesty and a willingness to be vulnerable. Remind yourself today that saying "Help!" every now and then isn't a weakness—it's an important step in recovery. Whether you need assistance with devising a meal plan or balancing your checkbook, by allowing others to give you the gift of their knowledge you help them feel important while lowering your own walls long enough to let others get close to you.

AFFIRMATION FOR THE DAY: Today I will acknowledge my limits and ask for help.

Only in prayer do we achieve the complete and harmonious assembly of body, mind and spirit which gives the frail human need its unshakable strength.
—Dr. Alexis Carrel

When we are feeling down, defeated or frightened, prayer is the fastest and easiest way we can regain strength and direction.

I used to avoid praying because I didn't think I did it "the right way." I compulsively bought books that explained to me how others did it and what kinds of reactions I could expect. I tried praying at certain hours in certain ways, but the process always felt contrived and unnatural.

Now, instead of designating a time and a place when I can connect with my Higher Power, I have many moments each day when I stop and either send a mental S.O.S. or I give thanks for something that has happened to me. When I see someone in pain or I learn of a difficulty another person is experiencing, I often take a minute to say a quick prayer for them.

Remember today that there is no one right way to talk to your Higher Power and that only you know what brings you the most peace. Don't worry about where you are or whether or not your eyes are closed—just do it. If we make a habit of asking for help and giving frequent thanks, we will always have the strength, guidance and connection with our Higher Power that we need to move through life confidently.

AFFIRMATION FOR THE DAY: Prayer is the battery that recharges me every day.

He who knows himself is enlightened.

—LAO-TZU

One of the most startling things I discovered when I first began to recover was that I had no idea who I was or what I truly wanted out of life. For so many years I had lived behind a carefully constructed facade that learning to just be alone with myself was very difficult.

When we put the food down we are suddenly faced with a number of hours that were once filled with bingeing, thinking about food and then worrying about what we had eaten. During this newfound time we have a golden opportunity to discover what really motivates us, what we like and where we want to go in life. Many of our revelations will be exciting and freeing. We must be aware, however, that some of the painful emotions and realizations that led us to binge in the first place may surface and that we'll need to be supported by friends and our own spiritual strength to avoid a relapse.

Be gentle with yourself as you enter this period of self-discovery. Avoid making rash judgments about who you are and how you relate to others. Let your path unfold gradually and allow others' wisdom and your own intuition guide you. You'll find that as you probe your inner spirit and become friends with yourself, food is simply not an option any longer and opportunities for growth are revealed to you daily.

AFFIRMATION FOR THE DAY: Today I'll remember that I may feel awkward getting to know myself without bingeing, but I'll soon gain grace, strength and assurance.

Then was Jesus led up of the spirit into the wilderness to be tempted of the Devil.
—Matthew 4:1

When I was new to recovery I always walked around with a fistful of change. I did this because I saw temptations to binge everywhere I looked, and many times the only thing that saved me was a dash to a pay phone to contact another recovering compulsive eater who helped me through the rough patch.

When we are just starting to recover from an addiction it seems the temptation to stray is everywhere. Although the pull lessens over time, it may remain with us forever as something we need to be conscious of. And our temptation will not always be for food; it could be for a number of things such as greediness, excessive spending and intolerant behavior. We just have to accept that we don't live in a glass bubble and that opportunities to veer off the path will always be an everyday fact for us.

Remember today that as a compulsive eater you are more prone to want immediate gratification than another person, and that your daily life of recovery needs to reflect that fact. Create safeguards that will prevent you from giving in every time you want something you know you shouldn't have. Whether it's a phone call, a prayer or a change of scenery, remember that the best defense is always a well-coordinated offense.

AFFIRMATION FOR THE DAY: Today I will remember that just because temptation exists doesn't mean I have to give in to it.

The best is yet to be.

—ROBERT BROWNING

A friend of mine who was out of work decided to try to imagine her perfect job. In her mind she saw herself working in the ideal atmosphere, at the right location and for a generous salary. Every day she tinkered with the details until she felt certain that she knew precisely what she wanted and could comfortably see herself fulfilling this dream. At that point she mentally turned the process over to her Higher Power and asked Him to help her find this position.

Almost immediately my friend was offered a good job. It wasn't quite what she wanted so she reluctantly turned it down, hoping a better one was around the corner. Soon she was offered another, even better-paying position, but still not the dream job. My friend stuck to her guns and turned this one down, too. A short time later her ideal position did manifest and she accepted it, grateful that she had not compromised her dreams and lost faith in her Higher Power.

When we really want something and visualize it in our mind, do we wait for it to happen or do we accept second-best because we don't believe we'll see our heart's desires come to pass? Try not to accept solutions today that aren't what you really want, because when you believe you deserve happiness and abundance, your Higher Power is often more than happy to oblige.

AFFIRMATION FOR THE DAY: Today I won't settle for less than I deserve.

You have the right to offer no reasons or excuses for justifying your behavior.

—ANONYMOUS

One day I read an interesting article about the problems people are having entertaining these days. The article said that it is impossible to throw a normal dinner party anymore because everyone has a special diet they insist on adhering to. The article quoted an exasperated host who complained that no one had eaten the main course at his recent party because it hadn't fit into various dietary restrictions. "Why is everyone so selfish?" he lamented.

I used to feel very bashful about explaining to a host or hostess why I couldn't eat a certain food that I knew might trigger my binge cravings, especially in early recovery. Deep down I thought I was being vain and selfish so a few times I let a dessert or creamy dish I didn't want be pushed on me, and later I found myself bingeing, wishing I had had the courage just to say, "No, thank you."

Our recovery is a matter of life and death and we can't forget it or think that the steps we have to take to remain abstinent are selfish. Other people don't necessarily have to understand or like our reasons for avoiding certain foods, so don't feel you always have to explain yourself or apologize to others. The more you can unlearn people-pleasing behavior and be assertive about your needs, the better you will be able to take care of yourself.

AFFIRMATION FOR THE DAY: Being selfish is different from being good to myself.

I'm mad as hell and I'm not going to take it anymore.
                                        —PETER FINCH IN *NETWORK*

The inability to summon up anger about our compulsive eating and to channel that anger into recovery is something that has hindered us in the past. We were more prone to overeat and compulsively exercise, purge or fast to make up for the extra calories than we were to use our energy to devise a healthful eating plan, attend self-help support groups or find new ways to fill our time.

"Hitting bottom" with our disease means that we are sick and tired of being sick and tired, and that we are angry enough to make those changes that will result in a new and better lifestyle. Apathy about our compulsive eating, whining to others about our lack of willpower, and laziness in visualizing a different life results in only one thing—the same old routine.

In recovery we need to get "mad as hell" before we can make any changes in our destructive lifestyles. We have to formulate our purpose and plan, and then—most important—follow through with it. For many of us this means eliminating the foods that trigger our binges and avoiding all mood-altering substances and behaviors. And although our goal is not to stay mad as hell, we will find that by correctly channeling our anger we can make useful and productive changes in our lives.

AFFIRMATION FOR THE DAY: I will use my emotions constructively rather than destructively.

Behold, I have set before thee an open door.
                      —REVELATIONS 3:8

When I was small I remember being told a story about a man who had to choose between two doors. Behind one was a beautiful woman and behind the other was a tiger that was hungry for its next meal. The man agonized over which door to pick and analyzed tiny details to try to figure out the right choice. Just as he made his decision, the story ended and the reader was left wondering which door had been selected.

Although I've never been in a similar life-or-death situation there have been many times when I've been faced with a variety of doors to choose from. Like the man in the story I'd analyze every detail and agonize over my decisions to the point of exhaustion and confusion.

I don't deplete my energy in the course of making decisions any longer. I have found that endless analysis and agonizing over my options doesn't always provide successful results. But when I survey my choices, pray for the best outcome and then take action, I am always in good hands. If you have choices to make today, resolve that you will ask your Higher Power for help and then act on your instincts. Not only will you save wear-and-tear on your mind and body, but you'll also eliminate the quality of indecisiveness that is so common to compulsive eaters.

AFFIRMATION FOR THE DAY: My Higher Power always leads me through the right door.

And I said to the man who stood at the gate of the year:
"Give me a light that I may tread safely into the
unknown," and he replied: "Go out into the darkness
and put your hand into the hand of God. That shall be
to you better than light and safer than a known way."
                                    —MINNIE LOUISE HASKINS

Often when we start a new year or celebrate a
birthday, we resolve to make the coming year different or better in some way. Usually what we want to
accomplish is new and foreign to us so we embark on
our journey with some trepidation.

My tendency when starting something new is to grab
onto someone who will show me the way because I hate to
make mistakes. When I have done this, though, I have
always lost my individuality in the process. Holding on to
another person and following a path that many others have
trodden is extremely safe, but it keeps you from having
your own unique experiences and prevents you from
branching off on to your own, unexplored paths.

As you mark the beginning of your new year, resolve to tread into the unknown with only your Higher
Power leading you. Wise friends can certainly help with
directions along the path, but make this your own
unique journey. When you have the courage to stick
your hand out into the darkness and plunge ahead you'll
know that your experience is uniquely yours, and that
your faith is the best guide you can have.

AFFIRMATION FOR THE DAY: When I allow my
Higher Power to lead me, my path is guaranteed to
be the right one.

*Most people believe they see the world as it is.
However, we really see the world as we are.*
                                        —ANONYMOUS

One day I was discussing my wounded feelings
with a good friend. As I detailed what I thought were
rude and condescending attitudes in others that were
aimed at hurting me, she laughed and shook her head.
"Gee," she said, "if those things had happened to me I'd
have come to completely different conclusions!"

How we choose to interpret people and life
around us depends on how we perceive an event. If
we see the world as cynical and uncaring, then we'll
always perceive others that way. If we can't forgive
people who hurt us, then we'll always be moaning
about how no one ever absolves us of our wrongs. And
if we're materialistic, greedy people we're going to
assume that everyone else is, too.

This lesson has been one of the hardest I've had
to learn in recovery. Once I realized that much of the
negativity I perceived in others was really internal, I
had to take responsibility for my emotions and stop
projecting them onto others. Analyze your own attitudes today and ask yourself if you aren't guilty of this
behavior. Until we can acknowledge the power we
have over creating the world around us, we won't be
able to shape the kind of life we want for ourselves.

AFFIRMATION FOR THE DAY: The world I see
around me is an accurate reflection of my internal
state.

Life is not just a walk across a field.
—BORIS PASTERNAK

One day I read a survey of thousands of American women who were asked what their fondest dream was. The answer was surprising; shockingly few mentioned the ending of war, a cure for a deadly disease or an end to homelessness. Well over 90 percent said what they wanted most was a no-diet, no-exercise way to lose weight.

I was once guilty of this Fairy Godmother approach to life. I often wished that someone would tap me on the head and magically take away my bulimia, make me happy and give me a body I could be proud of. I thought success should be effortless and my motto was, "I want what I want when I want it—right now!"

We need to remember that life, and particularly our recovery, is not just an easy walk across a field. Whenever we are trying to achieve something important we are going to have to expend time and energy, and we will often encounter significant difficulties along the way that test our commitment to reaching our goal. Although a no-diet, no-exercise method of losing weight might seem like the ultimate fantasy, we must remember that any worthwhile lasting changes always take work, and that that is what will make our victories rewarding.

AFFIRMATION FOR THE DAY: There is nothing worth striving for that doesn't take effort on my part.

It is always a mistake not to close one's eyes, whether to forgive or to look better into oneself.
—MAURICE MAETERLINCK

As valuable as it is for us to be alert, questioning and active during the day, it is equally important for us to have moments when we voluntarily close our eyes to reflect and rejuvenate ourselves. Some of us find this time easy to come by; others need to plan it into their day.

One way to schedule quiet time is to seek out a massage therapist who is specially trained to work with touch and healing. Compulsive eaters with negative body images usually benefit from massage therapy because it alleviates much of the fear we have about being touched and helps us become comfortable with our bodies. Many of us also find that the time spent in quiet relaxation is an excellent opportunity to focus on what we have done that week that we would like to do differently or better next time.

If massage therapy is out of your budget, at least let yourself be touched gently and soothingly on a regular basis by someone who has your best interests at heart. As you incorporate more of this type of loving, reflective time into your life, not only will you find your physical condition improving, but so will your acceptance of yourself and others.

AFFIRMATION FOR THE DAY: I will close my eyes today in meditation and not be afraid to look within.

Who reflects too much will accomplish little.
—JOHANN CHRISTOPH FRIEDRICH VON SCHILLER

There are times in recovery when I've noticed that I can be a bit like an animal preparing for winter. I'll scurry around from one self-help book to the next, storing up advice and wisdom just like a squirrel stores up acorns. At times my actions have been so compulsive, and I've gotten input from so many people, that I've become paralyzed and unable to act.

The biggest danger we face in spending too much time thinking about doing something rather than just doing it is that we accomplish nothing. We become grand thinkers and big talkers, yet we go nowhere.

One of the healthiest things I ever did one day was to clear off my bedside table stacks of inspirational and self-help books. Now when I go to bed at night I don't have a tower of alluring titles vying for my attention, trying to teach me how to be more spiritual, feel better about myself, be more assertive and love myself unconditionally.

Do you feel like your mind is on circuit overload with ideas and orders about how to think and behave? If so, strip the extraneous books, people and meetings out of your life and concentrate on just utilizing, not analyzing. After all, you want to be known as someone who walks the walk, not someone who just talks the talk.

AFFIRMATION FOR THE DAY: Today I will be action-oriented.

You cannot help men permanently by doing for them what they could and should do for themselves.
—ABRAHAM LINCOLN

One day I was at a meeting where a relatively recent newcomer to my recovery program approached me with a pretty but sad-looking woman in tow.

"Caroline," she said, "Amy is an old friend of mine who has been bulimic for eight years. I've persuaded her to come here for help and I know that she needs a sponsor. I think you'd be perfect. Will you do it?"

Feeling rather put on the spot, I couldn't help but say yes. My relationship with Amy floundered, though, because she rarely called me and her attendance at meetings was sporadic. Everything I tried to do to "save" her failed, and finally she dropped out of sight and I later heard that she'd returned to her bingeing ways.

Although initially my pride was hurt that Amy hadn't heeded my brilliant advice and flowered under my expert tutelage, I finally realized that she had simply not been ready to help herself yet. The lesson I learned was a good one: When we are tempted to "fix" another person, we must stop and remind ourselves that we are not miracle workers, and that the best way to help someone is to be available if and when they ever want to ask for help.

AFFIRMATION FOR THE DAY: As much as I might want to change someone else, I can only be responsible for my own actions.

There are two ways of meeting difficulties: you alter the difficulties, or you alter yourself meeting them.
—PHYLLIS BOTTOME

As we begin to change our actions, behavior and outlook on life as part of our recovery from compulsive eating, we may be surprised to find that some of the biggest roadblocks to progress lie within our own families.

For many years we have probably been people-pleasers and chameleons who became whatever others wanted us to be, particularly within our families. As we start to become more spontaneous and assertive, we're often surprised to find that the people we thought would be happiest for us resist our positive changes.

Today keep in mind that change within a family system is hard, and sometimes impossible. We have no control over that. What we can control, however, is how we choose to cope with it. If we slip back into our dysfunctional patterns and food abuse, we are only harming ourselves. However, if we decide to persist with our healthier life-style, we'll need to have outside support to help us with our commitment to abstinence.

Resolve today to work with your family in a loving way to help them understand your goals and new behaviors. Explain your recovery process and why their support is important to you. Sometimes you'll be gratified by their enthusiasm and desire to help, but if you don't receive that make sure you create a loving "family" that will provide the support you need.

AFFIRMATION FOR THE DAY: There is nothing I can't accomplish if I remain flexible.

Education is hanging around until you've caught on.
—ROBERT FROST

I am an honors graduate of a prestigious Ivy League school. All of my years spent learning trivial events of history, mathematics and foreign languages, however, were useless in helping me recover from bulimia.

Recovery from an eating disorder is not an exam you can study for. There are no books to memorize, classes to attend or tests to take. Rather, it requires patient observation of others who have what you want, the study of certain spiritual truths and a willingness to keep trying until you've "caught on."

There is a phrase in my self-help program regarding the speed with which people get into recovery, especially if they are hesitant at first: "Bring the body and the mind will follow." Remember today that the Phi Beta Kappas in the school of recovery aren't the richest, smartest or best-connected men and women; the ones who graduate at the top of the class are the ones who just keep coming back until they get the hang of it.

AFFIRMATION FOR THE DAY: It's how well I learn, not how fast, that matters in recovery.

I take my work seriously. I don't take myself seriously.
　　　　　　　　　　　　—JUDGE JOSEPH WAPNER

One night I was watching the news and I saw an interesting report about Japanese business schools. One of the requirements before graduating, I learned, was that each student do something utterly humiliating. Often this took the form of singing at the top of one's lungs in a crowded subway stop—usually a ridiculous song, too. The lesson was that once you learn to live through total embarrassment, you can handle any business setback.

Although we don't need to go to these extremes to learn not to take ourselves so seriously, there are ways we can become more free in spirit. One method is to do something that may seem unconventional, but that you secretly desire anyway—like getting an unusual haircut or wearing an avant-garde outfit to a stodgy party.

We all need to remember the difference between being earnest about our tasks and being overly earnest about who we are. Instead of meticulously planning our vacations, we should occasionally toss the guidebooks out the window and just go without a rigid schedule. We also need to be able to take risky, unpopular stands we believe in and not worry about what others think of us or how it might affect our image. Challenge yourself to be unconventional today and to do something unexpected. Once you can liberate yourself from the image of what you think you ought to be and do, you've taken a big step toward leaving people-pleasing and dull conformity behind.

AFFIRMATION FOR THE DAY: Today I will take a responsible risk.

*God is like an abstract painting which people inter-
pret in different ways.*

—SHAUN LOCKHART

One day I received a letter from a woman in her
forties who had been a compulsive eater since her early
teens. For over twenty-five years, she complained, she
had been a slave to food and had gained and lost thousands of pounds in the process of dieting. She knew that
to recover she needed some kind of spiritual redirection
in her life, but she couldn't get past her self-imposed
hurdle that God didn't love her. "If He truly cares about
me, why am I so miserable?" she asked.

All too often we make the mistake of thinking that
God is an all-powerful deity who makes or breaks our
lives with the lift of a finger. If we choose to identify
Him as a despot, we'll live in fear. If He's punishing,
we'll live in guilt. We have to remember that we are the
ones who make those decisions, and we are the ones
who endow our Higher Power with characteristics that
either make us feel loved or rejected.

If your Higher Power is still not your friend, ask
yourself why. Are you carrying around a childhood idea
that He is imposing and awesome? Did your parents
instill the notion that God is like Big Brother, always
watching and ready to punish? If so, take the opportunity today to see your Higher Power as an abstract
painting that you confer meaning on, and then assign it
the qualities you need to feel comforted, protected and
loved.

AFFIRMATION FOR THE DAY: Whether I feel the
warmth of a loving Higher Power or not is up to me.

When the tiger dies, he leaves behind his skin, but when a man dies, he leaves behind only his name.
—KOREAN PROVERB

When I was growing up, my parents sacrificed a great deal to ensure that their children had education at the finest schools money could buy. The reason, they often said, was that adverse circumstances could always cause you to lose your home, money and belongings, but an education could never be taken from you.

Just as your mind can't be forcibly taken from you, neither can the reputation you gain from the manner in which you conduct your life. If you are kind, honest, compassionate and thoughtful, your reputation will be sterling. Your word will mean something, your children will learn good qualities from you and you will know what it is to feel fulfilled and serene. When you die, your possessions may be divided up and sold, but your name will live on after you as a testament to the life you led.

What are you seeking to amass today? Is it nice cars, artwork and money? Or is it qualities of kindness, warmth and generosity that others will remember fondly when you are gone? Are you a tiger who will only leave behind its skin, or someone whose name will mean something positive in future years?

AFFIRMATION FOR THE DAY: Everything I own will eventually disintegrate. My reputation, however, will last forever.

All things are possible to him that believeth.
                                                    —MARK 9:23

Many of us who pray for good things for ourselves and others often get discouraged because our prayers are not immediately answered. We decide that our Higher Power is an angry, judgmental being who sits on a throne dispensing favors and that we are unworthy of those favors. We then decide to stop praying because we think it's useless.

One of the main mistakes we make when we pray like this is that we don't expect our petitions to be heard or granted. Although our mouths may move and the right words may come out, too often there is a small part of us that thinks, "This isn't going to do any good. This is a waste of time. No one cares about me anyway."

The key to having our prayers answered is to develop an air of expectancy. An analogy might be that when a woman is pregnant she is called an expectant mother. For nine months she prepares for the arrival of her baby, confident that she will give birth. What if we did the same with our prayers, and felt certain that they would be answered and that our troubles would be attended to?

During your prayer time today, experiment with creating your own air of expectancy. Try to erase any negative tapes in your head that tell you that your efforts are a waste of time. Then trust and expect the best. You'll discover that the more you believe that good is awaiting you, the sooner you'll find it.

AFFIRMATION FOR THE DAY: If there is something I really believe in, it will come to pass.

To understand truth one must have a very sharp, precise, clear mind; not a cunning mind, but a mind that is capable of looking without distortion, a mind innocent and vulnerable. Only such a mind can see what truth is.
—KRISHNAMURTI

For many of us our compulsive eating stemmed from an unwillingness to face the world squarely and accept conditions as they were. Bingeing altered our mood and our perception of events, temporarily making us insane. In this state we were no more able to understand the truth about something than a drowning person can think clearly.

Before we can understand and comprehend the truth about ourselves, we need to put the food down. If we decide to analyze our lives and the reasons why we developed a compulsive eating problem while we are still bingeing, we won't make any headway. Therapists say that trying to counsel someone who is still eating compulsively is about as effective as trying to work with an alcoholic who is still drinking. It is only when the abused substance is put down that the mind becomes more focused and pain can't be ducked any longer.

Work today on seeing life as it is, not through a filter of resentment, hurt and arrogance. If you don't think you are analyzing something honestly ask a trustworthy friend for her opinion. The more you can challenge your old way of thinking and adopt a different viewpoint, the easier it will be to develop an innocent, clear mind that knows what the truth is.

AFFIRMATION FOR THE DAY: Abstinence helps produce clear thinking.

*We know what a person thinks not when he tells us
what he thinks, but by his actions.*
                                    —Isaac Bashevis Singer

Try this exercise: Imagine a big white bear in your
living room, just sitting there. Now, forget about it.
Absolutely do not think about white bears anymore.

If you are like normal people, you will now think
about white bears in your living room with great
intensity. Try as you might, this will be an image that
will take over your thoughts and obsess you.

The same is true of food. If you are suddenly
struck with thoughts of bingeing and you sternly tell
yourself to forget them, chances are you will think
about nothing but eating forbidden foods and breaking your abstinence. And once the obsession over-
powers us, it's very easy to act on it.

The next time unwanted binge thoughts crop up
in your head, don't pretend they aren't there. Instead, ask yourself what is really going on that needs
attention in your life. Chances are that there is an
uncomfortable feeling or situation you are running
from that you need to address. Make a commitment
today to discuss any uncomfortable thoughts you have
because if you don't it won't be long until your actions
betray you.

AFFIRMATION FOR THE DAY: When I look into
the roots of my negative thoughts and obsessions I can
reach greater self-understanding.

An expert is one who knows more about less and less.
                                   —NICHOLAS MURRAY BUTLER

I once heard an amusing definition of an expert: "Ex—unknown factor; spurt—drip under pressure."

We all know people who fancy themselves experts about many things; we may even think that we are experts in some areas. The problem with most so-called experts, however, is that they tend to inflate the boundaries of their knowledge and pretend to know more than they do. It is only in times of stress when they are challenged that others see how much of their act is bluster.

I once saw this happen on an interview show. Two men in the same field were being questioned by a panel of reporters. One of the men was soft-spoken yet well versed in an arcane area of economics. He frequently said "I don't know" when asked to comment on theories he wasn't familiar with. The other man, by contrast, had opinions on everything. By the end of the show I distrusted everything the know-it-all said and believed the comments of the man who had the humility to admit he didn't have every answer.

The lesson here is that when we try to be experts on something, we are bound to drip under pressure eventually. There is always more we can learn or master about any subject, and others will find us more credible if we can admit what our limits are. Keep this in mind today, especially regarding your recovery. Stay open today, be humble and avoid being an expert.

AFFIRMATION FOR THE DAY: The less I think I know, the smarter I am.

The shoe that fits one person pinches another; there is no recipe for living that suits all cases.
—CARL GUSTAV JUNG

I have some friends who have chosen to remain childless. Their priorities are not to raise a family and sacrifice for them; they prefer to spend their money and time on spa vacations, nice houses, work and their friends. They appear to be happy, fulfilled and content with their decision, despite others' pointed comments about their self-indulgent behavior and luxurious life-style.

After I had my first child, I, too, joined the chorus urging them to consider parenthood before it was too late. I realized, however, after a long conversation with the wife, that I was the one being thoughtless, not them. My friend told me how she had had to assume responsibility for all of her younger brothers and sisters because her mother had died unexpectedly at a young age, and as a result she had chosen to enjoy her siblings' children rather than have her own. I suddenly understood that her decision not to have children wasn't "bad"; it was just that the shoe that fit me didn't fit her.

Remember today when you are tempted to criticize another person's life-style, behavior or belief that you don't necessarily know all the factors that have gone into their decision. Recovery means learning to be open-minded and nonjudgmental—two ingredients that are required in the recipe for a happy and successful life.

AFFIRMATION FOR THE DAY: If everyone thought and lived the same way, we would never learn anything from each other.

A watched pot never boils.

—A<small>NONYMOUS</small>

Too often in recovery we are guilty of looking over our shoulder to see how far we've come. Once we've realized the ramifications and seriousness of our disease and seen how much we've hurt ourselves and others, we want nothing more than to be completely healed—and quickly.

Just as it always seems like a watched pot never boils, if we are impatiently checking our progress every day wondering "Am I well yet?" we'll never be satisfied with how far we've come. One way we might sabotage our recovery is by jumping on and off the scale every day, hoping the numbers will change dramatically. Or we can have overly high expectations for our emotional growth that are only achieved after years of painstaking efforts.

Keep in mind today that the most significant improvements in our recovery are the ones that take time and that we cannot necessarily track physically. Make an effort today to just relax and let the healing process carry you along. Check your weight infrequently, glance over old journals once a year and don't expect miracles overnight. If you can simply do the footwork of recovery and avoid excessive introspection, you'll find that things happen most easily when you aren't waiting impatiently.

AFFIRMATION FOR THE DAY: Today I'll be patient about the speed of my recovery.

The absurd man is he who never changes.
—AUGUSTE BARTHÉLEMY

We all know people who seem to be caught in a time warp. For many years they have changed nothing about themselves or their lives because they are comfortable with the status quo. Many compulsive eaters are like this; afraid of rocking the boat or treading on uncertain ground, they remain mired in personal and professional ruts.

It's unhealthy not to go through transformations on a regular basis. Animals routinely shed their skins in the process of renewal, and our bodies—hair, blood cells, and skin, for example—are constantly dying and being replaced. Doesn't it make sense for us to frequently examine other aspects of our lives to see if we've become stagnant in some area?

Ask yourself today if you've outgrown something in your life that is no longer valuable to your well-being. It could be a friend, a meal plan, a hairstyle or even a job that you discover isn't suited to you any longer. Whatever it is, remember that change for a compulsive eater takes courage and energy, but that without it we are violating the natural order of life and denying ourselves the joy that comes with healthy and positive transformation.

AFFIRMATION FOR THE DAY: Today I will remember that it is unhealthy not to change.

In nothing do we lay ourselves so open as in our manner of meeting and salutation.
—JOHANN KASPAR LAVATER

Experts say that we form opinions about people within ninety seconds of meeting them. What do we usually base these opinions on? Handshake, eye contact, manner of dress, expression and attitude.

Many people with eating disorders betray their depression and lack of self-esteem immediately. Downcast eyes, limp handshakes, nervous laughter, ill-fitting clothes and cynical attitudes are common to us while we are still compulsively eating. Because we feel so isolated in our anger and self-loathing, we're incapable of even pretending that we're glad to meet someone new.

As we recover emotionally we have to remember that our physical appearance should match our progress. When shaking someone's hand today be firm and tell them that you are pleased to see them. Instead of looking down, make eye contact and smile. And there's no reason to still be dressing in your baggy binge clothes if you are in recovery, so bundle the old things up and give them away. Use those ninety seconds to your best advantage at every opportunity today and make sure that your behavior and appearance are accurate barometers of your internal progress and recovery.

AFFIRMATION FOR THE DAY: Today I will greet others with confidence, enthusiasm and good cheer.

*Some seeds fell by the wayside . . . because they had
no root, they withered away. But others fell into good
ground, and brought forth fruit, some an hundredfold,
some sixtyfold, some thirtyfold.*

—MATTHEW 13:4, 6, 8

I have a friend who has seemingly done everything
she can to recover from her eating disorder. For years
she has attended recovery meetings, read scores of
self-help books and been involved in attitudinal healing
groups. Yet she still struggles with bingeing, still wakes
up fearful and angry in the morning, and still alienates
people with her obstinate and self-centered behavior.

Whenever I see or hear her, I am reminded of the
biblical parable in which good seeds were scattered and
only took root where there was a receptive environment.
Physically we can go through the motions of recovery for
years, read the right books and say the right things, but
real growth can never take root until we are receptive and
willing to change. Until then it will be like throwing fertile
seeds on rocks.

If you are despairing because you are trying to
recover but nothing is clicking, hang in there. Keep
doing the footwork and praying for a tiny corner of
your mind to become open to change. All it takes is a
small window of opportunity for our recovery to grow.
If we truly want to stop eating compulsively and we're
willing to try to keep an open mind, some of the seeds
that are tossed our way will fall on fertile ground and
the right attitudes will eventually flower.

AFFIRMATION FOR THE DAY: Nothing can survive or grow in a mind that is filled with rocks.

God does not discriminate.

—LEAH RUTH DREYFUS

When I take my walks in the morning I am often struck by the evenness and self-sustaining rhythm of nature. For example, when apple trees drop their fruit, they do so randomly and all of the people and creatures that happen by are free to help themselves. Just as many apples fall to the right as to the left, and there are certainly no signs indicating that one particular clump of apples is better than another.

If we carefully observe the world around us we'll see that discrimination is not the natural order of things. Every one of us is born with certain talents and gifts that are unique to us and that are meant to foster our growth in some way. When we accept the conditions that exist and then do our best to improve ourselves, we reach our potential. If, however, we start to look around and perceive discrimination and favoritism in what other people have been given, we become paralyzed with envy and cannot move forward with our own lives.

Practice expressing gratitude today for your unique position in life. Instead of looking around and seeing that another person was born with more money, better looks or wiser parents, accept that you have been given just what you need for your life's journey. If you can allow yourself to join the ebb and flow of the natural world around you and see rhythm and beauty instead of competition and unfairness, your daily journey will be filled with more thankfulness and joy.

AFFIRMATION FOR THE DAY: I can't practice gratitude if I'm looking for the inequalities in life.

Anger helps straighten out a problem like a fan helps straighten out a pile of papers.
—SUSAN MARCOTTE

Most people with eating disorders grew up in families where anger was expressed inappropriately. Sometimes it was done violently with a lot of yelling and hitting; sometimes it was covered up and no one admitted they were angry. In either case, feelings can't be aired healthily in such systems, and family members often turn to addictions as a way of coping.

Anger is a dangerous emotion for compulsive eaters who have no background in handling it well or seeing others handle it well. However, we *can* learn to give ourselves permission to feel anger while at the same time reminding ourselves to express it in ways that don't damage us or others. Pounding a pillow, venting our feelings with a friend, writing in a journal and taking a walk are all healthy outlets for our frustration.

Remember today not to fear your anger. Being in recovery means you don't have to lose control over it any longer. When your emotions get hot, stop and assess the problem calmly, allow yourself to feel angry if it is warranted and then take steps to defuse it in an appropriate way. Don't confuse the specific incident by bringing in unresolved anger from other problems. Learning how to deal with our feelings honestly as they arise, without reacting in an extreme manner, is a difficult but important step of recovery.

AFFIRMATION FOR THE DAY: I will not speak or act in anger today.

A little learning is a dang'rous thing.
—ALEXANDER POPE

Do you know people who know a little bit about a certain subject, yet who are capable of holding forth for hours on it as if they were the world's experts?

I detest this kind of person yet I fell into this trap when I first started to recover from bulimia. Elated at my early success, I preached to others about the program I was in. No one was immune from my lectures. If I didn't eat sugar or white flour, no one else should either. Every bite my husband took was scrutinized and commented on. Thank goodness someone finally had the courage to tell me to be quiet for a while so that I could learn from people who had years of recovery under their belts!

The "pink cloud" of early recovery is a very dangerous time. Because everything is often going so well our tendency is to think that we have our problems licked and that we can save others. When this happens we have to be extra vigilant and restrain ourselves from being cocky know-it-alls because this is precisely the time when we are in most danger of watching our sanity, serenity and recovery evaporate.

AFFIRMATION FOR THE DAY: Today I will remember that there is always more to learn.

The buck stops here.
>   —SIGN ON HARRY S. TRUMAN'S DESK WHILE HE WAS
>   PRESIDENT OF THE UNITED STATES

Aren't we all guilty at times of seeing a person in need and of turning our backs, assuming that someone else will help? I see this happening every day—for example, motorists who need assistance sit disconsolately at the side of the road, hoping someone will stop and help, but it's often hours before anyone does. I've also watched homeless families on the streets, begging for money to feed their children. Too often people stride by, thinking that it's someone else's job to care.

Instead of passing the buck, we all should feel a sense of responsibility when we see a person in need. Although we can't shoulder the burdens of the world and save everyone, we can do our own part when we are able. If there's a blood drive because the local hospital has a shortage, roll up your sleeve and go donate. If there's a homeless shelter nearby, volunteer your time or take over some needed supplies. And if you see someone looking lost on a busy street, ask if they need help or directions.

Good Samaritans don't always have to be other people. If we can take the initiative instead of always walking away when we see someone in need, we'll learn how to give the empathy and kindness that we will undoubtedly need from others from time to time.

AFFIRMATION FOR THE DAY: Today I will accept responsibility for helping another person.

The touchstone of all growth is pain.
    —FROM THE TWELVE STEPS AND TWELVE TRADITIONS OF
                                    ALCOHOLICS ANONYMOUS

To escape pain in the past we usually sought solace in food and self-destructive behavior. We were unable to accept any unhappiness or setbacks so we bemoaned our bad fortune, wondering why our lives couldn't be easier and more to our liking. And when we couldn't make people, places and things conform to our wishes, we retreated with our tails between our legs, looking for sympathy.

Many of us in recovery have found that our emotional maturity was stuck at the age our compulsive eating began. In the process of trying to catch up and become adults we have found ourselves learning rather painful lessons that involve getting along with our peers, sharing, experiencing disappointment with dignity and not using food as a crutch.

We must remember that life is not always easy and that our recovery will be quite painful at times. But we need to also keep in mind that as difficult as some situations can be, a life of compulsive eating is infinitely worse. Try to appreciate the pain you feel today instead of avoiding it, because pain can be the best teacher.

AFFIRMATION FOR THE DAY: Instead of numbing myself with food, I will respond to pain today with maturity.

Courage is grace under pressure.
—ERNEST HEMINGWAY

Recovering from compulsive eating takes guts. It takes no courage to go on another diet, but it does require courage to address and change the spiritual, physical and emotional components of our disease that help make us feel inferior, insecure and angry.

At the self-help meetings I attend we say a prayer at the beginning that includes a phrase asking our Higher Power to give us "the courage to change the things we can." By saying this we are acknowledging that while there are some things we can do nothing about, there are others that we have some control over and that we need help with to make positive changes.

There are many things compulsive eaters need courage with in recovery. They might include giving up a binge food, making amends, asking someone for help and developing humility. Other situations requiring courage would be leaving an abusive relationship, openly stating our needs to others, and having faith in our Higher Power in the midst of dark times.

If you don't feel you have enough strength to do what needs to be done today, get on your knees and pray for it. You'll find that whenever you ask your Higher Power for help, the door will be opened for you to receive whatever courage, strength and insight are needed.

AFFIRMATION FOR THE DAY: It is up to me whether I respond to the pressures of recovery with dignity or immaturity.

Self-pity is one of the most unhappy and consuming defects that we know. It is a bar to all spiritual progress and can cut off all effective communication with our fellows because of its inordinate demands for attention and sympathy. It is a maudlin form of martyrdom, which we can ill afford.

—BILL WILSON

When I am down in the dumps and wallowing in self-pity, it is close to impossible for anyone to reach me. I reject friendship, offers of sympathy and healthy pursuits. I prefer to isolate myself and let my depression deepen.

We all fall into the "poor me" syndrome at times. It's perfectly normal to be there occasionally but if we wallow too long in this type of self-pity, we are apt to jeopardize our abstinence, as well as the patience and understanding of our family and friends.

What few of us realize is that when we put ourselves down—"If I had been wittier, he would have asked me out," or "If I were smarter I would have gotten that raise"—we are trying to make ourselves feel more powerful and in control. This is a very arrogant mindset.

Remind yourself today and often that self-pity is the fastest way to alienate your friends and undo your spiritual progress. If it still envelops you, force yourself to get out and interact with others and pray for the willingness to have your depression lifted. The sooner you can allow the light of reality to shine on your self-absorbed perspective, the more you'll be able to soak up the love and friendship that surrounds all of us.

AFFIRMATION FOR THE DAY: I am not useful to myself or anyone else when I am filled with self-pity.

Pray inwardly, even though you find no joy in it. For it does good, though you feel nothing, see nothing.
—MOTHER JULIAN OF NORWICH

We have all had episodes, unless we have been given the gift of extraordinary faith, when we received no joy from prayer. The words were like dust in our mouths, the belief that we were taken care of was absent, and closing our eyes was like staring into a black hole.

At times like these it is useful to read self-help accounts and spiritual literature about what other people have done when they felt abandoned in a spiritual wasteland. One woman who has inspired me in down times is Mother Julian of Norwich, a fourteenth-century mystic who retained her faith in a loving God and the power of prayer despite being surrounded by wars, pestilence, hate and destruction. Her faith was a beacon of light to many who consulted her in the solitary cell where she spent her days in worship. When I contemplate the true horrors of what life was like then, and how committed this woman was to her faith, it never fails to inspire me to renew my belief in the power of prayer.

If you can't summon the resources to pray and believe in a loving Higher Power today, don't despair and give up. Even the most devout have their moments of darkness and doubt, and if we can remain hopeful during these periods we'll find that they are what will give us strength and inspiration in the future.

AFFIRMATION FOR THE DAY: My spiritual beliefs are always enriched by my darkest times.

Love is listening and listening is love.
                                    —GERALD G. JAMPOLSKY, M.D.

One day I was trying to tell a friend of mine how I was feeling about our relationship. Every time I started to talk, she interrupted me. This went on for several minutes as I became increasingly frustrated. Finally, in total exasperation, I said, "Please let me finish my sentences!"

When we don't listen to other people and then try to tell them how they are feeling rather than letting them tell us themselves, we are insulting them. Everyone has their own truth and point of view and we must respect that. Not to listen to another's thoughts is like saying, "I don't love you enough to let you be you."

My outburst startled my friend and taught us both something. She had never realized how domineering her personality was, nor had I ever stopped to wonder if I was also guilty at times of walking on top of other people's words. Watch yourself today for signs of thoughtless behavior, such as not respecting other people's right to express themselves. One of the greatest gifts we give others is our willingness to listen without judgment or interruption because it conveys a greater sense of love and acceptance than almost any other act we can perform.

AFFIRMATION FOR THE DAY: Quiet, attentive listening equals unconditional love.

It's easier to write your principles down than to live up to them.

—BILL MOYERS

There is a man who is considered to be one of the greatest exponents of the twentieth century on the principles of love, healing and kindness. He makes a good living traveling all over the world and appearing on numerous shows, telling others how to behave if they want to live long, stress-free, fulfilling lives.

Imagine one reporter's surprise, then, when she went to interview this person and found him to possess none of the qualities he made so much money espousing. During the interview he was cold, curt and rude to his secretary. And although he preached the importance of human interaction, his eyes rarely met the reporter's, he didn't laugh once, and he didn't shake her hand when she left. Needless to say, the meeting was quite disillusioning.

We need to guard against the attitude shown in this story of "Do as I say, not as I do," because even small children can spot a phony a mile away. Instead of always telling others how they should behave, do a reality check on yourself first. Are the principles you support the ones you live by every day? If you're one of the people who can write your beliefs down yet not live them, then take some action today to be more consistent.

AFFIRMATION FOR THE DAY: When I only pay lip service to what is important to me, I fool no one but myself.

Habit is habit, and not to be flung out the window by any man, but coaxed downstairs a step at a time.
—MARK TWAIN

In recovering from our compulsive eating we must accept that we cannot and will not get better overnight. Although we all want to wake up tomorrow with normal food cravings and a healthy body, we have to remember that we did not develop our disorders in one day, therefore we will not recover immediately either.

If we are in a twelve-step recovery program, we must recognize that the steps come in order for a reason. Not only do we need to work through all of them to recover completely, but we must do them in the sequence they are presented. For example, if we admit our powerlessness over food with Step One then skip to carrying the message of recovery to others with Step Twelve, we will miss out on the middle steps of spiritual awakening and amends which are critical to our growth.

Even if we are not in a self-help group, the same caution holds. Don't try to tackle every facet of your compulsive eating and dysfunctional lifestyle at once. For example, if you are overhauling your diet, do it gradually. And if you want to improve your appearance, phase in your new look in stages. As slowly as you positively transform yourself, though, remain committed to changing because even small unaddressed problems you would prefer to avoid can grow to impede your recovery later.

AFFIRMATION FOR THE DAY: Today I will coax my bad habits down the stairs, one at a time.

No man ever said on his deathbed that he wished he had spent more time at work.

—ANONYMOUS

Therapists have coined a new phrase to describe people who spend inordinate amounts of time laboring to achieve success, power and prestige, yet who reach the top and feel empty and spiritually impoverished. These men and women are called "the working wounded."

Counselors find that the "working wounded" are often surprised by these feelings of depression when they reach their material goals, and their coping often involves mood altering addictions that temporarily make them feel better such as compulsive eating, extramarital sex, gambling and drinking. The real problems, spiritual and emotional, go unattended.

Do you think that success is making a good salary and rising in your company? What about spending time with family, friends and worthy causes that need volunteers? Do you even know how you'd fill your spare time if you weren't so obsessed with putting in long hours at work?

The Pennsylvania Dutch have a saying, "We grow too soon old and too late wise." Don't allow yourself to become wise too late about what real happiness consists of, because the sooner you can put your job into perspective, the less likely you'll be to succumb to unhealthy addictions.

AFFIRMATION FOR THE DAY: A paycheck doesn't always bring happiness or inner peace.

*To let go is not to cut myself off, it's the realization
that I can't control another.*

—ANONYMOUS

Letting go is one of the hardest things a compulsive
eater needs to do. It means we have to admit to ourselves
that we can't control the outcome of events or the actions of
other people. For people who are accustomed to running
the show, this is a rough learning experience.

One of the most difficult times I had in learning to let
go was watching someone close to me die. As she gradually
deteriorated and lost her zest for living, I tried to think of
ways to save her. Some of my strategies included dragging
her to the doctor against her will and emphasizing how sad
I'd be if she wasn't around anymore.

Needless to say, nothing worked. My plans all
backfired because they assumed that I could make
someone else do something to please me and fit my
script. It was only after she died that I realized how
much pain she had lived with and how little joy she'd
experienced in her physical condition. Trying to make
her live for me, I then saw, had been extraordinarily
selfish.

Learning how little control we have over people,
places and things is tough but necessary. Try to restrain
yourself today when the urge to dictate overtakes you and
remember that putting your Higher Power at the steering
wheel always ensures a smoother ride.

AFFIRMATION FOR THE DAY: Today I will "let go
and let God."

The sacrifices of friendship were beautiful in her eyes as long as she was not asked to make them.

—SAKI

Once I had a friend, or at least I thought I had a friend. We enjoyed a lot of lunches and phone conversations together but rarely made demands on each other.

Then some crises hit. Her life changed dramatically and she required a lot of support, love and time. I gave it as best I could, knowing that she would do the same for me if I was in a similar spot.

Then my hard times hit. I found myself juggling a lot of balls, but not well. Bad luck seemed to be my middle name. I turned to her for aid, especially after she kept asking, "Is there anything I can do to help?" Finally I admitted that I could use assistance with something, and although she agreed to help, never did.

It often takes a painful situation like this to show us what our friendships are made of. We like to think our buddies will be there for us in tough times, but when they're not, we're sadder and wiser. Ask yourself today if you believe in the sacrifices of friendship as long as you don't have to make them. If so, prepare yourself for some long, dry spells when misfortune hits because you'll never receive what you cannot freely give to others.

AFFIRMATION FOR THE DAY: Today I'll remember that friendship isn't always convenient.

If you love, you will suffer, and if you do not love, you do not know the meaning of a Christian life.
—AGATHA CHRISTIE

While we were eating compulsively many of us erected emotional walls around ourselves because we didn't want to be hurt by another person. Having experienced rejection before, we decided to close our hearts so that no person, place or thing could make us feel abandoned again. With us it was all or nothing—either we loved with our whole hearts or we did not love at all.

When we pretend to be rocks that are incapable of emotion we miss out on one of the greatest joys of being alive. Caring about others and allowing ourselves to be vulnerable are signs that our recovery is progressing. For as we give love, we receive it in turn. One sure law of the universe is that whatever you freely provide others will come right back to you.

Do you find yourself pulling away from someone because you feel you've gotten too close or revealed too much about yourself? If so, fight the urge to end the relationship. Recovery means learning to feel the intensity of love as well as the pain and insight it can bring us. If we can dare to express our honest feelings we will find ourselves drawing people to us who enrich our lives and awaken emotions that may have lain dormant for years.

AFFIRMATION FOR THE DAY: I am vulnerable when I love another person with my whole heart, but without that vulnerability I cannot experience the richness of life.

Humility is the fruit of inner security and wise maturity.
—CORNEL WEST

People who begin to live honest, spiritual and modest lives and who make amends for past wrongdoings usually experience a sudden upturn in fortunes. Some of the most common beneficial occurrences I've seen among recovering compulsive eaters are job changes, unexpected financial windfalls, newly rewarding relationships and positive attention from others.

When good times and prosperity hit it's easy to forget how low we once were. All of a sudden those desperate late-night binges, cash flow problems and meaningless friendships have become a thing of the past. We begin to take our newfound prosperity and recovery for granted.

When this happens we are one bite away from a binge. We are not only at risk of breaking our abstinence when we forget our years of pain from compulsive eating, but we are also in danger of losing the respect of others. If we become cocky and act superior to the people who have helped us find a better way, we are preparing ourselves for a nasty fall.

Take a moment today to acknowledge the blessings that have come your way since you started to recover. Make it a point to thank the people who have helped you regain peace of mind. And remember that as much as you may accumulate, humility is still your most valuable asset.

AFFIRMATION FOR THE DAY: When I am truly grateful for my growth, I lessen my chances of returning to where I once was.

A promise made is a debt unpaid.
—ROBERT WILLIAM SERVICE

Is your word good? If you promise something, do you follow through and do it? Or do you constantly make vague pledges to yourself and others that have come to mean nothing because of your track record of unreliability?

When we tell others we will meet them at a certain time, invite them for dinner, or do something for them, we should consider those promises unpaid debts. Although we might not attach much value to our words, others may wait expectantly for those events to happen. One widowed friend of mine says that countless people have said that they'll be inviting her for dinner "soon" to help assuage her loneliness. To her great sadness, though, no one has ever followed through.

Reliability and making our word good is an important lesson for compulsive eaters to learn. Listen to yourself today and see how many promises you make to others such as "I'll call you," "We can do that later," and "Let's have lunch soon." Make a mental note to follow up on even your small pledges and you'll discover that as you get into the habit of fulfilling your promises, your words will take on the weight of gold.

AFFIRMATION FOR THE DAY: Today I won't make promises I can't keep.

The soul is dyed the color of its thoughts.
—MARCUS AURELIUS

I read a rather interesting story in the paper one day that vividly showed the power of our thoughts. One man, a chain-smoker, was out with friends when one of them told the smoker that he was exhibiting all of the physical characteristics of someone with heart disease. As he carried on about the subject at great length, the smoker became increasingly worried and vowed to get a checkup soon. The next day he died of a massive heart attack.

Was this a coincidence? I think not. Although smoking is seriously detrimental to your health, this man probably became so obsessed overnight with the possibility of heart disease that he may have unwittingly contributed to bringing the heart attack on himself. This type of story is not unusual; countless inspirational books have been written about how our thoughts and beliefs influence our health, prosperity and well-being.

What are the thoughts you hold true about yourself? Whatever you honestly believe about your abilities, appearance and destiny is probably an accurate blueprint of yourself and your future. Think positively and see yourself in the body you want, going through a joyous day and feeling blessed. As you start to reprogram the inner tapes that limit you, you'll undoubtedly find that as we think, we are.

AFFIRMATION FOR THE DAY: When I see myself in a positive light, I am halfway there.

We must muster the insight and the courage to leave folly and face reality.

—ALBERT SCHWEITZER

One day I was reading a study of compulsive eaters and I was particularly drawn to the conclusions researchers had come to about the social impairment of compulsive eaters. Eating disorders, it said, were so devastating to self-esteem that even people in long-term recovery had difficulty socializing with others, and that learning normal human interaction was an arduous process that took these men and women years to master.

I immediately became defensive. I couldn't possibly be like these people they had studied. I had a responsible job, a good marriage and several years of recovery under my belt. Despite my bravado, though, a little voice inside me said, "Oh, yeah? Last week you hung up on someone you were mad at. And you pouted like a kid the other day when you didn't get your way. That's maturity?"

My realization that day that I still had trouble relating to people socially despite freedom from bingeing was a searing one. But it also relieved me to know that my awkward feelings were normal. Remind yourself today that our disease is like a burr with deep spikes that we can't totally remove in a short period of time. It's only when we have courage and patience to face the areas that need work that we eventually come to the place where we feel comfortable with ourselves and others.

AFFIRMATION FOR THE DAY: Today I will be realistic about the pace of my recovery.

The desire of perfection is the worst disease that ever afflicted the human mind.

—LOUIS DE FONTANES

There is a new group of people in the United States that worries therapists: "plastic surgery junkies." These people are obsessed with the quest for perfection and will undergo numerous operations at great expense to fix their nose, chin, eyes, ears and thighs. Not content with what nature gave them, they even are willing to have excess fat vacuumed out of their bodies and put implants in a variety of places.

The risk of this type of behavior is that the junkie will never be satisfied. There will always be something else they can find that needs "fixing." Although I have never undergone plastic surgery, I, too, have been a perfection junkie at times. For example, if I gave a well-received speech I would ignore the compliments and focus on the flaws, and if I improved one area of my body I would immediately find another one that seemed to need help.

When we are forever focusing on trying to improve what is outside, that is a clue that our inside needs work. Instead of doing fifty extra sit-ups to achieve the perfect waistline today, spend that time in quiet meditation asking for guidance. Love yourself for who you are, not for what you appear to be. And keep in mind that even the most expensive, beautiful car won't run well unless the motor under the hood is clean and rust-free.

AFFIRMATION FOR THE DAY: I'll never be happy if a "perfect" appearance is my main goal.

He restoreth my soul.

—PSALMS 23:3

In Hawaii there is an ancient mode of healing called *huna*. In this system, health is equated with energy and poor health is the result of lack of energy. A person whose energy has been restored from poor health is considered to be in harmony once again, and when two people are in love, they are thought to be blending their energies together.

The greatest depleter of energy is believed to be stress, which huna practitioners say brings on illness and depression. To counteract its negative effects healers prescribe a corrected diet, prayer, muscle work, breathing and other noninvasive surgical procedures.

When I was bulimic and constantly feeling stressed, I had no energy, either. Performing basic chores like brushing my teeth, being polite, paying bills and finishing a task often seemed overwhelming. But as I began to recover, changed my diet, prayed more and took better care of my body, my energy was restored. I remember being amazed at how much I could accomplish and how much better I felt when I looked after myself and focused on improving my health.

Identify the stressors in your life today and take healthy steps to eliminate or relieve them. Eat moderately, exercise, pray and breathe deeply. The more you can care for yourself lovingly, the more you'll discover that the greatest wellsprings of energy and peace exist within you.

AFFIRMATION FOR THE DAY: Today my energy will be directed toward positive actions that enhance my well-being.

Character builds slowly, but it can be torn down with incredible swiftness.

—FAITH BALDWIN

About five years after I had begun to recover from bulimia—a period during which I had made enormous progress toward building my self-esteem—I entered a difficult time when it seemed that all I heard from other people was "I don't like you," "You're wrong" and "No, thanks."

I tried to separate myself from these numerous rejections and remember that it wasn't me that was being rejected, it was usually my work, my ideas or a superficial characteristic of mine. But it was hard, if not impossible, to feel confident and happy during this period and I was amazed to see how quickly my years of deliberate character-building could be erased by the rampant negativity.

Like an oyster that builds a hard shell in violent waters, however, I eventually learned to build stronger walls of self-worth around me as a result of this difficult episode. Now when rejection and negative people converge on me, I tune them out and concentrate on what I know to be true and good about myself. Today if you feel your self-esteem slipping away because of some outside disapproval, think about the oyster. Remember that violent waters, rocks and predators are going to come after all of us at times during our recovery, but if we have hard shells that protect the tenderness and warmth inside, we won't lose sight of our internal worth.

AFFIRMATION FOR THE DAY: No matter how strong the winds of rejection blow today, I won't let them sweep away the walls of my self-esteem.

Do you know that conversation is one of the greatest pleasures in life? But it wants leisure.
          —AMY LOWELL

I have a friend whose company I enjoy, and whose conversations are often interesting, but who is on the bottom of my list of people to spend time with. Her problem? She talks too much.

Phone conversations with this person are exercises in frustration. Trying to get a word in edgewise is impossible, and when I am finally able to burst in with a thought, she reinterprets my words with, "What you are trying to say is . . ." I have even noticed in a crowd that if another person has the floor, she'll inevitably start a side conversation that gets more and more animated until she finally achieves her goal of capturing everyone's attention.

If we are guilty of talking too much or of always trying to draw attention to ourselves, we must try to curb this annoying tendency. Hogging conversations and not allowing others to express themselves is a pathetic way of saying, "Notice me! I'm important!" Remember today that you don't have to take it upon yourself to plug conversational gaps, and also that silence isn't just golden, it's the sign of a self-accepting person.

AFFIRMATION FOR THE DAY: When I am always talking I am never learning.

He is invited to great things who receives small things greatly.

—Flavius Magnus
Aurelius Cassiodorus

Have you ever done something for someone only to receive no thanks for your work? I have, and the unfortunate result has usually been for me to get angry at that person and resolve to avoid helping them again in the future.

Although our goal should be to give without expectation of reward or acclaim, it is human nature to want at least a pat on the back for a job well done. But as much as I personally always want thanks for my efforts, I find myself frequently forgetting to thank my Higher Power for the gifts I receive. It seems as though no sooner do I get something I've been hoping for than I focus on the next thing I want.

Why should we treat our Higher Power any differently than we'd like to be treated ourselves? If you stop giving when you don't receive thanks, don't you think your lack of gratitude might cause your own blessings to cease? Make an effort today to thank your Higher Power for everything you have in your life. Don't take anything for granted or write it off as a lucky break. If you can maintain an attitude of thanksgiving and wonder at the many gifts that flow to you, you'll ensure that your channel to prosperity, abundance and happiness remains clear and open.

AFFIRMATION FOR THE DAY: Every day brings many occasions for thanksgiving.

My solitude grew more and more obese, like a pig.
—YUKIO MISHIMA

We all need time alone to process our thoughts, escape from the bustle of our lives, and reflect on our actions. But as compulsive eaters we have to watch our tendency to isolate and avoid conflict and confrontation. We may think that we're doing something beneficial when we're alone with our thoughts, when we may in fact be running away from something we don't want to face.

I once thought it would be noble to be a nun. Cloistered, I would pray for the world and think good thoughts. As I matured in recovery, though, I realized that my fantasy had not been based on real conviction; it had been a sly way to escape from my responsibilities. I recognized that valuable growth would only take place if I tried to practice spiritual principles in a more challenging environment than a religious retreat.

When we begin to avoid the real world through long periods of solitude, we aren't doing ourselves any favors. Are you balancing your quiet time with active participation in life? Don't allow either one of these aspects to overshadow the other because, like the yin and yang of traditional Chinese medicine, too much of one side—even if it is beneficial—has the potential to upset the balance of our recovery.

AFFIRMATION FOR THE DAY: Isolation is the darkroom in which I develop my negatives.

One must not always think so much about what one should do, but rather what one should be. Our works do not ennoble us; but we must ennoble our works.
— MEISTER ECKEHART

I have some friends who make very impressive "To Do" lists every morning. By the time the day is over they have usually checked everything off and feel a great sense of accomplishment. I have observed, however, that sometimes in the interest of getting things done quickly their halfhearted efforts bring about shoddy results.

Do you fall into this category? Is it more important to you to compile a lot of results each day rather than do a few things very well? Pay attention to what you seek to accomplish today. Is there a task that can be eliminated in favor of spending more time on something really important—like putting off mending a shirt to read a book to your child?

Keep in mind that compulsive people have a tendency to begin many things and then do only some of them well. Today take on only what you can give thoughtful attention to and be more concerned with the quality of your work than the quantity. You'll find that when you slow down and go through your day mindfully, you'll feel more fulfilled than frazzled tonight.

AFFIRMATION FOR THE DAY: Today I'll ennoble my work instead of trying to make my work ennoble me.

There is only one good, knowledge, and one evil, ignorance.

—SOCRATES

One evening I attended a dinner where I listened to a number of conversations that became quite heated at times. The subjects involved a variety of topics from politics to religion to issues of personal freedom.

Some of the people had well-reasoned, thoughtful arguments, and it was clear that they really understood the issues involved. Some of the others, however, did not have the knowledge required to debate, yet they were the ones who were the loudest and most insistent about their views. They were also the ones who went home at the end of the evening fuming if others didn't agree with them, obviously nursing grudges against anyone who opposed them.

When we are coming from a place of ignorance we are likely to cover up our lack of knowledge with belligerence, anger and boasting. When we take the time to have knowledge about something, however, we can make reasoned decisions and not necessarily involve our egos in our stands. Today make sure that you have the facts you need to buttress your beliefs and actions. If you choose to remain in ignorance, however, you run the risk of alienating others and having your personal growth stagnate.

AFFIRMATION FOR THE DAY: When my beliefs are rooted in ignorance I cannot make wise choices for myself.

Whatsoever things are true, whatsoever things are honest, whatsoever things are just, whatsoever things are pure, whatsoever things are lovely, whatsoever things are of good report, if there be any virtue, and if there by any praise, think on these things.
—PHILIPPIANS 4:8

There is a world-famous violinist who exhibited enormous musical talent as a young boy. Just as he was starting to master the violin, however, he was struck with polio. Despite the doctors' gloomy predictions he continued to play beautifully, even with his handicap, and now he brings joy to millions with his skills.

There are many people like this man who choose to develop their strong points instead of focusing on their weak ones. These are the men and women who ignore their infirmities and hone the talents they do possess, like the people who are born without hands yet who learn to write and paint with their toes and mouths.

Every day we have the choice to dwell on the good facets of our lives and play them up for all they're worth, or on the negative, sad aspects. We become what we believe to be true so make it a point today to focus on the positive and uplifting things about yourself and then go about refining them, praising them and being grateful for the things that make you special.

AFFIRMATION FOR THE DAY: Today I will dwell on my strengths, not my weaknesses.

Acceptance of what has happened is the first step to overcoming the consequence of any misfortune.

—WILLIAM JAMES

To begin recovery from our eating disorder we must first accept the fact that we have a serious disease. Talking euphemistically about starting a new diet, going on vacation or beginning a new job as ways of addressing our eating problem won't help us. Taking "the geographic cure"—changing external conditions in the hopes that internal conditions will change—will also only prolong our difficulties.

One night a young woman called me, ostensibly for help with her anorexia. As we talked I could see that she had not accepted on any level that she was very ill and needed help. She spoke proudly of her daily exercise routine, the amount of weight she had lost and the miniscule number of calories she allowed herself every day. It was clear that she wasn't ready to recover.

Until this young lady accepts that she needs help with her disorder, I doubt her condition will improve. What about you? Have you accepted that you have a disease, not just a weight problem? Do you know deep down that a superficial physical change won't address your underlying emotional and spiritual deficiencies? Remember today that recovery begins with honesty and that once we accept the truth about our condition, we have taken the first and hardest step toward wholeness.

AFFIRMATION FOR THE DAY: If I don't acknowledge the seriousness of my eating disorder, my recovery will be illusory and short-lived.

No man is free who is not master of himself.
—EPICTETUS

There was a period in my life when I allowed myself to be a victim. Instead of knowing what I wanted and then acting on that, I was constantly being buffeted about by the actions of other people. Because I let myself feel so helpless, I became very depressed which lowered my immune system and resulted in constant sickness. The night I landed in the emergency room with excruciating stomach pains was the night I decided to do something about it.

I started by taking back control of my life. Instead of waiting to see what someone else might say or do, I decided what direction I wanted to go in and then I channeled my energies appropriately. I made a list of things I had always wanted to accomplish and then set out to find ways of experiencing them. As my ability to take action and be the master of my own destiny increased, so did my happiness, sense of well-being and energy.

Until we can take the initiative in our own lives we will never know freedom. We'll always be waiting for someone's approval or "the right time"—neither of which may ever occur. Decide what it is you want today and then do something concrete to take you there. This small, but critical, step can mean the difference between relapse and vibrant recovery.

AFFIRMATION FOR THE DAY: Today I will act, not react.

Be sure your sin will find you out.

—Numbers 32:23

Again and again as I read the newspapers and hear stories on television, I see that people rarely get away with wrongdoing. Even with the most carefully planned crimes there always seems to be a glitch that results in the capture of the guilty party. Sometimes it takes years, but justice usually prevails.

For many compulsive eaters life before recovery was littered with sins large and small. Our errors may have been shoplifting, abuse of power, infidelity, embezzlement or just consistent lying to others. Even when our transgressions were not immediately discovered, in most cases our consciences were heavy with guilt which prevented us from having peace of mind.

This is why the process of amends is so critical to recovery from compulsive eating. When we return to people who have suffered as a result of our past behavior and ask for their forgiveness, we wipe our consciences clean. We also free up our minds to focus on creating a new life.

Is there a "sin" you have committed that you haven't yet atoned for? Do you spend needless time obsessing about being found out at some point in the future? If so, be bold today with your amends. Write the letter, send the check or approach the person to whom you are indebted. Our recovery entitles us to freedom from guilt, which we can claim with humility, courage and a willingness to admit imperfection.

AFFIRMATION FOR THE DAY: When I don't atone for my transgressions I am in a prison of my own making.

Loneliness is the first thing which God's eye nam'd not good.

—JOHN MILTON

I have a good friend who is a very gifted athlete. Every sport he tries he soon excels at, but he is incapable of enjoying any of them. His problem is that he quickly becomes competitive with himself and others and feels compelled to clock his time and monitor his progress, only being satisfied if he's better, faster and stronger every day.

As compulsive eaters we usually fall prey to this mind-set ourselves. We want to be the best in everything we do—attractiveness, wittiness, schoolwork, our job—and we view anything less as failure. Because we are so wrapped up in this competitiveness we can easily become very lonely and isolated. Other people aren't seen as friends or colleagues; they are seen as potential conquests or competitors.

To recover we have to remember that when we view life as a big race where there are only winners and losers, we are going to feel lonely. Yes, we may be successes in some people's eyes if we rise to the top of the totem pole, but is it worth the price we pay in family time, friendship and serenity? Remind yourself today that we need to be one of the crowd every now and then, because when we feel compelled to know more and accomplish more than our peers all the time, we can't experience the support and love of true fellowship.

AFFIRMATION FOR THE DAY: When I set myself apart from others through competition, the only real loser is me.

We can build a community out of seekers of truth, but not out of possessors of truth.
— THE REVEREND WILLIAM SLOANE COFFIN

Frequently I'll receive letters and phone calls from people who have read my articles or heard me speak and who want to change my mind about something. They don't agree with my attitude on spirituality, recovery from compulsive eating, or a variety of other subjects, and through threats, anger and gentle persuasion they'll try to convert me to their point of view.

When we are guilty of the attitude that what we believe to be true is the only answer, we display a fear that a way of thinking could exist that is better than or different from ours. And while we may think we are skillful marketers of our views, others usually find us alienating, judgmental and close-minded.

The world cannot exist peacefully if everyone feels that their ideas are the only ones that are worthwhile. After all, if we possess the absolute truth, how can we grow, learn from others and change? Remember today to be a seeker, not a possessor, of knowledge, particularly with regard to your recovery from compulsive eating. Allow yourself to be open to fresh ideas and new viewpoints that can expand your insights and give you the humility to be a part of the world, not apart from it.

AFFIRMATION FOR THE DAY: I am in harmony with others when I am willing to learn from them.

We should not pretend to understand the world only by the intellect; we apprehend it just as much by feeling.
—CARL GUSTAV JUNG

One of the greatest hindrances I faced in learning to believe in a Higher Power was my education. Because I couldn't grasp the presence of a universal, loving force intellectually, I refused to believe in it. To me, if something wasn't concrete, visible and explainable in scientific terms, then it did not exist.

Turning off my head and learning to trust the stirrings of my heart was very difficult because it meant letting go. I had to give up the arrogant notion that humans should be able to prove everything, even the occurrence of miracles, for them to be real. Learning to trust my intuition, not just my mind, led me to see that my Higher Power wasn't necessarily a burning bush; He could make His presence known to me through warm feelings, unconditional love, beneficial coincidences and strange bursts of joy.

If you are feeling unconnected to the world around you, there is a good chance that you have not yet begun to trust your feelings. As you interact with people today, try to consciously feel your heart opening up to them. Let yourself experience warmth when you gaze on a beautiful landscape or do something that brings you pleasure. As you begin to marry your rational and sensitive sides you'll find yourself more at peace with the world around you.

AFFIRMATION FOR THE DAY: I can only learn to love with my heart, not my head.

We must cultivate our own garden.

—VOLTAIRE

It is so easy to see the mistakes other people make in their lives. It's easier still to point out to those people that they are dating the wrong person, hanging the wrong picture on the wall and wearing a color that is unbecoming. The costs of this behavior are steep; not only does it keep us from noticing our own very obvious flaws, it also ensures that no one will want to have anything to do with us.

One day I heard a woman say at a self-help meeting that she used to actively intervene in her daughter's life and tell her how to clean her house, raise her children and run her marriage. When her daughter had stopped calling and allowing her to visit, she had been puzzled. Wasn't it a mother's duty to point all these things out?

As a result of this and painful experiences with others, this woman said she had learned to keep her nose out of family's and friends' affairs. "Someone said to me, 'If it doesn't have your name on it, don't pick it up,'" she commented with a laugh. "Since I've tried to do that it's amazing how much better people seem to like me!"

We can all learn from this story. We have enough to straighten out and work on without having to jump headlong into others' lives, particularly when we haven't even been asked. Remember today to pick up only what has your name on it, and you'll see not only how much more your presence is appreciated but how many weeds need attending to in your own garden.

AFFIRMATION FOR THE DAY: When I mind my own business I always have my hands full.

Time is a dressmaker specializing in alterations.
—FAITH BALDWIN

Recovery from compulsive eating is an ongoing series of changes and new experiences. But change can be very frightening to a person who is comfortable doing the same thing every day, eating the same meals and talking to the same people. Any shift in the norm presents unknown outcomes, and rigid, controlling people like us usually cannot tolerate any uncertainty or doubt.

We mustn't let ourselves become complacent in our recovery programs. Losing weight and creating a new appearance isn't going to be enough to sustain growth and serenity in the long run. We must constantly be challenging ourselves, looking for ways to improve and not shrinking from difficult and uncomfortable situations and changes. Just like muscles that atrophy when they aren't used, our spirits and well-being will wither when they aren't exercised and pushed to the limits occasionally.

Take your cue today from the Starship Enterprise in *Star Trek*. Seek new lands and explore fresh opportunities. Going "boldly where no man has gone before" will always open exciting horizons to us and ensure that our recovery remains fresh and energizing.

AFFIRMATION FOR THE DAY: Today I will seek change.

Nothing happens to anybody which he is not fitted by nature to bear.

—MARCUS AURELIUS ANTONINUS

I once heard that when God closes a door, He opens a window. I have come to believe this because of the many times I have found myself backed into a corner, facing personal disaster, and a "window" has been opened for me.

I first learned of the miracle of "windows" when I complained to someone about a desperate financial situation I was in. He comforted me by telling me that many years earlier he and his wife had huddled in bed one night with their dog and two babies because there wasn't enough money to pay the gas bill. At the moment of their greatest desperation, he said, they inherited some money that had solved their financial problems.

Since that time I have witnessed similar types of "windows" in my own life. Time and time again when all hope seemed lost and I had no options left, something unusual happened that saved the day. Others have told me of being fired and having a better job present itself shortly, receiving gifts of money when bills needed to be paid, and getting unexpected advice that solved a serious problem.

Whenever my back is to the wall and I'm starting to get scared that I'm not going to be okay, I try to quiet myself and remember all the times my Higher Power has reached down and opened a window for me. I find that when I can focus on opening windows, not slamming doors, I can see solutions where none may have seemed present before.

AFFIRMATION FOR THE DAY: Miracles can happen when I have faith.

We are healed of a suffering only by experiencing it to the full.

—MARCEL PROUST

Fears in us will continue to grow as long as we don't confront them. That is why when we fall off a horse we are counseled to get right back on. When divers hit their heads on diving boards while practicing a new stunt, their coaches often have them do the same dive again. The lesson, it seems, is to quickly nip your fears in the bud by doing precisely what you don't want to do.

My tendency in the past was to avoid dealing with my fears. Needless to say, after a while I started to feel like I was walking around in a straitjacket. I stopped trying new things, refused to challenge myself in any way and became a one-dimensional person. I was so afraid of being hurt that I tried to surround myself in a protective cocoon, which prevented any growth or maturity.

Today I know that my fears only disappear when I have the courage to confront them. I have learned that stage fright only goes away when I am out in public. Fears of being a failure don't dissolve until I take risks. Remember today that many of your sufferings are magnified by your misperceptions of your abilities, and that slaying these mental dragons is often as easy as resolving to fight them.

AFFIRMATION FOR THE DAY: Doing what I fear most is the solution to eliminating that fear.

I am not bound to win, but I am bound to be true. I am not bound to succeed, but I am bound to live up to what light I have.

—ABRAHAM LINCOLN

How do you define success? When I was bulimic I never felt successful enough—which at the time meant thin enough, pretty enough and rich enough. If I had been asked to name successful people they would have been prosperous men and women who had nice houses and secure jobs.

Since I have been in recovery, though, my definition of success has changed. The people I now consider most worthy of emulation are those whose top priorities are spiritual contentment, family harmony and a zest for their work. I've also heard respected business leaders insist that if these are also the goals of the companies they run it is almost impossible not to create a profitable organization.

Write down your definition of success, as well as the names of people whose lives you admire. If you find yourself listing wealthy business tycoons and glamorous stars as opposed to more ordinary people whose values are solid, then any success you achieve will be fleeting and unsatisfactory. Remind yourself frequently today that we all need goals to strive for to make our lives meaningful and give us purpose, but that our greatest success and happiness always come when we try to make our inner light shine as brightly as possible.

AFFIRMATION FOR THE DAY: When I honor my individuality, I am always a success.

Genuine beginnings begin within us, even when they are brought to our attention by external opportunities.
—WILLIAM BRIDGES

Some of the most beneficial changes I've made within myself have been the result of extraordinarily painful encounters. For example, once I was talking to a friend of mine and she playfully called me a "yegg." I laughed along with her, not knowing what it meant. When I finally looked it up I was mortified; it meant "thief."

When I was bulimic, I was indeed a thief. Too embarrassed to buy laxatives, diuretics, syrup of ipecac or food in the quantities I needed, I usually resorted to stealing. My stealing, however, didn't stop at those items. I often helped myself to my friends' gum, tapes and other possessions without a second thought.

As embarrassing as my "yegg" moment was, the comment was part of an escalating number of realizations that something was very wrong with me. By confronting me like that, my friend helped me start to come to terms with my unreliable behavior. She set the stage for me to make amends to all those I had stolen from and been dishonest with.

Sometimes the external events that point to change are painful, but ultimately they are blessings. Remember today to be alert to and thankful for the nudges we get from others—whether they are enjoyable or not—and to have the courage and willingness to use them as positive tools for transformation.

AFFIRMATION FOR THE DAY: Today I will seize an opportunity to start something new within myself.

Winners never quit and quitters never win.
                                        —ANONYMOUS

Many compulsive people have a tendency to start a lot of things and finish few of them. I didn't realize that this was my habit until I noticed one day that I had four books on my night table that were in various states of progress, I had a similar number of needlepoint projects halfway completed, and there were several half-ironed items of clothing hanging in my closet that I had been too impatient to finish.

In recovery we have to remember that quitting will ensure that we never win. The way we approach relationships, projects and daily activities is a good barometer of our persistence, and we can be certain that our commitment to abstinence will be halfway if that's the way we feel about everything else in our life, too.

Are you guilty of leaving a lot of things undone? If so, resolve to see at least one thing through today. If you start a memo at work, finish it. If you begin an article, read the whole thing instead of skipping around. And if you are tempted to end a relationship, make sure that you have exhausted all the possibilities to make it work. Remember that when you quit before the race is over, you may never know what you might have won.

AFFIRMATION FOR THE DAY: Today I won't be a quitter.

The best mirror is an old friend.

—ENGLISH PROVERB

One day I read about a well-known public figure who had gotten himself into such a bad situation with tax evasion, gambling and drug smuggling that he was certain to go to jail. The article detailed his rise over the years and discussed how he had found himself gradually associating with more and more dangerous and disreputable people. His childhood friends spoke despairingly of how they had attempted to help him and warn him about his behavior, but how he had ignored their advice and avoided them.

As compulsive eaters we are often guilty of this same trait. When I was bulimic I avoided anyone who tried to point out that I was becoming moody and dishonest. Often these were my oldest friends who could see how much I had changed. To keep from recognizing the truth, I surrounded myself with newer friends who didn't know me as well, and who often shared my food compulsion.

Ask yourself today how many longtime friends you still have. If you have gradually cut them all out in favor of people who haven't known you long, you have eliminated a helpful tool in recovery. Start trying to reestablish your old ties, perhaps through amends to them for neglecting the friendship. If you can remain in contact with people who have seen you grow, change and mature over the years, you'll always have someone who can help you hold up a mirror to yourself and see an unvarnished image of what is really there.

AFFIRMATION FOR THE DAY: My oldest friends are often the most honest with me.

The price we have to pay for money is paid in liberty.
—ROBERT LOUIS STEVENSON

Many of us labor under the false assumption that money is going to buy us security and happiness. When I was eating compulsively I often fantasized about becoming wealthy enough to take marvelous trips and own many beautiful things, which I was sure would make me happy and chase away the bulimia.

I have learned, however, that true security and peace cannot be purchased. I have watched friends scramble to make ever-larger salaries which they spend on homes, boats and club memberships. Before they know it they are locked into hedonistic lifestyles that require vast sums of money to maintain, and they find themselves working ever harder to just keep up with their neighbors. I find them to be among my most unhappy and dissatisfied friends.

As recovering people we need to remember that true serenity and self-worth don't come from money, they come from liking ourselves and feeling the power of a spiritual presence within. Ask yourself today if your goals consist of just making money and owning pretty things, because if they are, you will indeed lose your liberty. Keep your priorities in order—recovery, spiritual growth and moderation in all things—and you will never feel hemmed in or chained to anyone or anything.

AFFIRMATION FOR THE DAY: Today I will remember that wealth can be as much of a prison as poverty.

Better a sinner who knows he is a sinner than a saint who knows he is a saint.

—YIDDISH PROVERB

There is something very appealing about people who know that they are deficient in some way, who admit it and who take steps to correct the problem. This stands in stark contrast to those who think they're perfect in every area: They're fine the way they are and everyone who disagrees with them is wrong.

This compulsion to appear flawless can take a heavy toll. For example, one day I received a call from a young woman who was severely bulimic yet who refused to seek help for her problem. Her reason? She was the epitome of success at her college—head cheerleader, homecoming queen, president of her sorority and the girlfriend of the biggest "catch" on campus—and she felt that preserving her image was more important than openly admitting that she needed help.

Give the burden of perfection to your Higher Power today and have the humility to concede that you have limitations that require attention. When this is difficult for you, it's likely that you are frightened of the vulnerability that comes with exposing your anger, fear or shame. If this is so surround yourself with a "family" of loving, supportive people who allow you to be human and imperfect without judging or abusing you, and who can supply you with the kindness and warmth you need to learn to give yourself, as well.

AFFIRMATION FOR THE DAY: It takes wisdom to know and admit that I'm not perfect.

He who helps in the saving of others,
Saves himself as well.

—HARTMANN VON AUE

Time and again I've seen that the people who do
not make significant progress in recovery are the ones
who share little of their struggles and triumphs with
others. They may have a variety of reasons for not
reaching out: They don't want their families to know that
they have an eating disorder or they have failed at
recovery before and are embarrassed that they might
fail again. Whatever the reason, it's a good rule of thumb
that the less you reach out to others—whether to help
them or confide in them—the less likely it is you'll have
lasting recovery.

One of the main problems we have when we try
to fight our battles alone is that we don't have the
opportunity to benefit by helping others with similar
problems. I know that I've often had binge cravings
taken from me when someone has called for help with
a difficulty. By the time I've finished listening to them
I have renewed my own commitment to recovery and
forgotten about my desire to eat.

If you are having trouble with your abstinence
today, ask yourself if you are isolating because you just
don't feel like helping anyone else. We need to remember that our own salvation is strengthened by reaching
out to others because it is by sharing their struggles that
we often save ourselves as well.

AFFIRMATION FOR THE DAY: The best way to
help myself is to help another person.

There are two cardinal sins from which all the others spring: impatience and laziness.

—FRANZ KAFKA

One night after I gave a talk at a college about my recovery, I found a beautiful but sad young woman waiting for me by the exit. She begged for a few minutes of my time so that she could share her unhappiness with me and hopefully find some answers to her problems.

I soon learned that this woman had already spent several months in various hospitals trying to recover from her eating disorder, but that she was discouraged about her progress. She thought that she "should" be completely healed of her binge compulsion already and was beginning to despair that she'd never fully recover. She also admitted that she wasn't following the aftercare plan that had been carefully designed for her because she was "too busy" to go to group therapy or self-help meetings.

If we want to recover from compulsive eating we must remember that hard work and patience are crucial to our progress. We aren't going to expunge old habits and transform ourselves into moderate, flexible people overnight, and coming to terms with this fact is necessary if we hope to experience solid and lasting change. Focus today on the little, positive steps you are taking instead of how far you need to go, and remember that persistence and patience are two of the qualities we need most in our important journey to wholeness.

AFFIRMATION FOR THE DAY: When I am unwilling to invest time and energy into achieving a goal, I will never reach it.

It is harder to preserve than to obtain liberty.
—JOHN CALDWELL CALHOUN

There is a well-known liquid diet in America that is famous for helping men and women lose a lot of weight quickly, but that almost always results in the eventual regaining of the weight. Many of the people who succeed with this diet ruefully admit that it's keeping the pounds off that's the challenging part, not losing them.

Isn't this always the case when we attain a goal of some kind, particularly if we have achieved it quickly? Sometimes I'll find that I am very motivated while I am in pursuit of something I want, but that once I succeed it is easy to backslide and erase my gains. Staying where I want to be frequently takes far more determination and energy than I may have expended in getting there.

Remember today that if you have already achieved several years of solid recovery, you may have to be more vigilant and careful about what you do than someone who is new to the healing process. For example, the compliments that rolled in about your appearance when you first started to change may have ceased and you need to find other ways to boost your self-esteem. Most importantly don't neglect to preserve any newfound qualities of humility, gratitude and spirituality because once complacency sets in, your hard-fought gains are liable to slip away.

AFFIRMATION FOR THE DAY: Today I'll remember that anything that is easily gotten is easily forgotten.

Being alone is a markedly different experience than being lonely.

—CLARK E. MOUSTAKAS

When I was bulimic I was intensely lonely. I had no real close friends nor did I confide in anyone. My life felt like a bubble that I couldn't break out of and that no one could enter, no matter how hard either side tried.

In recovery I have learned the difference between being lonely and being alone. At first I confused the two and surrounded myself with people and distractions so that I wouldn't return to my previous solitary life-style. I finally realized that I had to have some free time just to reflect on the changing me if I were to develop the insight that would enable me to continue growing. Aloneness, I saw, was what I required to stay in touch with myself; loneliness was a state of mind I chose when I was incapable of reaching out to others and accepting myself.

Do you spend enough time alone with yourself? Or are you uncomfortable with your thoughts because they are so new and intense, and you aren't sure how to deal with them? No matter how awkward being alone might feel to you, don't run from it. The time we spend in daily prayer, meditation and reflection is what will continue to push us forward in recovery, and it is also what allows us to erase the feelings of loneliness that once haunted us.

AFFIRMATION FOR THE DAY: I need to remember that although loneliness can bring about aloneness, solitude does not have to make me feel lonely.

Nothing in life is more wonderful than faith—the one great moving force which we can neither weigh in the balance nor test in the crucible.

—Sir William Osler

When many of us started to recover we floated on what is called "the pink cloud." Our weight seemed to come off effortlessly, purging was no longer an option and moderation in all areas of our lives seemed to come naturally. We also felt—sometimes for the first time—a strong connection with our Higher Power.

Then, however, the crash came for many of us. We clashed with our families, were fired from jobs and got divorced. Often we had full-blown relapses and found ourselves turning to food again to dull the pain we were experiencing.

When bad times hit—as they almost always will—faith is tough. We decide that our Higher Power doesn't like us and is punishing us. Prayer and meditation, which were so much fun when life went our way, are now impossible. We make a conscious, yet irrational, decision that we don't care about recovery and that we want our old friend, food, back.

We must reject this self-pitying attitude when we have our normal share of crises. If we really try we can think of all the times we felt the presence of a Higher Power when we had lost hope, and how often prayer and meditation had been a soothing balm when we were troubled and confused. Remember today that life isn't always easy, but that with steadfast faith and a lot of courage, we can gracefully weather any storm that comes our way.

AFFIRMATION FOR THE DAY: My faith is an internal flame that I must fan daily.

The world has enough for every man's need but not enough for every man's greed.

—MAHATMA GANDHI

As compulsive eaters we have had histories of greedy behavior, particularly with food. Often we weren't content with reasonable portions and found ourselves taking extra helpings to try to satisfy the emptiness within. What I often found puzzling was that many of my worst binges started with modest amounts of nourishing food that just multiplied, leaving me angry, ashamed and depressed.

Our greed was probably not limited to our food intake. Many of us have coveted friends' promotions at work, neighbors' houses and vacations, and others' good fortune. Our problem has been that we feared never having enough of anything to be happy, so we gathered as many material things around us as possible, regardless of whether we needed them or not.

As we recover we must frequently remind ourselves that our Higher Power always provides enough for us, and that when greed rears its ugly head it is not an indication that we need more food or possessions, but that a deeper hunger within needs to be satisfied.

AFFIRMATION FOR THE DAY: I always have what I need, but not always what I want.

What is food to one, is to others bitter poison.
—Lucretius

One of the worst mistakes a compulsive eater can make is to copy someone else's daily meal plan bite for bite in an attempt to emulate their success or to lose weight. I know, because I tried this several times but always wound up discouraged and feeling like a failure.

Soon after joining my self-help group I found a person who seemed to have her life in order. I decided to copy her macrobiotic diet but found it didn't work for me.

Not only did I quickly tire of tofu and rice, but I found myself panicking at the thought of eating out where I couldn't order my special foods. I experimented instead with moderation in a variety of foods, and discovered that it fit my active lifestyle better and kept me from feeling deprived.

Remember today that there is no one meal plan that will work for everyone. Our best course is to take suggestions from people who are in recovery and then see how they fit with our lives. Whether this means completely eliminating certain "trigger foods," eating everything in moderation, or having numerous small meals each day, allow yourself the freedom to find your own way to abstinence. Keep in mind, too, that one of our goals is to be comfortable around food, not terrorized by it, and that anything that facilitates this is right for us.

AFFIRMATION FOR THE DAY: My meal plan has to work only for me, not anyone else.

All that we are is the result of what we have thought. The mind is everything. What we think, we become.
—BUDDHA

There is a doctor who runs a pain clinic where his patients are only allowed to discuss their pain with the physician during certain hours. They are instructed to think happy, healing thoughts at other times because the studies show that the more you concentrate on something, the more real it becomes.

What images of yourself fill your thoughts? Do you see yourself as vibrant, happy and whole? Or do you picture yourself as a perpetual loser who is unworthy of health, prosperity and spiritual abundance?

Remember today that your thoughts have more power over who you are and how you behave than you probably realize. If you are giving energy to images of an overweight body, bingeing and depression, train yourself to visualize moderation and happiness instead. Make it a point to set aside a period each day when you will think all of your negative thoughts at once, and be done with them for the next twenty-four hours. Then think positively. Don't forget that as helpful as abstinent meals and support group meetings are to recovery, one of the most powerful tools for transformation we possess is our mind.

AFFIRMATION FOR THE DAY: Whatever I can visualize, I can achieve.

Nothing pays like restraint of tongue and pen.
—FROM THE TWELVE STEPS AND TWELVE TRADITIONS OF
ALCOHOLICS ANONYMOUS

You're angry: The florist forgot to deliver roses to your husband on your anniversary, a supposed friend is spreading vicious and untrue rumors about you, and your boss has dressed you down in front of your colleagues.

You pull out a sheet of writing paper or pick up the phone prepared to do battle. You are really going to give these so-and-so's a piece of your mind. They will be so impressed by your persuasiveness, clarity of thought and intelligence that they will immediately admit their fault. *Wrong.*

There is nothing that causes people to dig their heels in the mud and insist on their innocence more than being attacked. Getting back at someone will ensure you of only one thing—bitterness and bad feelings will multiply, and you will get the reputation of being a thin-skinned, short-tempered monster.

The next time you are angry enough to try to get even, resist the impulse to call or write the offending party. Sometimes it's best to do nothing, or to wait until an opportunity arises in the future to gracefully set matters straight. Remember, too, that the old saying "Least said, soonest mended" contains a great deal of truth that we'd be wise to heed.

AFFIRMATION FOR THE DAY: Today I won't let my anger get the best of me.

When thou doest alms, let not thy left hand know what thy right hand doeth.

—MATTHEW 6:3

One day I read about a very wealthy man who wanted to take on a well-known actor as a client. In lieu of charging a fee he suggested instead that the actor donate money to various causes in his name. When reporters got wind of this scheme and asked why the money wasn't just given anonymously, the wealthy man replied, "There's no point in doing good works unless everyone knows who did them."

It goes without saying that this man had an enormous ego and a dire lack of humility. If we only give to charity or do nice things in order to be applauded and recognized, we are doing them for the wrong reasons. And as compulsive eaters who generally lack humility, we need to practice the art of giving without receiving—that is, doing charitable activities with our right hands without letting our left hands know about it.

Do something for someone else today and don't broadcast the fact. Give your time, your love or your money to a worthy cause without thought of acclaim or payback. If you do this religiously, you'll always find that you will be the one who derives the greatest and most lasting benefits from your largesse.

AFFIRMATION FOR THE DAY: When I am generous and let others know about it, my gift is tarnished.

*Do not repeat slander; you should not hear it, for it is
the result of hot temper.*

—Ptahhotpe

As compulsive eaters we are not known for our
high self-esteem, especially while we are actively
practicing our disease. As a result of this, many of us
fall into the trap of putting others down and gossiping
because it is a quick and dirty way to feel superior, if
only for a minute.

At one time I could always be counted on to
know and repeat the latest gossip on others. Naturally, the type of people who gravitated to me were
similar in nature and we used to delight in trashing
other people's reputations.

This attitude is not compatible with recovery. I
learned quickly that slander was not just detrimental
to others, it hurt me by dragging down my self-
esteem. Low self-esteem breeds depression, which
usually results in compulsive eating.

Once I decided to work on not gossiping I
noticed how distasteful it really was. Not only can a
false rumor destroy someone's reputation, but you
begin to wonder what the gossip is saying about you
when your own back is turned. Make it a point today
not to pass along rumors and unsavory speculation.
Bone up on worthwhile and interesting subjects
instead and remember that not gossiping won't make
you boring, it will only make you more likable.

AFFIRMATION FOR THE DAY: It is just as easy to
praise someone as it is to put them down.

Things cannot always go your way.
—Sir William Osler

I used to become petulant and angry when I didn't get my way. Like most compulsive eaters I was accustomed to having everything suit me, and sometimes that meant forcing my will on others. Although we may be able to live this way for a period of time, sooner or later we are going to come up against something bigger and stronger than us that we can't mold to our liking.

The first time a compulsive eater is made aware of his or her powerlessness is an aggravating and unsettling experience. For some it is encountering a person who cannot be manipulated or sweet-talked into giving us what we want; sometimes it's realizing that Mother Nature is going to foil our plans for an outing or vacation; and sometimes it is being unable to control natural events like birth, sickness and death.

Whatever our epiphany, recovery depends on learning that our will isn't omnipotent and that we can't always control people, places and things to our liking. Remind yourself frequently today that life was not created to go your way or anyone else's all the time, and that our maturity and growth involve accepting the limits of our powerlessness and making the best of the hand life deals to us.

AFFIRMATION FOR THE DAY: Life is so much more manageable when I accept that I can't dictate its terms.

The worst sin towards our fellow creatures is not to hate them, but to be indifferent to them: that's the essence of inhumanity.

—George Bernard Shaw

I was once struck by a story I heard about a wealthy lady who had her house cleaned every day by her maid. One day she had guests over and the maid didn't show up so the house was dirty and disheveled. The wealthy lady flew into a tirade when the cleaning woman called, and only after she had vented her spleen did the maid have the opportunity to explain sadly, "My husband died last night and I wasn't able to call you."

Many of us forget that other people have thoughts, feelings and lives that are important to them; we see them only in terms of their value to us. It's less complicated and easier to be indifferent to their troubles because too often we focus only on ourselves and our own needs.

Do you avoid caring about other people's lives because it takes too much energy? Are other people only important to you if they can give you something? If so, fight your indifference today by remembering that everyone you come in contact with has their own concerns and feelings, and that the essence of humanity involves learning to be considerate of someone other than yourself.

AFFIRMATION FOR THE DAY: Today I will put myself in someone else's shoes when I'm tempted to judge them.

It is only our own thoughts that hurt us. It is only our own minds that need to be healed. We are not victims of the world that we see.

—A COURSE IN MIRACLES

For us compulsive eaters, our minds are sometimes our greatest enemies. We frequently misperceive other people's intentions and actions, constantly seeing ourselves as victims of the world. When we feel this way it is easy to slip into a blaming mode, believing that everyone is at fault but us.

When we see ourselves as victims we are acting from a place of fear. Most commonly this occurs when we feel that someone has threatened our self-esteem. Instead of looking at why our self-confidence is so fragile, we go on the attack and fight who we perceive to be our enemy. By always reacting this way we don't allow ourselves to develop open-mindedness, unconditional love or trust.

When I began to recover I was amazed to realize that most of my enemies were in my own head. I never gave others the benefit of the doubt; I attacked first and asked questions later. Ask yourself today if you behave this way, too. If you are tempted to be cynical and always see others as threatening to you, try to look at the situation differently. Once you can move away from the notion of yourself as a victim of the world, you'll find that you are capable of healing your mind and of seeing life in a new, more harmonious way.

AFFIRMATION FOR THE DAY: My thoughts can often hurt me more than events themselves.

You gain strength, courage and confidence by every experience in which you really stop to look fear in the face. . . . You must do the thing you think you cannot do.

—ANNA ELEANOR ROOSEVELT

"I can't" is one of the saddest and most self-limiting phrases in the English language. When we think that we are incapable of trying something we are admitting defeat before the battle has even begun. Enough experience of folding our hands and walking away from challenge is sure to make us into frightened, limited, conventional people.

To learn what we are capable of we have to identify our fears and attack them one by one because that is the only way we will chase them away. One friend of mine who stopped getting promotions at work because she was afraid to learn word processing finally took the bull by the horns and sat in front of a computer with a beginner's book. To her surprise she found that not only did she enjoy computers, but she was good at them. Today she teaches others what she was once so frightened of.

Identify something today that scares you and make the commitment to try it, at least once. Visit the dentist, admit you're wrong about something, go to a movie by yourself and pass up your favorite binge food. When you can do this you'll find that your fears are never as crippling as you think they are, and that you are capable of accomplishing far more than you might have previously given yourself credit for.

AFFIRMATION FOR THE DAY: The fastest way to build self-confidence is to look fear in the eye.

The best things in life are free.
                    —LEW BROWN AND BUDDY DE SYLVA

Several surveys of office workers have consistently shown an interesting finding: Salaries are one of the least important criteria in feeling job satisfaction. In fact, the reasons most often cited as critical in deciding to stay or quit had nothing to do with money. Workers said that if they felt they were important, got verbal feedback for a job well done and had input into the company's direction, they were happy. Building loyalty and self-esteem, it seems, doesn't have to cost a penny.

A lot of compulsive eaters tend to think that the more they spend on someone, the better a friend that makes them. Actually, the opposite is true. Letting someone know you love them and care about them can take the form of a phone call, a note or just a hug. Although it certainly takes more time and effort to help people when we don't just buy a gift or write a check, we'll find that we can do more good and feel better about ourselves if we remember that some of the greatest presents we give to ourselves and others are free.

AFFIRMATION FOR THE DAY: When I give others my time and my love, I give a precious gift.

*If a man does not make new acquaintances as he
advances through life, he will find himself left alone.*
                                    —SAMUEL JOHNSON

I used to think I needed no one in order to be
happy and fulfilled. Therefore whenever I made
friends I always kept certain aspects of my personality
and needs to myself because I didn't want to ever rely
on another person to comfort me, assist me or give me
strength.

My attempts to remain rocklike and independent
crumbled when I began to recover from compulsive
eating. I discovered that if I was to make any headway
I had to learn from others how to cope with life and its
frustrations without turning to food. Although every
fiber in my body fought against asking for advice,
assistance and love, I found that without them my
recovery was impossible. Alone I had no resources to
draw upon; in a community of friends I had vast
amounts of experience and comfort available. The
only price of getting this help was having the humility
to ask for it.

A poet once said, "No man is an island," and I
would add to that, "Nor should he try to be." Because
even though we may be able to fly solo for a short
time, sooner or later we will all find that without the
companionship and love of others we can't travel far
and will eventually crash.

AFFIRMATION FOR THE DAY: Today I won't be an
island.

To be confident is to act in faith.

—BERNARD BYNION

There are times when we all feel useless and unworthy. When I am like this I am hard-pressed to list my strengths or assets. The only thing I can concentrate on is how many mistakes I've made, how many people dislike me and what parts of my body are especially unattractive.

When we lack self-confidence we have to force ourselves to remember that we do have positive qualities, and that not everyone is going to like us all of the time. If our feelings of worthlessness are especially strong, we can call a friend and ask what they think are our best traits and then really absorb what they say. Sometimes we may hear compliments that surprise us, and that, too, will help us feel better about ourselves.

Confidence is a word that is derived from two Latin words meaning "with faith." Remember today that we can't help but be confident when we believe wholeheartedly in what we're doing. If you can be your own biggest fan and not look for outside approval, you'll be surprised by how much you can accomplish.

AFFIRMATION FOR THE DAY: When I believe in myself, others do, too.

Question: How does one go about finding oneself?
Answer: Listen.

—Anonymous

Many people complain that they don't have a
sense of what they are supposed to do in life, in their
profession, or in their personal relationships. They
find themselves careening from one unsatisfying situation to another, hoping that the next change will be
the one that fulfills them. Despite frequent and
well-meaning attempts to find happiness, peace of
mind remains elusive.

For centuries, many religious and spiritual dis-
ciplines have taught that meditation is the finest way
to gain enlightenment. As compulsive people, we
may have considered this avenue to self-understanding but rejected it because we didn't feel we
could do it perfectly enough, long enough, or with
enough dedication to have ethereal experiences.

Throw away your ideas today about what perfect
meditation is because there is no one "right" way. Just
make it a point to still your mind and let your
thoughts wander for a few minutes every day. Ask
your Higher Power for messages and guidance and
then really try to listen. You'll find that when you can
decipher the still, small voice within you'll always
hear the right answers.

AFFIRMATION FOR THE DAY: When ever I pause
to really listen, I will never fail to hear the voice of
truth.

It is not enough to do good; one must do it the right way.
—John, Viscount Morley of Blackburn

When I was new in my recovery someone handed me a set of daily goals that included a challenging one: do something nice for someone else without getting found out.

For a compulsive eater who reveled in attention this was a very difficult task. I had never done anything truly unselfish; I always made sure others knew about it. My gifts were often elaborate and I would ask the recipient whether or not they were pleased. Others like me say they were fond of making sure they even mentioned the price of the gift so that everyone would know how much had been spent.

Although I initially didn't understand how good deeds could help with recovery from compulsive eating, I soon learned that feeding expired parking meters, paying for several cars behind me at toll booths and giving anonymous bouquets of flowers successfully obliterated binge thoughts. Above all, I found that the humility of not being able to tell anyone what I had done helped dismantle my "Notice Me!" attitude.

If giving does not come naturally to you, start small. Say a prayer for another's welfare or put in a good word for a co-worker who wants a promotion. As this behavior becomes second nature, unselfish giving will soon be as normal as breathing and you'll wonder why it took you so long to discover the fulfillment it brings.

AFFIRMATION FOR THE DAY: I will perform an anonymous good deed today and not let anyone else know about it.

*April prepares her green traffic light and the world
thinks Go.*

—CHRISTOPHER MORLEY

Spring is a glorious time during which the earth
begins her yearly transformation from winter barren-
ness to colorful blossoms and lush greenery. It is hard
for most people to be depressed when the days are
getting longer, birds are beginning to sing, forsythia is
blooming and trees are budding.

When someone is eating compulsively, though, the
change of seasons often passes joylessly, if noticed at all.
Beautiful days are often spent in a food hangover with
the shades drawn and the covers pulled over one's head.
Instead of reveling in the loveliness of nature the compulsive eater usually worries about wearing swimsuits
and revealing summer clothes, then begins an unbalanced diet which creates mood swings and depression.

Resolve that your attitude toward spring this year
will be healthy and positive. Concentrate on enjoying
outdoor activities as the days lengthen and sunshine is
more abundant. Lighten up your diet as fresh fruits and
vegetables become more available. And above all, as
nature renews itself and the world becomes bright and
fresh once more, take time to renew your commitment
to a recovering lifestyle and greet each day with the zest
and joy that once were denied you.

AFFIRMATION FOR THE DAY: The seasonal renewal of nature reminds me that I am continuing to
grow, change and renew every day, too.

Laugh and the world laughs with you; weep, and you weep alone.

—ELLA WHEELER WILCOX

People used to think I was terribly mature, even as a young girl. The truth of the matter was that I took everything so seriously, especially myself, that I never laughed or found joy in anything. It's also easy to appear mature when you look somber all the time and when "play" is a word that has no meaning in your life.

When we start to recover, we usually start to lighten up and allow ourselves to be childlike at times. Although we can't gloss over or forget the gravity of our disease, being able to see the funnier moments in our difficult pasts, or even during the trials of recovery, can help us accept ourselves and our lives better.

If you feel you are too "mature" to be light-hearted, then you are setting yourself up for a life of loneliness. Find something to laugh about today, even if it's something that only you find amusing. Surround yourself with people who are fun and self-effacing and let yourself shake off some of the adult armor that prevents you from connecting with others and enjoying the gaiety of a recovering life.

AFFIRMATION FOR THE DAY: I know I am getting well if I can laugh genuinely and easily several times today.

Life is just one damned thing after another.
—FRANK WARD O'MALLEY

There are times when I've looked at other people's lives and wondered how they could go on in the face of some of the catastrophes that have befallen them. For example, one friend's husband killed himself in a depression, leaving behind mountains of unpaid bills and other obligations. Another friend's daughter was killed with her fiancé by a drunk driver as they were preparing for their wedding.

I asked both these people later how they had managed to go on living, working and functioning after such immense tragedies. Both had uttered the same reply: "I don't know. I guess you just do what you have to do." They emphasized the importance of taking each day as a single unit and not thinking about the future. They also said that they had been surprised to find that they possessed far more inner strength than they had thought possible.

The world is going to contain unpleasant surprises for all of us, and what we'll usually discover is that somehow we're going to cope with those setbacks, whether we think we can right now or not. Accept today that life is just "one damned thing after another" and work on developing unshakable confidence in the strength that flows from your Higher Power. Once you know that that support is always there for you, your life will be infinitely more manageable.

AFFIRMATION FOR THE DAY: My inner resources are always deeper than I think.

[We] *made a decision to turn our will and life over to the care of God as we understood Him.*
— STEP THREE OF OVEREATERS ANONYMOUS

For people in a self-help group such as Overeaters Anonymous, "taking the third" is one of the greatest acts of self-love in recovery. By asking a God of our own understanding to comfort and care for us, we are saying, "I love myself enough to ask for help and to trust that it will be given to me."

What many find hardest about this step is being able to remain serene in the belief that they are being cared for. They see that life isn't working out to their specifications and they will jump back into control, trying to make things go their way. When this happens to me I inevitably create problems and confusion, reminding me once more that my Higher Power is wiser than I am, and that He knows my needs better than I do.

Remember today that the act of turning your will and life over to a Higher Power is not something you do just once; sometimes it's an exercise we have to go through many times each day. Although it may take years before our stubborn, independent natures can yield to something greater than ourselves, we'll always find that relinquishing control results in better, more productive, results.

AFFIRMATION FOR THE DAY: Putting my Higher Power in the driver's seat is a freedom, not a restraint.

Where there is no vision, the people perish.
                                        —PROVERBS 29:18

I once worked with a man who was world-renowned for his sweeping vision of urban life. I was fascinated by how grand his dreams and observations were. There wasn't anything he thought couldn't be accomplished with optimism and faith in the power of the human spirit.

For every ten ideas this man had, nine didn't work. But there was always one that was bolder and contained more genius than anything previously considered by his peers. He was never discouraged by his "failures"; he just focused on bringing to fruition the one concept that was workable.

The greatest lesson I learned during my years with this person was that creativity and growth require vision. Allow yourself today to have a vision of where you are going and what you hope to accomplish. Don't be deterred if some of your dreams don't bear fruit and if other people laugh at you. Place no limits on your imagination and remain optimistic, because without your vision a large part of you will, indeed, perish.

AFFIRMATION FOR THE DAY: When I can't dream big dreams, I have no faith in my abilities or my Higher Power.

Keep your sunny side up.
> —LEW BROWN AND BUDDY DE SYLVA

There is a new field in medicine called "psycho-neuroimmunology." Roughly translated this means that your inner thoughts and emotions affect you physically. Researchers have documented cases of patients who appear to be able to overcome life-threatening diseases by focusing on positive thoughts, seeing themselves as healthy and mentally chasing away negative beliefs.

This technique can benefit us in our recovery. For too long we have given time and energy to nurturing images of ourselves as weak, defeated and imperfect. Instead of finding good things about ourselves to concentrate on, we have frequently focused obsessively on our perceived flaws and mistakes.

Start today by finding the "sunny side" of yourself and meditating on it. If you don't feel there is a sunny side, act "as if" and pretend that you already possess the trait you desire. You'll find that as soon as you can see yourself in a positive, loving way, it won't be long before you are precisely the type of person you once only dreamed of becoming.

AFFIRMATION FOR THE DAY: If there is a quality I wish to embody, I will "fake it till I make it."

I was early taught to work as well as play; my life has been one long happy holiday. Full of work and full of play—I dropped the worry on the way.
　　　　　　　　　　　　—JOHN D. ROCKEFELLER

One day I received a letter in the mail from a woman who was recovering from an eating disorder. She was a subscriber to a newsletter I publish for people with eating disorders, and although she thought the articles were helpful she felt a key ingredient was missing: a column called "Focus Off Food." She emphasized that too often our lives revolve around eating or not eating, and that in recovery we needed to focus on new hobbies and pastimes that have nothing to do with food.

Her point is well taken. We can't really say we are free of our food obsession if we are still talking about food, spending a lot of time in the kitchen and incessantly reading recipe books or restaurant reviews. How long do you think an alcoholic could stay sober working in a bar, discussing the fine points of decanting wine? Not very long I don't think.

As part of continuing to take the focus off food in your life, pick up some new hobbies to fill the spare hours during your days. Although my eating disorder took away the pleasure I once received from some activities, I have replaced them with new ones like needlepoint and yoga. Other friends of mine have taken up jazz dancing, scuba diving and playing the guitar as part of their recovery. What can you do today to take the focus off food?

AFFIRMATION FOR THE DAY: When I know how to incorporate play into my day, I deemphasize food and eliminate worry.

People who love soft words and hate iniquity forget this, that reform consists in taking a bone away from a dog. Philosophy will not do this.

—JOHN JAY CHAPMAN

There's a limit to how far reading great thoughts and listening to inspirational sermons will take you when you are trying to change yourself. Words are just words until they are put into action. It won't do us any good to read self-help books or motivational pamphlets unless we go that extra step and actively incorporate the recommended principles into our lives.

To reform ourselves we do need to take away some of our "bones." Like stubborn dogs, many of the behaviors that hinder our recovery are similar to bones that we hang on to because they make us comfortable, not because they're good for us. We also aren't sure whether the replacement will satisfy us or bring us pleasure, so we hold fast to what we already have as long as possible and resist any attempts to change.

Decide today to give up one of your "bones." Identify a comfortable habit that you know isn't entirely beneficial for you but that you haven't had the courage to get rid of yet. We need to remember that just as children eventually leave behind safety blankets and favorite toys, maturing and moving forward means outgrowing people and attitudes that no longer serve us well.

AFFIRMATION FOR THE DAY: Positive change usually involves making painful sacrifices.

In quietness and in confidence shall be your strength.
—Isaiah 30:15

So often our lives are filled with disruptions and noise. We get in the car and immediately turn on the radio. We enter a quiet house and turn on the television. When we face a lull in our day, we pick up the phone and call someone.

Being alone and at peace with our thoughts is one of the most useful things we can do for our recovery because when we are quiet we have the opportunity to renew our bond with our Higher Power and to review any situations in our lives that need attention.

When I was younger I participated in an outdoor survival course which included a three-day, three-night "solo." During this time we were to see no one, eat nothing and drink only water. The goal was to get to know ourselves better. All I remember doing was making endless lists of food I wanted to eat.

Now I use my quiet time more wisely. Instead of filling the air with music or unnecessary talk, I try to get in touch with my inner self. I let myself dream without distraction and just allow my thoughts to come and go as they may. Sometimes I am surprised by my insights and reactions, but I am always enriched by them.

Give yourself the gift of quiet time today and don't be frightened by it. Learning to be comfortable with ourselves is a goal of recovery, and this can only happen when we create opportunities to be alone.

AFFIRMATION FOR THE DAY: When I am quiet and confident, I radiate strength.

Embrace simplicity.

—LAO-TZU

Compulsive eaters love to complicate things. We often gravitate to the center of family problems, office conflicts and difficult situations. We seem to need to project the confusion and disharmony within onto the people and events around us because we may never have known anything but chaos in our personal lives, and the idea of simple solutions isn't exciting enough.

As hard as it may be for us, recovering from compulsive eating means learning to "keep it simple." This applies not just to our food plans but to our responses to crises and other events in our lives. If we take a moment to center ourselves before we respond to events and ask ourselves what the most direct and simple course of action is, we'll find that life is infinitely less complicated and troublesome than we once thought it was.

Examine your life and your surroundings today. Is your house cluttered and in disarray? Do you overdress and wear too much makeup? Are all of your friendships fraught with strings, conflicts and unresolved emotions? If so, pare down to the essentials today and try to understand why you prefer confusion to harmony. When you begin to decipher this dilemma you will have opened the door to self-understanding and serenity.

AFFIRMATION FOR THE DAY: The less I own and the fewer things I desire, the simpler and easier my life will be.

We must get rid of fear.

—THOMAS CARLYLE

How many of us, when facing a big problem, quiver in fear and retreat? Overwhelmed by the enormity of the problem we usually find some excuse to ignore it, hoping it will disappear or that someone else will take care of it.

One successful businessman I know keeps a big thistle plant in his office to teach new hires how to deal with this issue. During their first meeting together the man asks the new employees to go over and pluck a thistle from the plant. Usually they recoil in fear when they tentatively touch the prickles but, with encouragement, they find that grabbing the thistle boldly and ignoring the momentary pricks leads the thistle to painlessly crumble in their hands.

This story can help us as we face fearful situations in our lives. If we cower when we start to address a problem because it hurts, our fears will be the masters of us. But if we grab our dilemmas with both hands, we'll always find that the solutions are less painful than we might have thought and that our problems always will crumble in the face of boldness and courage.

AFFIRMATION FOR THE DAY: When I seize my difficulties with both hands, I crush them effortlessly.

My yoke is easy, and my burden is light.
—MATTHEW 11:30

In the past my tendency was always to think that my life and my troubles were far more momentous than anyone else's. It was precisely this type of self-centered thinking that kept me enmeshed in self-pity and my eating disorder for a good number of years.

If we take a moment to expand our horizons, we will find people who have much greater crosses to bear than we do. In the newspaper there are countless stories about families who have lost their homes and all of their possessions in a fire, children who have died in accidental shootings, and people who have been laid off in middle age with families to support and no immediate prospects for employment. Reading articles like these makes it possible to put our woes into perspective and give thanks for what we do have.

Serenity and joyful recovery come from accepting the crosses we have been asked to bear and in making the best of whatever they are. Now, whenever I feel myself slipping into the "poor me" frame of mind, I remind myself that my load is far lighter than the one many others carry, and that my Higher Power will only give me what He knows I can handle.

AFFIRMATION FOR THE DAY: Instead of fighting my crosses, I will bear them with the strength I know I possess.

The path is one for all, the means to reach the goal must vary with the pilgrims.
—THE TIBETAN DOCTRINE

I once had a close friend whom I spoke with daily and shared many ideas, hugs and dreams with. Our friendship ended, however, because she informed me one day that I was probably not going to have a happy afterlife because we didn't share the same view on religion. She urged me to convert to her faith so that I would be "saved" and assured of going to heaven, and so that she wouldn't have to worry so much about my salvation anymore.

I didn't believe then, and don't believe now, that there is only one path to spiritual enlightenment. I find it difficult to accept that a loving God only favors certain religious traditions, particularly when some of the tenets separating various faiths are so minor.

How do you feel about your spirituality? Do you think you have a corner on the God market? Do you spend more time trying to convert people to your way of thinking than in trying to improve yourself? Remember today that there are as many paths to abstinence as there are to spirituality, and that the only way that is the "right" way is the one that works for you.

AFFIRMATION FOR THE DAY: Today I will remember that pilgrims walk down many different paths.

The most decisive actions of our life . . . are most often unconsidered actions.

—ANDRÉ GIDE

The saddest words in the English language are "I wish I had . . ." They bespeak frustration at not having had the courage to try something new, as well as remorse about the past. The people who utter these words have usually locked a desire or dream deep inside and never done anything about it, only to be filled with regret in later years that they couldn't bring themselves to take a risk.

Don't let this happen to you. Instead of pushing a dream away, try to find a way to manifest it. There will always be safety in numbers and conventional actions, but it is the people who dare to be different who have the ability to change the course of their lives and make their hopes come true.

Even if you fail at trying something you dearly want to do, you'll know you gave it your best shot and you won't set yourself up to wonder in future years what you might have accomplished with a little more courage. What are your secret, unconsidered actions? Do they nag at you, begging you to give them a shot? If so, try today to honor your inner desires because you just may find yourself taking a decisive and life-changing step.

AFFIRMATION FOR THE DAY: Today I will take an unconsidered action.

The quest for perfection is spelt paralysis.
—WINSTON CHURCHILL

One of our most common shortcomings as compulsive eaters has been the notion that everything we undertook—whether it was schoolwork, raising children or dieting—had to be perfect. Our unrealistic standards allowed no deviation for slips. So when we were less than perfect we vented our frustrations and anger on ourselves and those around us.

To desire perfection is to plan for failure. Babies who learn to walk only do so after falling down repeatedly. A child doesn't avoid hot stoves until he is burned. And every great commander who has won battles has lost skirmishes along the way.

Our motto needs to be "Progress, not perfection." Our expectations for ourselves need to be flexible enough so that we can have a slip with our food plan, or an angry outburst, without feeling like a failure. We must remember that it is our task to work on self-improvement on a daily basis, but that when we start with a goal of perfection, we are guaranteed to be paralyzed.

AFFIRMATION FOR THE DAY: Today I will accept myself just as I am.

Be nice to people on your way up because you'll meet 'em on your way down.

—WILSON MIZNER

There was a celebrated trial of a wealthy man in California who was once accused of not paying his taxes and of billing his employer for all sorts of personal items and services. A mean and imperious person, this man had humiliated and made fun of scores of men and women on his way to the pinnacle of the Los Angeles social and business scene.

It was these men and women who ultimately did this person in because so many of them took delight in testifying against him. Had he been a little kinder over the years it's conceivable that it may not have been as easy to convict him. As it was, he had bruised so many egos and behaved so poorly that they were only too happy to cut him down to size.

Remember this lesson because recovery often brings an upturn in our lives, and be careful of how you deal with your newfound triumphs. If you become curt, selfish and self-important with people because you suddenly feel superior and better than them—beware. The same people you give short shrift to now could easily be the ones who will be in a position to help you later. Also keep in mind that our successes are frequently due to luck, others' help, and our Higher Power—not just our own efforts—and that we must not forget to be grateful and generous as we begin to experience the joys of prosperity that often accompany recovery.

AFFIRMATION FOR THE DAY: Gratitude and humility are essential to my recovery.

*Seek ye first the kingdom of God and his righteous-
ness, and all these things shall be added unto you.*
—MATTHEW 6:33

To be happy we have to have our priorities in order.
But many of us don't even know where to start—we aren't
sure if our recovery, our jobs, our families or our friends
should be at the top of the list. All seem equally important
to us and we feel that giving any one of them short shrift
will pave the way for disaster.

I've learned through trial and error that my greatest success and happiness come when my top priority is
carrying out what I feel my Higher Power wants me to
do. Listening to Him takes many forms; sometimes I
meditate, sometimes I heed inner promptings and
occasionally a special person will enter my life and guide
me in certain areas. When my spiritual side feels
connected I need less and love more. My troubles only
seem to arise when I ignore this aspect of recovery and
think only about concrete, material things that will
boost my ego.

If you are feeling directionless today, seek first
what your Higher Power wants for you. Silently ask
what it is you need to do and where you need to be,
and then pay attention to the answers you receive.
Although you may not initially agree with or like the
"messages", you'll find that heeding your inner wisdom is the best way to have "these things . . .
added unto you."

AFFIRMATION FOR THE DAY: My Higher Power
knows what I need to feel fulfilled, and if I listen, I'll
know, too.

Beauty in things exists in the mind which contemplates them.

—David Hume

One night I was idly watching a national beauty pageant that made my blood start to simmer. Although the contest ostensibly valued talent, the focus of the judges was on physical perfection. The commentators even noted that most of the contestants had undergone cosmetic surgery, relentless dieting and extreme exercising to reach this supposed pinnacle of American attractiveness.

Although I, too, used to see beauty only in thin, long-legged, symmetrically perfect women, or dark, handsome men, now I see attractiveness in people who may not rate that second look. Today I find that a genuine smile, a giving nature and the ability to be a loyal friend better define the word "beauty" to me.

Make a list of people you consider attractive. If your focus is still on outward appearances rather than inner qualities, it will prevent you from nourishing your inner spirit. Keep in mind, too, that if you want to be honorable, kind and giving, those have to be the qualities you most value in others.

AFFIRMATION FOR THE DAY: Real beauty has nothing to do with my measurements, my looks or my weight.

Play it down and pray it up.

—ANONYMOUS

We compulsive eaters usually have one tendency in common: When faced with difficult dilemmas we hang on to them relentlessly. Instead of relaxing our grip on the problem we resolutely try various solutions—all man-made—which often make the situation worse. Instead of conceding defeat and asking others for help, we're liable to continue this way indefinitely, unaware of how much we are harming ourselves.

Wiser souls know it's a waste of time to flail about looking for answers ourselves. These men and women choose to get out of their own way, turn the problem over to a Higher Power and await guidance. Some use a "God Box" for this exercise, which involves writing worries down on paper, putting them into a container and then seeing what happens. God Boxes can come in all shapes and sizes; some people use a paper bag, some a Bible and others an old coffee can. It is the process of letting go, not the container itself, that is important.

Resolve today to let go of whatever is bothering you. Allow yourself to admit that you don't have all the answers and that turning the problem over to your Higher Power—through a God Box or some other way—will always give you the solutions and peace of mind you are seeking.

AFFIRMATION FOR THE DAY: Today I'll pray it up.

If at first you don't succeed, try, try again.
—WILLIAM EDWARD HICKSON

All of us have at one time or another felt that prayer was useless. Maybe we have repeatedly prayed for a successful outcome to a thorny business or personal problem, yet not seen any results. As a result, we've begun to believe that God doesn't exist.

There was a time when I faced overwhelming difficulties that threatened to destroy everything I had worked for years to create. I saw doors closing all around me and began to panic. In desperation I called a prayer line where a man reminded me that when we pray, we must do so with the attitude that our problems will be solved. I uncomfortably realized that as hard and as often as I had prayed, I had done so with a heavy heart and the certainty that nothing I did mattered. I had expected no solutions, thus I had received none.

We have to remember that we not only should be persistent with our prayers, but we also must expect good to happen. When I feel stymied and unsuccessful in my contacts with my Higher Power now, I don't give up. I just readjust my attitude and try again—sometimes a day or two later. When I can do this I find that the old slogan "Persistence breaks resistance" comes true every time.

AFFIRMATION FOR THE DAY: When I pray and expect solutions, they always come, even if they aren't what I had anticipated.

To build a better world, build a better you.
—ANONYMOUS

I have a friend who is active in all kinds of "save" movements. She works to save whales, trees, battered women and the environment. Virtually all her free time is spent on one cause or another, and rarely does she ever devote time to nurturing herself.

I wish I could say that my friend is a happy, fulfilled person—but she's not. Her appearance is frequently disheveled and she carries around twenty extra pounds which she continually complains about. The lack of time to exercise keeps her from feeling healthy and vital, and she says she often finds herself taking her frustrations out on her husband and children.

Is toiling away on various social issues more important than working on yourself and your own well-being? I think not. If my friend felt better about herself, her family relationships and her body, she would contribute far more to the world than she does now because every person whose path she crossed during the day would benefit from her serenity and self-confidence. We need to remember as we recover that if we want to improve the world we must start with our most valuable contribution—ourselves.

AFFIRMATION FOR THE DAY: As important as it is to help others, I must help myself first.

Touch is metamorphosis.

—JOHN CHEEVER

When I was bulimic, the idea of touching another person in friendship was alien—even scary—to me. I felt so isolated and alone in my disease that I found it impossible to relate normally to others and resisted the notion that holding someone's hand as I prayed, or giving them a loving hug, could help me.

Much research has been done on the healing power of touch in recent years. Hospital patients who are touched by their nurses and doctors recover more quickly than patients who receive no contact, and shoppers who are briefly touched when they are paying for their groceries report higher feelings of self-esteem later than those who are deliberately not touched. Touching also brings physical benefits such as lower blood pressure and calmer heart rates.

Make sure that you get enough physical contact today to enhance your well-being. Hug a friend, get a soothing massage and touch someone gently in a way that lets them know you appreciate them. As you allow your energy to mingle with that of others and you reinforce your positive emotions through contact, you may find any lingering feelings of isolation and lovelessness disappearing.

AFFIRMATION FOR THE DAY: When I am afraid to touch or be touched, I cut myself off from genuine love.

There is no such thing as "best" in the world of individuals.
—HOSEA BELLOU

One of the most common handicaps we compulsive eaters struggle with is the need to be special and different. We aren't content to be one of many in anything we do, therefore we constantly find ourselves avoiding challenges and opportunities because we prefer to be the big fish in a small pond.

I know a woman who tried to leave the small pond without success. All her life she had received awards and accolades that led her to believe that she was destined to be the tops in whatever she chose to do. It was a rude awakening for her to find herself at a big corporation where there were a number of men and women who had similar, if not better, qualifications. No longer the standout she had always perceived herself as, this woman began to lose interest in her job because she wasn't obviously "the best" anymore. It wasn't long before she joined a smaller firm where she was the only person in her field and could feel special again.

We need to remember that there are going to be a lot of people we will meet and work with during our lives who are more professionally skilled, better-looking and smarter than we are. Our response doesn't need to be envy, scorn and a retreat to a cocoon where we can feel unique. In recovery, we can learn to be mature and to accept that we are all special and different in our own ways, and that instead of judging ourselves and others as "winners" or "losers," we can all just participate in life together.

AFFIRMATION FOR THE DAY: Today I'll remember that I can be the best I can possibly be without having to feel superior to everyone else.

If you do not find peace in yourself you will never find it anywhere else.

— PAULA A. BENDRY

I once thought inner peace flowed from the acquisition of fine clothes, big homes, nice children, and foreign trips. Because of this mind-set I used to jump from job to job and achievement to achievement, certain that happiness was right around the corner with the next big raise or pair of beautiful shoes.

My former attitude reminds me of a woman I know who carried around feelings of inferiority and resentment for years. She started to think her husband was her problem, especially after she ran into a childhood sweetheart one day who made her feel attractive and desirable. Soon she was having an affair, but instead of feeling better about herself, she felt worse. The inner peace she had sought was now more elusive than ever, and she finally saw that she was the person who needed to change—not her husband.

When we catch ourselves thinking that we'd be happier if we owned certain things or had ego-boosting experiences, that's a good sign that our inner spirits need healing. If you are lacking self-esteem and self-love today, don't make the mistake of thinking that being on the cover of a magazine, getting a raise or winning a sports event is going to fulfill you. Peace within never comes from externals; it only comes to those who invest time, patience and hard work into challenging, confronting and resolving contradictions inside themselves.

AFFIRMATION FOR THE DAY: There is no person, place or thing that can substitute for the serenity I can find inside myself.

Thunder, wind and earthquakes instantly evoke a sense of unfathomable power. But sometimes, the simplest things contain equal amounts of God: babies, fingernails, bugs, Popsicle sticks, smiles, tears.
—KEITH HARING

One day I did a poll of my friends and asked them when they had felt closest to their Higher Power. One man told me it had been while watching his son's birth, another told me it had been late one night when an odd sense of peace had descended upon him while grieving his mother's death, and an older woman swore that in the quiet lull after thunderstorms she felt most at one with her God.

I once thought that church was the only place one felt the presence of a Higher Power. I've learned from wise, spiritual people, however, that often our Higher Powers are closest to us when we're least expecting it—for example, while washing dishes, taking a walk, feeling helpless or experiencing a new sensation.

As you go through your day today look for the small manifestations of your Higher Power. The sunrise, your children, a friend's smile and an abstinent meal are all miracles that carry the stamp of a loving universal presence. Broaden your restrictive view of a Higher Power if you can only feel His presence at designated times, because the joy and comfort of the God of our understanding is available to us at all times during each day in a variety of situations.

AFFIRMATION FOR THE DAY: Today I will see my Higher Power in ways that I may not have previously considered.

To be able to say how much you love is to love but little.
—PETRARCH

I know someone who says she "loves" everyone. No one is immune from her affection; she loves her mailman, boss, children and casual acquaintances. The word, which is special to me, seems to have lost its worth to this woman, and what she doesn't realize is that everyone she claims to love feels like just one of the bunch.

On the flip side, I listened to a friend complain one day about how her husband never took the time to say he loved her. When she asked him why, he responded that she should know how much he cared about her because he supported the family, took out the garbage, gave her birthday presents and didn't cheat on her. He felt that saying the word "love" was just redundant.

Do you identify with one of these scenarios? Are you too generous with the word "love," perhaps because you don't know how special and intimate it can be with a close circle of people? Or do you fear that just saying the word makes you too vulnerable to exposing your inner emotions?

When you use the word "love" today, use it judiciously. Remember that your affection is a precious gift that is not to be bestowed lightly, but one you do need to share with the people who mean the most to you through words and thoughtful actions.

AFFIRMATION FOR THE DAY: When I can express my love for the people who are important to me, I feel my heart open.

You can be a child only once—but you can be immature forever.

—Anonymous

When we start to recover from compulsive eating we usually discover that we stopped maturing at whatever point our disease overtook our actions and emotions. While others were learning to cope with life and its tribulations, we were busy eating and hiding. The result, we now find, is that we have immature personalities in adult bodies.

When I started to recover from bulimia at the age of twenty-two, I felt and acted like a wide-eyed adolescent. Normal socializing of teenage years, learning to deal with rebellious feelings and discovering who I was had all passed me by. I had no idea how to form and articulate my opinions, I was afraid that disagreement would always lead to others disliking me, and I usually felt tongue-tied and flustered in social situations.

We have a choice to make when we start to recover. We can either stay stuck in our immaturity or we can take the difficult, but necessary, step of becoming responsible adults. If you are feeling immature and lost today, you are going through a common stage of recovery. Don't give up; find people who have the qualities and behaviors you want and stick close to them. Although the language and interchanges of normal adult actions may feel odd at first, if you persevere you'll find that it won't be long before your chronological age and your emotional age catch up with each other.

AFFIRMATION FOR THE DAY: It is my choice to grow up or remain an adolescent.

*If you want to be miserable, think about yourself, about
what you want, what you like, what respect people
ought to pay you, and what people think of you.*
—Charles Kingsley

The 1980s were commonly called the "Me Decade"
in America. A lot of people placed undue importance on
satisfying themselves, making a lot of money and feeling
good at the expense of others. As compulsive eaters
many of us probably behaved this way, not just during
these years, but throughout our entire lives.

Although we may know intuitively that self-
centeredness isn't good for us, there is also medical
evidence showing that it may shorten your life. Researchers have found that people who use the words "I,"
"me" and "my" a great deal are more apt to develop
heart disease than their less self-absorbed peers. Self-
centered people view themselves as separate from
others which leads to social isolation, depression and
hostility—all known contributors to heart disease.

If we see this trait in ourselves, a prescription could
be replacing "I" and "me" with "you" and "we" more
often. There is another fast way to forget your own
problems: get involved in helping someone else. Call a
friend, write a letter or do some volunteer work. It's
amazing how quickly our own problems and concerns
can recede in importance when we take the time and
energy to think of someone other than ourselves.

AFFIRMATION FOR THE DAY: If I am feeling
miserable, it's unlikely that I'm concerned about
anyone else's welfare.

Train up a child in the way he should go, and when he is old, he will not depart from it.

—Proverbs 22:6

When I came home from the hospital with my first child, I remember looking down at his tiny blond head one night and feeling overwhelmed by the enormity of being a parent. I worried that I wouldn't be compassionate enough or wise enough to give him the tools he needs to be successful and happy in life.

Too often we compulsive eaters fear that we won't be good enough role models, that we'll make irreparable mistakes and that we aren't up to the challenge of being selfless and mature. If we are from dysfunctional families we may be concerned that some of the negative experiences we had will be repeated in our own homes.

Although some of our fears may be well-founded, being a parent is a golden opportunity to practice giving unconditional love to both your children and yourself. Recovery brings self-awareness, which enables us to create the type of loving home we may not have had as children but that we can choose for ourselves and our own children now.

If you have the blessing of being a parent, allow yourself to feel the same love for yourself today that you feel for your children. When you say "I love you" to them, say it to yourself as well. You'll find the more you share your affection and kindness with your family and friends, the more you will be able to give it to yourself.

AFFIRMATION FOR THE DAY: I can be a loving, wise and fair parent to my children if I am that way with myself.

Instead of heavy duty, try putting yourself on the gentle cycle.

—ANONYMOUS

One day while doing my laundry, I was struck by the fact that I had never changed the setting on my washing machine. I washed all of my clothes—delicate, colors and permanent press—on the heavy duty cycle, and always used the hottest water possible. Needless to say, I had ruined some beautiful things over the years.

The way I once washed my clothes is analogous to how I used to treat myself. I was always hard on myself and found it difficult to cut myself any slack. If something didn't go my way I blamed myself for being stupid, lazy or ineffective. It never occurred to me to forgive myself for my mistakes, or to see that I wasn't always the one at fault.

Although I still don't handle the laundry perfectly, I do try to put myself on the gentle cycle more often now. I don't automatically assume that I'm a failure if something I'm doing doesn't work out, and I don't harshly berate myself when I've been wrong. Remember today that just as our clothes require a variety of settings on a washing machine, we, too, have to give ourselves delicate treatment at times.

AFFIRMATION FOR THE DAY: Today I will be gentle with myself.

*Yea, though I walk through the valley of the shadow
of death, I will fear no evil for thou art with me.*
—PSALMS 23:4

When we are experiencing troubles, it's hard to
remember that there is a Higher Power with us,
protecting and watching out for us. Times of sadness and
great stress usually provoke me to rant and rave about
how unfair life is and how my Higher Power doesn't care
about me.

One day I read a story about how a man grappled
with this issue. He was a habitual jogger who usually
exercised at daybreak. One morning he left a bit earlier
than normal and found his familiar path illuminated only
by street lamps. He started to notice that as he approached the lights his shadow would grow larger, then
disappear in the full glare of the lamp, and finally
reappear as he padded back out into the darkness. It
occurred to him that his Higher Power was like his
shadow: sometimes large, sometimes small, sometimes
visible, sometimes invisible, but always attached
whether he could see it or not.

This story helped me a great deal because my
faith often wavers, disappears, and then reappears at
various times, testing my belief in the God of my
understanding. I have found like the jogger, though,
that if I can stay on my feet and keep running through
the dark times of my life, knowing that my Higher
Power is invisible to me yet still right there, His
presence will be known to me again before long.

AFFIRMATION FOR THE DAY: Today I will remember that like my shadow, my Higher Power is
never far away.

All I want to do is stay home with my dog. He loves me. He waits for me to come home. He jumps up and I give him a cookie. What more could a man want?
—CHARLES M. SCHULZ

Many of us have the erroneous belief that once we obtain something material we will finally be happy. Sometimes it's a car, sometimes it's a new relationship, and sometimes it's a new wardrobe. When we do get what we want, though, inevitably we tire of the new diversion, become dissatisfied, then start the "if I only had that, I'd be happy" cycle again.

I used to think that any one of the following items would bring lasting happiness: attending a good college, getting married, having a fulfilling job, losing weight, owning my own house and having a baby. Over the years I achieved all of these things, though, and not once did I experience permanent fulfillment. I could have easily gone on for years identifying and going after other external goals had a wise woman not confronted me and encouraged me to focus instead on nourishing my self-esteem, spirituality and independence.

If we have a strong grounding and accept ourselves fully, big-ticket items won't be the things we seek to feel good about ourselves. Simple pleasures like rocking a baby to sleep, sitting on a beach at sunrise or doing our jobs well will give us the peace and good feelings that we once thought came from expensive possessions and external acclaim. Strive today to find your contentment in the small, often unnoticed, moments of your day and remember that the ones that usually bring you the most satisfaction are often free.

AFFIRMATION FOR THE DAY: The simplest pleasures often bring me the most joy.

God setteth the solitary in families.

—PSALMS 68:6

A lot of people call or write me to ask how I learned to overcome bulimia. When I tell them that my biggest aid came from participating in a self-help group for compulsive eaters, their response is usually, "Oh, I hate groups. I could never do something like that."

That used to be my attitude, too. When my bulimia was in full flower I was isolated and avoided all contact with people. Because I had such trouble even admitting to myself that I had an eating disorder, the idea of discussing it openly in a group was unthinkable. But desperate, miserable, and with nothing left to lose, I had given the self-help group a try only to find that it became the most important factor involved in saving my life.

If we are serious about recovering from compulsive eating, we have to take some measures that we may not like and one of these may be going to group meetings where we can listen to and interact with people who understand us. Remember today that if you are feeling "solitary" and alone, there are lots of other people out there who are fighting the same battle as you are, and that building a "family" around yourself is one of the most effective ways there is to heal, dissolve shame and develop self-acceptance.

AFFIRMATION FOR THE DAY: I can't feel isolated when I have a recovering "family" around me.

Even God cannot change the past.

—AGATHON

When we begin to recover from our eating disorders, most of us are mortified by memories of our past behavior. Now that our minds are clearer and our moods are steadier, we can evaluate our previous actions with more clarity. And when our angry words, immature behavior and petty jealousies come to mind, we are often filled with a burning desire to undo the past.

When I first started to recover I was overcome with sorrow at the many years I had lost while in the grip of my eating disorder. It was devastating to think about the high school and college years I could never replace, the friendships and activities I had ignored in favor of a binge, and the social outings I had skipped because I felt bloated or wanted to exercise away extra calories.

I've since learned that crying over the past is a waste of time. We can't undo the past; all we can do is forgive ourselves and others for mistakes, change, and then move on. Losing ourselves in a morass of if-onlys and what-ifs is a sure way to prevent ourselves from moving into a new and richer life, and from appreciating all of the steps and missteps that have brought us to a place of recovery today.

AFFIRMATION FOR THE DAY: Where I am today is more important than where I was before.

You cannot teach a man anything. . . . You can only help him to find it within himself.

—GALILEO GALILEI

One day a man called to talk to me about his wife's eating disorder. He wanted to know what to do to help her lose the forty or fifty extra pounds that were plaguing her and ruining her self-esteem. "I don't bring home sweets, I tell her I love her, and I never compare her to other women," he said. "But she keeps eating when I'm not around and won't stop. I don't know what to do!"

After an hour of talking, he began to realize that the problem was out of his hands. As much as he wanted his formerly slim and attractive wife back, he was powerless to make her do something she wasn't prepared to do. In fact, he saw for the first time that he was enabling her behavior by making excuses for her absences from parties, catering to her moods and keeping his frustrations to himself. He finally decided to address his own codependency issues instead of trying to change his wife.

Are we just like this man? Do we think that we can make another person do something just because we want it to happen? Remember today that trying to change another person to suit us is always going to be futile and pointless, but that with work we can change our own reactions and attitudes so that our desire to remake other people lessens or disappears completely.

AFFIRMATION FOR THE DAY: The only behavior I can control is my own.

Failure is, in a sense, the highway to success; inasmuch as every discovery of what is false leads us to seek earnestly after what is true, and every fresh experience points out some form of error which we shall afterward carefully avoid.

—JOHN KEATS

All of us have failed at something at some time, whether it is a diet, a marriage or a job. As compulsive eaters, however, we are prone to take setbacks much harder than others because we tend to be perfectionists who expect to do everything correctly the first time. We also are often incapable of separating the failure of a project from a sense of failure as a person.

To achieve at anything we are going to have to fail every now and then. Well-known historical figures such as Winston Churchill failed subjects in school, yet went on to make their mark in politics. And inventors frequently speak of the hundreds of failed products they tested before finding one that was useful.

Are you brooding today about something you feel you have failed at? Have you resolved never to try the same thing again because you felt humiliated by not being a winner? Don't allow this type of self-pitying attitude to drag you down. Assess the experience that is gnawing at you and glean whatever wisdom you can from it. Be proud that you had the courage to try something new and risky, and remind yourself that the highway to success is always fraught with potholes, curves and dead ends.

AFFIRMATION FOR THE DAY: I have no failures, only valuable learning experiences.

I'm not going to "should" on myself today.
—ANONYMOUS

The way we perceive stressful situations can often determine our physical condition. For example, one recently divorced friend of mine with two children who was looking for a new job developed a host of troubling problems: jaw pain, stomachaches, migraines and high blood pressure. After she was diagnosed as suffering from a stress overload and ordered to find time to relax, meditate and send herself positive messages during the day, her condition improved dramatically.

What really helped my friend most was learning to recast her past in a different light. Instead of telling herself that her divorce had made her unworthy, she told herself that she wished she hadn't had to undergo such a difficult situation but that she would not define herself as damaged goods because of it. As my friend began to view her experiences in a more positive way, her self-esteem rose and her stress level decreased.

Avoid the words "should," "always" and "never" when you are analyzing situations in your life. These words can "catastrophize" an event, making it into a bigger deal than it really is and harming you in the process. Remember today to monitor your self-talk because it is what you say to yourself, not what others say to you, that has the greatest effect on your health, outlook and mental well-being.

AFFIRMATION FOR THE DAY: Too often I am my own worst critic. Today I will give myself nice reviews.

Why do some people always see beautiful skies and grass and lovely flowers and incredible human beings, while others are hard-pressed to find anything or any place that is beautiful?

—LEO BUSCAGLIA

There are two distinct kinds of people: those who only see dark clouds and those who see rainbows after storms. We compulsive eaters usually fall into the first category, especially while we are active in our disease. We have become so accustomed to feeling bad that it's natural to extend our pessimism to everything and everyone around us.

We have to remember, though, that we do have a choice in what we think about and focus on. It's our decision to zero in on newspaper stories about rapes, murders, cruelty and war and decide that life is hell, rather than to dwell on tales of kindness, miracles, Good Samaritans and love, and conclude that the world can be a wonderful place.

Thinking positively rather than negatively is a skill that doesn't come naturally to everyone; it often has to be deliberately fostered and practiced. Try these exercises: When you meet someone today, focus on what you like about them rather than what you dislike, and if you experience a disappointment find at least one aspect of it that will benefit you. Don't worry if sunny thoughts initially run contrary to your nature because once you start to see rainbows, it isn't long before they are the first thing you notice.

AFFIRMATION FOR THE DAY: Today I will see beauty and kindness around me.

There are no wrong notes.

—THELONIOUS MONK

It's very easy to become obsessed with doing the "right" thing, and to act based upon getting others' approval. This may mean wearing only what certain magazines deem "in," reading only the books that get stellar reviews, and decorating your home just as you've seen it done in a stylish magazine.

When we live this way we stifle our own internal spark of individuality. By catering to everyone's tastes and whims but our own, we become paralyzed. We forget that there is nothing "bad" about our tastes, only that we may have different ideas and longings than others.

Look inside yourself today and see if there is some urge you've pushed down because you think it's "wrong." Make a "Fantasy List" of activities you've put off, books you've wanted to read and places you'd like to go. If you visit the seashore every summer but really long to go on an architectural dig in a foreign country, start making plans to do so. Don't worry that your mother, spouse, co-workers or acquaintances might disapprove or think you're out of step with the rest of the world. Honor your uniqueness and it will honor you.

AFFIRMATION FOR THE DAY: Different is not the same as wrong.

Music has charms to soothe a savage breast,
To soften rocks, or bend a knotted oak.
—WILLIAM CONGREVE

Some of us instinctively know what to do when we feel hot, bothered and frustrated—we flip on the radio. Although blasting rock and roll may be a way to empty our minds and avoid thinking about problems, other types of music have the ability to soothe us, make our breathing even and facilitate meditation.

Many hospitals now use music therapy for depressed and anxious patients. Ten to fifteen minutes of calming sounds have been shown to induce happiness and release pain-killing endorphins in the body. I found this to be the case when I was in labor with my first child; favorite classical music pieces played over and over helped reduce my fear and made the experience more bearable.

Today make sure to create at least one soothing interlude when you can relax and listen to peaceful music. If you don't have enough time to close your eyes for a brief period, at least, substitute silence or classical music for some of the rock 'n' roll you might favor. If you're like most people, this experience will cool a hot temper or distract you from unpleasant thoughts while at the same time restoring your sense of equilibrium and serenity.

AFFIRMATION FOR THE DAY: When I make time for peaceful music in my day I am taking care of myself.

Dese are de conditions dat prevail.

—JIMMY DURANTE

As compulsive eaters we tend to be dreamers. We have trouble facing reality and will frequently pretend that things are going smoothly when they're not.

If we want to recover we must have a firm grasp on reality. We can't pretend we haven't binged when we have, we can't say our family life isn't dysfunctional if it is, and we can't lie our way out of uncomfortable situations when we ought to face an unpleasant truth.

The first step in recovering from an eating disorder is admitting that we have one. To skip this fundamental action means we aren't in touch with reality, because the person who doesn't believe he or she needs help is the person who hasn't grasped the progressiveness and destructiveness of compulsive eating.

Look at yourself in the mirror today and honestly ask if you have really admitted to yourself the extent and seriousness of your disorder. Have you started to cut corners, tell half-truths and skip steps that were important to you in early recovery, but that seem tedious and unimportant now?

Don't live in a fantasy world. If you've been avoiding something that needs addressing, do it now. Acknowledge painful truths and then feel the liberation that always follows when problems emerge from the shadows and are seen in the light.

AFFIRMATION FOR THE DAY: I make the most progress in my recovery when I am realistic about my goals, my obstacles and my commitment to wellness.

A busy mind is a sick mind; a slow mind is a healthy mind; and a still mind is a divine mind.

—INDIAN SAYING

Frequently I catch myself doing a lot of things all at once, yet completing none of them. A common scenario in my typical day involves me starting a letter, abandoning it midway because I think of a call I need to make, and then filing documents while I am on the phone. When my mind races this way I am incapable of doing anything well, or of experiencing clarity of thought.

There are many ways to still a racing mind. Breathing exercises and positive affirmations are two well-known antidotes. I've also found that morning meditation is an extremely effective way to calm my thoughts, keep my priorities straight and maintain serenity.

If you feel yourself doing multiple things today yet performing none of them effectively, remind yourself that this is the surest way to get into trouble. Slow down, force yourself to focus completely on whatever is before you, and then finish it. When the temptation to hurry and take on more than you can reasonably handle crops up, stop and breathe slowly. Allow the tension to leave your body and remember that it's not important how much you accomplish, but how well you do it. Although it may feel odd to not live frenetically, the more you can incorporate periods of stillness and clarity into your day, the more serenity and satisfaction you will experience.

AFFIRMATION FOR THE DAY: When my mind is too busy, my Higher Power can't reach me.

Fear is the sand in the machinery of life.
—E. STANLEY JONES

So many of us never realize our full potential because we are too afraid—too afraid to ask for a raise, too afraid to assert our rights and too afraid to try something new. Our reasons for letting fear stop us are many and varied: "I'll never succeed," "No one likes me" and "It doesn't matter anyway."

It's all right to be afraid at times. We are all born with fears that help us survive and protect ourselves from harm. Newborn babies, for example, are instinctively frightened of heights and loud noises. But problems arise as we get older and adopt self-limiting fears that keep us from trying new experiences and taking risks. Instead of going through life looking for ways to challenge ourselves and expand our horizons, we become timid creatures who look for the safest, easiest way to slide by.

Do you have a healthy amount of fear or an unhealthy amount? Do you find yourself unable to assert yourself, try a new hobby or ask someone you like on a date because you can't stand rejection or uncertainty? If so, take the first step to overcoming fear today by just admitting it to yourself. But don't stop there—take the action that frightens you. If you never take risks, try new endeavors or experience uncertainty, your life is destined to be predictable and dull and you are always going to find sand in the machinery of your life.

AFFIRMATION FOR THE DAY: When I let fear and worry dictate my actions I'm unable to move forward.

Life by the inch is a cinch—life by the yard is hard.
—ANONYMOUS

Many times in my recovery I have surveyed my
character defects and other areas of my life that
needed work and felt overwhelmed by the task ahead
of me. Because I have always been one to want
something immediately—expecially when I was
bulimic—I despaired of ever having the patience to
make positive, lasting changes.

It was a friend of mine who bicycles professionally who helped me most with this problem. He said
that when he is going up a steep hill, he deliberately
doesn't stare at the top. He looks only at the few feet
directly in front of him and consequently finds that he
is less exhausted when he reaches the summit. "If I
spend the whole time focusing on how steep the hill
is, I feel more tired and less confident about my
ability to get to the top," he explains.

Is there something you want to accomplish but it
seems like the hill you have to climb is too high? If so,
cut your journey down to a manageable size today.
Focus only on what is directly in front of you and just get
through that portion. Like the Chinese saying that the
longest trip begins with the first step, you will discover
that you can do anything by the inch successfully, but
that when you start trying to go by the yard, your
journey will seem longer and harder than it really is.

AFFIRMATION FOR THE DAY: Today I will attack
my tasks in small increments.

It is one of the secrets of Nature in its mood of mockery that fine weather lays a heavier weight on the minds and hearts of the depressed and the inwardly tormented than does a really bad day with dark rain sniveling continuously and sympathetically from a dirty sky.

—MURIEL SPARK

I have been through periods of depression so dark and intense that it has seemed there was no solution but to run far away so that I could escape all of my responsibilities. Frequently it was on soft spring mornings or sparkling and crisp autumn afternoons that I was at my worst. I felt as if my Higher Power was putting a wonderful feast in front of me and saying, "You can't have this—you're not good enough."

When we are extremely depressed we have to try, hard as it is, to stay in touch with friends and look for that tiny opening that will enable us to start pulling ourselves out of our darkness. Avoiding the phone, skipping self-help meetings and refusing to see anything but the worst in people and life will keep us down and beaten.

If you are steeped in depression today, seize every opportunity to fight it. Enjoy the nice weather, read something uplifting and dress attractively. Above all, remember that you have as much power to weigh down your soul as you do to unburden it.

AFFIRMATION FOR THE DAY: It is my decision whether I allow nice weather to torment me or to energize me when I am down.

Forgiveness is the key to happiness.
—A Course in Miracles

We all know that we need to forgive other people if we are to erase the bitterness and hatred that poisons our soul and leads us to such self-destructive habits as compulsive eating. But forgiveness is often the biggest challenge we face in recovery because we don't know how to do it and we aren't even certain why it is necessary to our well-being.

Some of us may even feel that we need to be forgiven by our Higher Power before we can build a new life. We think that our Higher Power is like an angry parent who is quick to punish and withhold favors because we have been "bad." But this is an erroneous view because a loving Higher Power is not a parent and He doesn't ever judge or condemn us.

See yourself today through the eyes of your Higher Power. Try to love yourself unconditionally with all of your flaws and inconsistencies, and to forgive yourself when you are judgmental of your shortcomings or those of others. You'll find that honest forgiveness brings the gift of peaceful acceptance and greater harmony in your dealings with others.

AFFIRMATION FOR THE DAY: When I can't truly forgive, I can't truly love.

Priests are no more necessary to religion than politicians to patriotism.

—JOHN HAYNES HOLMES

Have you turned your spiritual life completely over to the guidance of another person? Does this person influence the way you dress and behave? Do you feel that the only way to know your Higher Power is through this person's interpretation?

I have a number of friends who would answer yes to these questions, and who approach religion with fear. For a variety of reasons they feel that they aren't good enough to enjoy the love of a Higher Power, that they have to attend church religiously or else their Higher Power won't be with them, and that they are fundamentally evil people who need another's intervention to "save" them.

Remember today that your Higher Power is always with you and that you don't necessarily need to see someone special or go to a holy place to feel the warmth of His love and acceptance. No one person among us is so gifted that he or she alone can interpret God's will for us, and we must bear in mind that just as we take responsibility for our recovery, we must also take responsibility for the quality of the relationship with our Higher Power.

AFFIRMATION FOR THE DAY: Today I'll remember that if I'm feeling distant from my Higher Power, I'm the one who's moved.

Draw your salary before spending it.

—GEORGE ADE

We compulsive eaters usually spread ourselves too thin and take a number of things for granted. We promise our time to too many causes, spend our paycheck before receiving it, and count on things happening before they actually do. It's no wonder that we often find ourselves overdrawn—not just at the bank, but in time and energy.

Recovery means learning realism and delayed gratification. Although it's not fun, we must remember that we can't always have what we want immediately, nor is our energy unlimited. If we persist in eating whenever the mood strikes us, buying whatever catches our fancy, and blithely promising to help anyone who asks us, we're going to wind up bingeing, bankrupt and exhausted.

Ask yourself if you're overcommitted and impulsive, and if you're still trying to be all things to all people. If so, this is insanity. Before promising anything to anyone today take a step back and ask yourself if you can afford to do it. Is that snack worth it? Do you really have the time to help with another charity? If you buy those clothes can you pay the rent?

If "no" answers any of these questions, take a hard look at your life and analyze your resources. If you can't learn to hold off spending your time and money before you have set aside enough for yourself, you will always feel out of control and powerless.

AFFIRMATION FOR THE DAY: Today I will not exhaust my resources.

Humor is an affirmation of dignity, a declaration of man's superiority to all that befalls him.
—ROMAIN GARY

There are times when nothing goes right in our lives, when fate seems against us and when Murphy's Law reigns supreme. When this happens we have choices as to how to react; we can retreat inward, lick our wounds and feel sorry for ourselves, or we can laugh about our predicaments and simply accept them.

One friend of mine visited a healing retreat one week where she said the focus was on learning how to deal with misfortune. She was taught that there is no "good" or "bad" situation—there are only "challenges." How we choose to approach those "challenges" is what defines them for us, and the application of humor and optimism can make virtually anything a positive occurrence.

Keep this in mind today as you contemplate the difficulties that face you. Raging at the heavens or falling into an abyss of depression will not help you deal with a situation over which you are powerless. Try instead to find humor in your challenges and you'll discover that when you can laugh about your difficulties, you will have taken a big step toward triumphing over them.

AFFIRMATION FOR THE DAY: The load I carry is made lighter with laughter.

It is not easy to find happiness in ourselves, and it is not possible to find it elsewhere.

—AGNES REPPLIER

Are we guilty of looking to other people and situations to fulfill us? I used to be that way. I was sure that each new city, new boyfriend, or new job would cure my compulsive eating and make me happy. Unfortunately, despite every change I made my bulimia and despair went right along with me.

There's a lot of hard work to recovery and to being content and happy. It means examining what drives us, why we jump to certain conclusions and why we repeat painful patterns when we ought to know better.

What makes you happy? If the answers that spring to mind are money, possessions, a new romantic relationship and successful children, then you'll never be satisfied. Real happiness only comes with acceptance of ourselves and our limitations, and appreciation for what we do well. Anything else only brings fleeting fulfillment that vanishes as quickly as it arrives.

Spend time today finding the joy that lies within and consciously identify what it is you do that brings real warm feelings of joy and passion. Whether it's caring for someone you love, devoting time to a hobby, or just being alone with nature, the more you know how to activate your own internal happiness, the less time and energy you'll waste looking for it elsewhere.

AFFIRMATION FOR THE DAY: Today I will look to myself and not others for my happiness.

The desire of perfection is the worst disease that ever afflicted the human mind.

—LOUIS DE FONTANES

The first time someone called me a perfectionist I was secretly thrilled. I thought it meant that I had a strong character and discriminating standards others admired. It wasn't until I started to recover that I realized that my perfectionism was really a character defect that would be a hindrance to living a happy, abstinent life.

Perfectionism is part of the reason I became bulimic; I wasn't satisfied with being an average shape. Goaded by advertisements featuring skinny models and countless diet articles in magazines, I began early to abuse myself with anorexic, then bulimic, behavior so that I could achieve the "perfect" body. My attitude led me to live a tightly controlled life where everything had to be just right, including grades, the way I spent my day and how I was seen by others.

To recover from compulsive eating we need to address the issue of how perfectionism impedes our growth. For example, if our weight goals are unrealistic and our meal plans are too rigid, we are setting ourselves up for failure. We must keep in mind that by shooting for the stars we can often achieve wonderful goals, but that when we always go for the moon we are likely to wind up discouraged and empty-handed.

AFFIRMATION FOR THE DAY: When I try to be perfect I forget that my individuality is defined by my imperfections.

Union gives strength.

—AESOP

Like a lot of compulsive eaters I tried numerous times to recover by myself from bulimia. I read books, joined diet programs, made promises in my diary and resorted to self-destructive schemes to alleviate my bingeing. Nothing ever worked, however, and my disorder progressed over time.

Entering a self-help group where I could discuss my food obsession with others was what finally launched me into recovery. Although it seemed silly at first, I found it enormously helpful and empowering to talk to others who shared my compulsion and learn how they managed their lives without succumbing to food, negative emotions and other unhealthy behaviors during times of stress, sadness and change.

When we try to combat our eating disorder alone we foster the illusion that we are powerful enough to recover from a very complex condition without any outside help. If this is our attitude, who will our role models be? Who will applaud us for the small, but important, changes we need to make? Who will give us insight into, and help with, our daily challenges?

Remember today that as individuals we will have trouble making a dent in our compulsive eating but that with a strong circle of understanding friends and the backing of a Higher Power, there is nothing we can't accomplish.

AFFIRMATION FOR THE DAY: My recovery is enhanced by the courage, wisdom, and insight of others like myself.

*Hold a picture of yourself long and steadily enough in
your mind's eye, and you will be drawn toward it.*
                                        —HARRY EMERSON FOSDICK

I noticed one night when I was watching the
Olympics that the world's top weight lifters always
paused to psyche themselves up before making a
huge lift. Inevitably the ones who took a moment to
close their eyes, see themselves being successful and
say a few positive affirmations were the ones who
came out on top.

I started to observe other winning athletes—
gymnasts, swimmers and runners, for example—who
did the same thing. They closed their eyes, ignored
the crowd noise prior to their performance, and then
prepared themselves for victory.

This visualization technique is indispensable for
us as we go about living in recovery. If we close our
eyes in the morning, imagine ourselves going through
the day successfully and use positive affirmations, we
will be victorious in our tasks, as well. We will find
that whenever we are able to plan our work, then
mentally see ourselves performing triumphantly, we
are always able to work our plan.

AFFIRMATION FOR THE DAY: Whatever I see in
my mind's eye I can accomplish.

Worry affects the circulation, the heart, the glands, the whole nervous system. I have never known a man who died from overwork, but many who died from doubt.
—CHARLES H. MAYO

When we shop most of us stock up for the future. We buy bulk containers of food, paper goods and toiletries—usually enough to last a week or more. Although we may be unaware of it, the primary reason we hoard things is fear: the fear that we will run out of something and be inconvenienced.

When we worry like this we stress our bodies in ways we may not even realize, and also exhibit a disbelief that our needs will be provided for by our Higher Power. One extraordinary woman named "The Peace Pilgrim" has made it her life's mission to prove that we are always taken care of when we have faith in God. To show this she has renounced all of her possessions and now tours the world, subsisting on whatever she is given each day. Although she starts every morning without any idea where her food or lodging will come from, she has never gone without either one.

Although most of us can't go to the same lengths as this woman to prove the existence of an almighty provider, we can try to trust our Higher Power more than we do now. For example, we can stop worrying incessantly about how future bills will get paid and how our children will turn out when there's nothing we can do at this moment to affect those outcomes. Make it a point today to start trusting more and letting go of the future and you'll be surprised by the pleasurable results.

AFFIRMATION FOR THE DAY: Worrying costs much and accomplishes little.

Demands made upon other people for too much attention, protection, and love can only invite domination or revulsion in the protectors themselves—two emotions quite as unhealthy as the demands which evoked them.
—FROM *THE TWELVE STEPS AND TWELVE TRADITIONS OF
ALCOHOLICS ANONYMOUS*

As compulsive eaters we need to be aware of our tendency to smother other people with affection, advice and most important—expectations. All too frequently in the past we have demanded an excessive amount of time and attention from others and been petulant, immature and unreasonably hurt when we didn't get what we thought we deserved.

To recover from our eating disorder we need to learn to let go. We need to let go of our need for constant reassurance, excessive stimulation and being the center of attention. We need to release overly high expectations of our friends, who can probably never live up to our demands. And we have to avoid setting unrealistic expectations of ourselves, which will only lead to disappointment, depression and relapse. Just like flowers can't grow without the right balance of water and sunlight, remember that healthy relationships require equilibrium between giving and taking.

AFFIRMATION FOR THE DAY: When I expect too much from myself and others, I can't accept people, places and things as they are.

When you feel grateful for something others have done for you, why not tell them about it?

—ANONYMOUS

I have a friend who has worked at the same company, for the same man, for over thirty years. Her pride and joy is her work, and she often stays late and goes in on weekends to ensure that everything has been done correctly and that the coming week will flow smoothly. Her one regret, she often tells friends, is that she feels unappreciated. Money and perks aren't what she wants—just a hearty thank-you every now and then for a job well-done.

Aren't we all guilty of taking kindnesses for granted at times? I have always been meticulous about thank-you notes and gratitude for a job well-done in the office, but I've often been lax on the home front. Somehow I find it easier to skip a thank-you at home when a favor is done than I am elsewhere, simply because I assume— sometimes incorrectly—that the people who know me best know I'm grateful.

Today remember that everyone appreciates gratitude, even if it is for something small. Make an effort to thank a co-worker who has helped you, a receptionist who has taken a message for you and a person who has held a door for you. At home take pains to notice if someone has made your bed, your dishes have been washed or a pet has been fed. Treat everyone exactly as you want to be treated and remember that the words "thank you" are among the easiest and most appreciated ones we can possibly utter.

AFFIRMATION FOR THE DAY: Being ungrateful is one of the most unbecoming and self-limiting character defects I can have.

There is nothing either good or bad, but thinking makes it so.

—WILLIAM SHAKESPEARE

All too often we have seen our world in black and white without any shades of gray. This has been a direct result of our inability to experience moderation with food, emotions and destructive actions. My personal responses to situations when I was bulimic were always extreme, and thus I found myself either exultant or extremely depressed much of the time, with many of my feelings revolving around how fat or thin I thought I was that day.

A life of recovery usually brings us a more realistic and level way of looking at things. We find that we are less prone to judge something as "good" or "bad," and that we can accept it "as is."

Remind yourself today that it is a gift to see the shades of gray in your life. If you feel yourself starting to be inappropriately negative or positive, find a friend who will help you with a check on reality. Allowing events to unfold naturally without unnecessary judgments will give us the freedom to see the perfect plan our Higher Power has for us.

AFFIRMATION FOR THE DAY: I can choose to see everything that happens to me today as a positive step toward a better life.

Let us forget and forgive past injuries.
—MIGUEL DE CERVANTES

I used to be plagued continually by mental reruns of hurts, slights and cruelties I felt I had endured throughout the years. As much as I tried to forgive people and practice unconditional love, I still occasionally found myself flashing back to scenes that gripped me with feelings of anger and revenge.

The person I turned to for help with this was an older woman who had undergone sexual abuse as a child, physical abuse in her first marriage and had had a child killed in a drug-related argument. Despite all this she radiated serenity and thankfulness for even the little blessings in her life.

She said her secret to peacefulness was to write down any troubles and fears, talk honestly about them with a friend or spiritual advisor, and then either make amends for her behavior or forgive the person who had harmed her. "When I do this I can look back, but not just stare," she said.

We compulsive eaters often have trouble coming to terms with our past, but must if we are ever to enjoy the present or anticipate the future. Do what you can to heal old wounds, but also realize that what's done is done. Allow yourself the freedom today of closing the door on the past because this is what will free you to move confidently into a bright and hopeful tomorrow.

AFFIRMATION FOR THE DAY: It is only when I make peace with what is behind me that I can set my sights on what lies ahead.

People are lonely because they build walls instead of bridges.

—Joseph F. Newton

Before I became involved in a self-help group for compulsive eaters I shunned the idea of any gathering being helpful in recovery from bulimia. Like most people with my disorder I isolated myself from others, especially during a binge and afterwards. I couldn't imagine that getting together with people like myself and discussing mutual problems and solutions could be comforting or instructive.

But when I became beaten down and unwilling to spend any more money on diet plans, I reluctantly started to attend meetings and found myself improving by leaps and bounds. I've since learned that self-help groups for any problem are considered powerful medicine, and also that people who socialize with others are generally healthier, happier and more resourceful than those who are loners.

Whenever you feel yourself starting to isolate—avoiding friends or not answering the phone—remind yourself of the power of reaching out. Frequently we'll find that even the deepest depression or sadness can be alleviated by talking to a sympathetic person who genuinely cares about our well-being. Remember also that the same energy we expend building walls around ourselves can just as easily be channeled into building bridges and friendships that strengthen and heal us.

AFFIRMATION FOR THE DAY: Today I will choose not to be lonely.

Almost all our misfortunes in life come from the wrong notions we have about the things that happen to us. To know men thoroughly, to judge events sanely is, therefore, a great step towards happiness.

—STENDHAL

I have a friend whom I would dearly love to shake at times. She is always seeing slights and hurts where none are intended. She is sure that people are discussing her in a nasty way if she walks into a room and they fall silent. She is also incapable of telling me a story where she isn't the poor victim of circumstance or the butt of cruel jokes.

At first I took up her cause and tried to fight some of her battles because I believed her "poor me" stories. What I soon found, though, was that she usually tampered with the truth in her version. It became apparent to me that she was ultra-sensitive and lacking in self-esteem, and therefore her view of simple occurrences was tainted.

How can we learn to "judge events sanely"? We can start by giving people the benefit of the doubt and not always assuming the worst about them. We can be less judgmental and more forgiving. And we can spend more time helping others than obsessing about ourselves, our flaws and how others perceive us.

Work today on viewing life and yourself in a balanced way. Don't rush to conclusions or extreme positions too quickly, and do seek outside opinions often. When you can stop seeing yourself as a victim, you won't have to be one again.

AFFIRMATION FOR THE DAY: I see others clearly only when I see myself clearly.

He who never made a mistake never made a discovery.
—SAMUEL SMILES

A young lady called me one day in tears, loudly wailing that she was a failure and was doomed forever to a life of bingeing. When she calmed down I asked her why she was so certain that she would never be free from compulsive eating. She then told me that the previous night she had given in to temptation, driven to a convenience store and bought the biggest bag of her favorite binge food that she could find. She had then spent the rest of the night eating.

We talked a bit about slips and relapses and I assured her that I, too, had had my share of difficult times as I had forged my path toward recovery. I told her that despite my feelings of failure and worthlessness when I had fallen off the wagon, I had learned good lessons from all of my slips and that they had been my most valuable teachers. Like a child who learns not to touch a hot stove, my "burns" had shown me which foods, people and places were detrimental to my recovery.

Today remember that we will all probably veer off course at times during our recovery, but that what's really important is how we choose to deal with those painful experiences. When you can accept that your path won't be perfect and not allow your slips to overshadow or halt your progress, you'll inevitably develop the wisdom and tenacity needed for long-term recovery.

AFFIRMATION FOR THE DAY: Today I will learn from my mistakes, not berate myself for them.

Never give up then, for that is just the place and time that the tide will turn.

—HARRIET BEECHER STOWE

"I've never understood the game of poker," a friend said to me one day. "It doesn't make any sense to put your money in the pot then fold your hand."

Folding our hand, however, is what many of us do in times of stress. We're on the brink of accomplishing something we have worked hard for, then something comes along to challenge us. Rather than risk a loss, we cash in our chips and settle for less than we had hoped for.

It is precisely at times like these that we have to dig our heels in the mud and stand firm. I've always found that when I'm ready to give up because of some seemingly insurmountable problem, if I hang in there just a bit longer the tide turns in my favor. It's almost as if my Higher Power is throwing one last roadblock in my way to see how really serious I am about reaching my goal.

If you are facing a challenge today that feels like the straw that will break the camel's back, make yourself stand firm. Call upon all the faith and determination you possess and don't give up. If you can bravely withstand that one last tidal wave that threatens to crush you, you may find it is the one that finally causes the tide to turn.

AFFIRMATION FOR THE DAY: Winners never quit and quitters never win.

Expectation is the breeding ground for disappointment.
—ANONYMOUS

There was a period in my life when I felt my friends were dropping away like flies. It was a particularly busy and difficult time for me both professionally and personally, and my feelings were hurt when people either didn't recognize it or didn't seem to want to help me through it.

A friend shared her philosophy of life with me one day that helped me put this situation in perspective. She said that she always hoped for the best in people and in life, and that she never stopped imagining wonderful things happening to her. However, she tried to keep her expectations reasonable so that she'd would avoid crashing into disappointment if she didn't achieve her goals. Previously she had set too-high standards for herself and others which had been difficult to meet, consequently she had always been discouraged and dispirited by the results.

Remember today that there is nothing wrong with expecting the best in life; don't, however, be overly distraught if things don't work out according to your plans. People may not have the time or energy to help us when we need it, but that calls for understanding not judgment. Similarly, situations may not unfold as we had hoped, which means we must try alternate courses of action, not that we should completely give up. Try to be flexible and you'll be that much surer you won't break.

AFFIRMATION FOR THE DAY: As long as I have rigid ideas about how my life and the people in it should be, I won't be happy.

> *Last night at twelve I felt immense,*
> *But now I feel like thirty cents.*
> —GEORGE ADE

Speaking up, telling someone off, and getting revenge can feel great—but only for a short time. Often I have felt "immense" when getting back at someone who has hurt me, only to feel antsy and remorseful soon afterwards. Inevitably, when I replay the encounter in my head, I am not just embarrassed, I'm able to see the other person's viewpoint for the first time.

Getting back at people is never worth the momentary zing of pleasure you receive while doing it. Although you may think that you're defending your honor by attacking someone who has hurt you, there's a certain dignity in remaining silent and allowing events to just take their course. I've also found that if I can restrain myself long enough to let my Higher Power even the score, I limit the damage I am capable of inflicting on myself.

We are all going to feel hurt and anger at times but we must learn to release those emotions in ways that don't come back to harm us. Write in your journal, take a walk or call a trusted friend when you're longing to lash out at someone. If you can find healthy ways to defuse your anger, you will lessen the chances of jeopardizing your hard-won emotional balance and recovery.

AFFIRMATION FOR THE DAY: Today I will not do anything that will make me feel like thirty cents tomorrow.

Smiles are free and easy to give.

—ANONYMOUS

There is a simple action you can take that can make you and others feel wonderful at no cost—smiling. Dale Carnegie's best-selling book, "How to Win Friends and Influence People," emphasizes this point by saying that a genuine smile is one of the surest ways we can lift our mood, chase away negative thoughts and bring happiness to others.

When we are eating compulsively it's hard to smile or feel good about anything. At my bulimic worst strangers used to walk up to me on the street and say things like, "Lighten up! Nothing can be that bad!" In my mind, though, my body and my life *were* that bad.

I knew my recovery was taking hold when a friend surprised me by commenting one day that I was smiling more and seemed to be at peace with myself. Some of the ways I projected this were by smiling at lonesome-looking old people, waving at a small child in a passing car and unexpectedly hugging someone I cared about.

Enrich another person's day today at no cost by being happy and sharing it with a smile. Not only will you be taking care of yourself, you'll be unselfishly helping others without looking for a reward.

AFFIRMATION FOR THE DAY: My outward appearance is an accurate reflection of my inner condition.

As the body without the spirit is dead, so faith without works is dead also.

—JAMES 2:26

Many of us have wonderful ideas about how to live our lives. We believe that we should not do unto others what we don't want done to us. We believe in honesty and high morals. We believe that turning to a loving Higher Power will help us in times of need and that this same Higher Power would never let us down. But how many of us actually live our beliefs?

I know some people who have humanitarian philosophies that they cannot put into practice themselves. These are the ones who haven't spoken with their parents in several years because of an argument, yet who talk about the beauty of forgiveness. They are also great believers in exercise but never do it themselves. When I hear someone like this talking I get the impression that the person she is trying hardest to reach, in vain, is herself.

Ask yourself today if your living philosophy is consistent with your actions. Do you think volunteer work is wonderful but you don't have time for it yourself? Do you believe people should tolerate their children's mistakes, yet somehow always find yourself judging your own harshly? Step back today and take a hard look at what you say and what you do. You may find that the beliefs you are most vocal about are the ones you have yet to put into practice yourself.

AFFIRMATION FOR THE DAY: When I am preaching loud and long, there is a good chance that I ought to be the main audience.

Do not take life too seriously. You will never get out of it alive.

—ELBERT GREEN HUBBARD

I have a tendency to take myself and my work too seriously. The phone rings constantly and mail streams in daily from people begging for help with their eating disorders. I often get wrapped up in the problems I hear about and do everything I can to help others into recovery. When my efforts bear no fruit sometimes I'll brood for hours, wondering what I could have said or done differently.

I have had to work hard to curb this predisposition to take everything so seriously. I remind myself daily that a serene and composed friend of mine once told me that her motto is "Life is a garment to be worn loosely." I also try to keep in mind what I've heard are the two rules of a happy life: Don't sweat the small stuff, and remember that everything is small stuff.

If you find yourself slipping into a brooding, serious mood today, make a concerted effort to lighten up and put your worries in perspective. Nothing is ever as bad as we think it is, nor will we be any closer to serenity if our energies all go into obsessing about problems. Learning to be a bit more carefree about life doesn't come easily, but with practice we'll find that it can be a garment worn loosely about us.

AFFIRMATION FOR THE DAY: Today I won't sweat the small stuff.

It is easier to resist at the beginning than at the end.
—LEONARDO DA VINCI

How many days in the past have we awakened with good intentions about our meal plans, only to find ourselves bingeing at the end of the day and telling ourselves that tomorrow will be different?

When I first began recovery I carried a pamphlet from my self-help group in my purse entitled "Before You Take That First Compulsive Bite." The wisdom contained in it was simple but profound: Find ways to avoid starting to eat compulsively because once you start, there is no guarantee you will ever stop. From experience I knew this was true because I had countless memories of thinking, "I'll just try one bite of this frosting" or "I'll take a tiny taste of this ice cream," only to then find myself overcome with a desire to eat anything and everything in sight. Sometimes I had been able to resist; more often, though, I had not.

Remember today that when you are confronted with a situation where your resolve is slipping, or someone is encouraging you to try "just one bite" of something they have made, turning your thoughts elsewhere is almost impossible once you have given in. At such difficult times it's critical to reinforce the importance of recovery, and to remember that no matter how much abstinence we have achieved, we are always one bite away from a binge.

AFFIRMATION FOR THE DAY: When I have frequent slips in recovery, it's a sign that I don't take my eating disorder seriously.

By fighting you never get enough, but by yielding you get more than you expected.

—ANONYMOUS

Have you ever noticed that when you disagree with someone you can remain deadlocked in an argument indefinitely with both sides hardening into defiance? But that when you yield—even a little bit—you can usually come to a middle ground for resolution? Successful negotiators have always capitalized on this technique as a way of bringing warring parties to peace, and it's a good one we can use to end warring within ourselves.

As compulsive eaters we have been renowned fighters, especially when it came to deciding how we were to recover. We have fought multiple solutions and offers of help because we didn't want to admit that someone else might be right about our condition. Giving in to others, or even to suggestions of a self-help program, was unthinkable because that would have been an admission of weakness.

Recovery, however, means yielding and admitting that we aren't always right. When I finally threw in the towel with my eating disorder and asked for help from others, my life started anew and creative solutions blossomed. I try to remember this lesson when I find myself resisting change in any part of my life, because I know that if I can let go even the littlest bit, then I have paved the way for a resolution that will bring me peace.

AFFIRMATION FOR THE DAY: My toughest struggles are usually with my ego.

Now good digestion wait on appetite, and health on both!

—WILLIAM SHAKESPEARE

Often my binges began as a result of anger, depression and fear. I never enjoyed what I ate when I was in this state because I wasn't eating for pleasure, I was eating to stuff down uncomfortable feelings.

In recovery we need to learn a different attitude toward food. It is no longer a weapon to be used against ourselves. We must strive to make our meals enjoyable, relaxing times that are not fraught with tension and anger. We also need to be careful not to assign food too much importance; it is not a reward, it is just nourishment.

Many people with strong recovery say it is helpful to say a brief prayer before eating, or to just pause and empty their minds of distracting thoughts. At some inpatient eating disorder units, one meal each day is even devoted to "gentle eating"—a time during which patients put their utensils down between bites and chew slowly while listening to meditative music.

When we eat in a relaxed state we also digest our food faster and more efficiently than those who eat under stress. Take the time today to appreciate everything you put into your mouth and give thanks that you can choose healthy foods now, not just junk binge foods. Make it a goal not to eat while standing up, riding in a car or doing something else distracting. Mindfulness while eating is a wonderful way to promote mindfulness during the rest of our day.

AFFIRMATION FOR THE DAY: Today I will have a clear, peaceful mind during my meals.

I may be in an uncomfortable situation but it is necessary in order for me to grow.

—ANONYMOUS

I firmly believe that when there is something we need to learn that will better us in some way, we consciously or unconsciously cause a situation to occur that will teach us an important lesson. This fits with the well-known saying, "When the student is ready, the teacher appears."

We compulsive eaters tend to be very stubborn people who ignore warning signs that something needs to change until it is almost too late. Then we are thrust into a particularly painful and challenging spot that forces us to examine ourselves because we have no other choice. In this way I have been able to face and tackle some of my most self-destructive and negative attitudes and behaviors. Remember today that discomfort never feels good but that it always leads us to a stronger, better place. Keep in mind, too, that resistance to change is usually a sign that you are on the verge of an important breakthrough and that your Higher Power feels you are up to the challenge.

AFFIRMATION FOR THE DAY: When I avoid pain, I avoid growth.

Be cheerful while you are alive.

—PTAHHOTPE

Someone close to me had her marriage called off a few short months before it was to take place. She went into a funk; she felt unloved and discarded. Would she ever meet anyone again who wanted to marry her? Was there something wrong with her? Would she ever have children?

Traumatic events like this happen to all of us. Everyone periodically has something occur that sets them back emotionally for a period of time, and grieving is a normal and natural response. If we try to pretend that we feel no pain and that we need no support, we only hurt ourselves. But, by the same token, our grieving must have a reasonable time limit or we run the risk of alienating those around us and hurting ourselves emotionally.

One way to move through the grieving process more easily is to train ourselves to find the silver lining in our difficulties. As a friend said to me once, this involves having a stronger "uplook" than outlook. When we can look up to our Higher Power and trust that what happens to us is in our best interests, we are better able to handle disappointments with maturity and under-standing.

Try to be a person with a strong uplook today. Choose optimism and graceful acceptance over depression and anxiety. Remember, too, that the more joy and love you radiate, the more you'll attract.

AFFIRMATION FOR THE DAY: It is just as easy for me to look up as it is to look down.

How sickness enlarges the dimensions of a man's self to himself.

—CHARLES LAMB

When we are practicing our disease of compulsive eating it is hard to think about anyone but ourselves. The world seems to revolve around us—what we look like, who our friends are, what they think about us, when our next binge will be, and so on. We also like to think that we are the authorities on everything, even things we know nothing about. The polite term for this behavior is grandiosity.

When we begin to recover we find the "dimensions" of our importance shrinking. Suddenly we discover that most people have never cared about our looks, our friends or our opinions after all. To our great surprise, the world has never even revolved around us!

These painful revelations are often the beginning of the end of our grandiosity. Self-importance, however, is a persistent character defect that is likely to reappear periodically no matter how much we acknowledge it and work to eliminate it. Be very conscious today of the little ways you puff yourself up. Instead of calling attention to yourself, make it a point to compliment others often. The more you are able to see yourself realistically and without any illusions, the greater will be the distance between you and your disease.

AFFIRMATION FOR THE DAY: I am liable to eat compulsively when my grandiosity and feelings of self-importance get out of hand.

> *The miserable have no other medicine*
> *But only hope.*
>
> —WILLIAM SHAKESPEARE

There is an old Mexican story about how the devil wanted to go out of business one day so he decided to auction off his instruments. Most of his tools looked shiny and unused; only one was obviously well-worn. When someone asked him about it, he cackled and responded that it was his favorite tool because he used it to tempt people to despair. Once he got them to despair, it was easy to make them give up hope, he said.

Feelings of despair and hopelessness are common to compulsive eaters. Sometimes this is due to a history of mood disorders in our families and sometimes it's because we're constantly setting unrealistic goals for ourselves and falling short of them. When life seems hopeless, it's easy for us to decide that recovery is too much work and that we're just going to throw in the towel and start eating again.

We don't have to live this way any longer. No matter how bad we think our lives are at the moment, there is always hope for us. We can find it at self-help meetings where we meet recovering people like ourselves and when we consult with friends and professionals who give us perspective on our troubles. Fight your despair today by reaching out, praying and affirming a positive outcome to whatever troubles you. You'll find that when you can summon hope, however small, you won't lose the battle.

AFFIRMATION FOR THE DAY: Hope is the best medicine for my misery.

What others say of me matters little. What I say and do matters much.

—ELBERT GREEN HUBBARD

I used to run my life to get other people's approval. It was more important to me to know that someone else thought I was a good, nice person than it was for me to think that of myself. My outlook, so to speak, was stronger than my inlook.

This type of attitude leads to nothing but frustration. I found that the more I tried to get other people's approval, the less self-respect I had. And even when I did manage to please others, I'd always hear of at least one person who disapproved of me and that one person's approval would be what I focused on. I started to feel a bit like a dog who eternally chases his tail and is never satisfied.

We are never going to feel good about ourselves if what other people think and say can create and destroy our self-esteem. Although people-pleasing is a very deep-seated and hard behavior to change, it must be addressed for recovery to take place. Ask yourself these questions: Are you taking on projects you can't handle only to get a pat on the back? Are you trying to be all things to all people because you think it will make you more likable? If the answer is "yes," force yourself to do something today just for you and not for another's benefit. When you can learn to value your own opinion more than anyone else's, you'll have the self-esteem that's needed for true healing.

AFFIRMATION FOR THE DAY: If other people don't like me it is their problem, not mine.

If you pray, why worry? And if you worry, why pray?
                                        —ANONYMOUS

For many of us, prayer comes very awkwardly. When people in recovery told me that I needed to pray to a God of my understanding for guidance, I obsessed about my prayers being ill-conceived and trite. I also worried that someone else would catch me "in the act," so to speak, which would destroy my carefully constructed facade of self-reliance.

At first my prayers were convoluted and self-seeking. I prayed for what I thought I should have, not for what was best for me. When I didn't get what I wanted I was like a little girl stamping her foot and pouting about the unfairness of it all. In the intervening years, however, I've learned better. The prayers that take the worries off my mind now are the simplest, like "Help!"

For prayers to be truly effective, however, we have to have the faith that they are heard and responded to. When we have this profound trust in our Higher Power, we are incapable of getting too worried about anything that happens to us because we know that everything happens for the best, and that we'll always be given the strength to deal with whatever befalls us.

Today ask yourself if your prayers are giving you the comfort and peace of mind that they should. If not, why are you wasting your time, and where is your faith?

AFFIRMATION FOR THE DAY: Faith and fear can't live in the same house.

God never deceives, but man is deceived whenever he puts too much trust in himself.

—THOMAS À KEMPIS

Think for a moment about a newborn baby. It knows what it wants—food, nurturance and sleep—and it communicates its needs by crying loudly and insistently. When this happens, assistance always comes in the form of a bottle, a bed or a comforting presence. Thus, by speaking up the baby gets its needs met.

As we grow older we forget this lesson. We start to think that it's better to rely on ourselves and to shun help so that we aren't indebted to anyone else. We learn not to cry out and our needs go unmet as we struggle on, alone and miserable.

There is an American proverb: "A man who is his own doctor has a fool for a patient." Resolve not to be a fool today. Admit that you need help, particularly with your compulsive eating, and accept the strength and guidance you can receive from your Higher Power and others. When you have the humility to ask for what you need, you might be surprised to find that, as with a newborn baby, assistance will always appear in some form.

AFFIRMATION FOR THE DAY: Self-sufficiency in recovery is not always an asset.

Who sees all beings in his own self and his own self in all beings, loses all fear.

—THE UPANISHADS

We compulsive eaters have secret fantasies that we are unique individuals whom no one else can relate to because we're so special. When we are active in our disease we are sure we are the "worst" binger in the world, and when we are in pain we think that no one else has ever felt the same sorrow we are experiencing.

If we insist on isolating ourselves in our own little cocoons of uniqueness, we will never recover. For it is only by seeing ourselves in others, and in seeing others in ourselves, that acceptance lies. If you know that other people have experienced your troubles and survived, then you are given the tools to address your own fears. And when you observe another's character defects and recognize them in yourself, you are able to strip away self-deception and make positive changes. Isolation and uniqueness will not afford us these benefits.

Try today to experience connectedness with everyone you meet. Look for the similarities between you, not the differences. When we can overcome the barriers we erect between ourselves and others, we will finally be able to feel the healing balm of compassion and empathy that bonds us with our fellow man.

AFFIRMATION FOR THE DAY: Instead of nourishing my feelings of differentness today, I'm going to find common bonds.

People think luck is something that comes to them, but it never does. You have to go out and catch it, and grab it with your own two hands.

—I. M. PEI

Are we guilty of sitting around and waiting for our Fairy Godmother to appear, wave a wand, and make our wishes come true? Do we resent others' success because they were born into wealthy families and given all of the advantages that we may have to work for? Are we fond of saying, "Some people have all the luck!"?

While luck is inarguably a factor in creating success, many of the people who seem to have been born "lucky" have also worked hard to get where they are. They will admit that serendipity has gotten them a leg up on their competition, but they will also point out that hard work has enabled them to exploit their good fortune.

Don't waste your time envying "lucky" people and waiting for your big break today—go out and make it happen. If you work diligently enough to make your dreams come true, you'll usually find that you have positioned yourself in the right place to grab that brass ring when it comes your way.

AFFIRMATION FOR THE DAY: Today I'll create my own good fortune.

If you are serious about the sufferings of mankind, you must perfect the only source of help you have—yourself.

—JEROME FRANK

Frequently I receive calls and letters from anorexics and bulimics who want to help other eating disorder sufferers and would like to know how to go about writing books, making speeches and connecting with people like themselves. These men and women are always well-meaning but often have little or no recovery to share with anyone. Although they understand the medical causes and effects of their behavior, they usually have been unable to translate talking about recovery into living in recovery.

One day I was watching a talk show and the subject was eating disorders. One of the guests was a twenty-nine-year-old, fifty-nine-pound bulimarexic. If I had closed my eyes and just listened to her I would have thought she was the "guest expert." She exhibited tremendous knowledge about her condition and was able to discuss the finer points of her medical problems. What was painfully obvious, however, was that despite her stated goal to help others, she couldn't yet help herself.

Be aware of any tendencies you have to help mankind before you have helped yourself. It is far easier to tell others what to do than it is to do it yourself. Focus your energies today on improving yourself and you'll find that your ability to assist the people you want to reach is strengthened immeasurably, and that instead of looking for them, they will find you.

AFFIRMATION FOR THE DAY: Today I will save only myself.

*The more you depend on forces outside yourself, the
more you are dominated by them.*
— HAROLD SHERMAN

When I first began my recovery from compulsive
eating I received a wonderful lesson by working with a
very overbearing person. Because I still had little
confidence in my own creativity and abilities, I allowed
her to take on some of my more challenging tasks. The
more I let her do, the more she tried to take from me.
It wasn't long before I had gone from being grateful for
the help to being resentful of her domination.

This is probably what happened to us compulsive
eaters with food, too. At first we turned to moderate
amounts of food at odd times to help ease feelings of
fear, sadness, and grief. Before long we found ourselves
bingeing frequently on larger amounts, angry that food
had developed such a grip on our actions and emotions.
What had once been a friend was now the controlling
enemy.

To be in control of our lives we need to eliminate
our dependence on outside forces—not just food. When
we rely on friends, possessions and compulsive actions
to satisfy us, our contentment will never last. If this
behavior describes you, work today to nourish the
qualities of faith, self-love and optimism that will prevent external forces from defining your happiness and
instead bring you the quiet confidence and serenity you
deserve.

AFFIRMATION FOR THE DAY: I can't build my
inner strength if I only react to other people, places
and things.

And God said, Let there be light; and there was light.
—GENESIS 1:3

Centuries ago doctors prescribed sunshine as a way to help their depressed and listless patients feel better and recover faster from illnesses. Although no one has even been certain why getting outside into the fresh air and light is so healing, this advice has continued to the present day.

Some compulsive eaters take this advice too far. They become obsessed with getting the perfect tan and will neglect family, friends and errands in favor of sunning themselves. One recovering bulimic told me that she was once so concerned about bronzing herself that she missed her father's funeral. Other bulimics have told me about skin injuries they have sustained by spending lots of time in tanning parlors.

Keep in mind today that as restorative as sunshine can be to our disposition and outlook, we must practice moderation so that we don't hurt ourselves or neglect other areas that need attention. If we can balance our responsibilities with enough fresh air, warmth and sunshine we'll find that it's impossible to allow depression or confusion to rule our thoughts for very long.

AFFIRMATION FOR THE DAY: Today I will let sunlight shine on me and my affairs.

Your life is what your thoughts make of it.
                            —MARCUS AURELIUS ANTONINUS

I once heard a story about a master carver who could take an unfinished block of wood and whittle it into the lifelike rendition of an animal within hours. One day as he was carving the figure of a grizzly bear, his apprentice asked for a block of wood so that he could do the same.

The young man went into another room where the master heard him working furiously. After a while he came back discouraged with his whittled-down block in his hands. "Master," he said dejectedly, "there is no bear in my piece of wood."

The lesson for us in this story is clear. We cannot create anything without first seeing it in our minds and having a mental blueprint. Great things—like carved grizzly bears—cannot come into being until we have visualized them first as reality. Remember today that our lives are like blocks of wood and that we are master carvers who can create whatever we desire, as long as we have some idea of what it is we hope to accomplish.

AFFIRMATION FOR THE DAY: If I have the ability to picture what I want, I have the power to create it.

Your profession is not who you are, it is only a costume.
—ANONYMOUS

I frequently read about men and women who retire from their jobs and then suffer great depression and even death. Because they have identified themselves for so long as members of a company and they have neglected to nurture other interests, being out of work can feel like dying. Their "costume" is gone and they don't have any other clothes to put on.

This is also true of people who feel a need to wear jackets that announce where they work, or who plaster their cars with stickers proclaiming where they or their children go to school. Because they aren't content just being themselves, they are compelled to let the world know they "belong" to some special group.

If we are depending on designer labels, our jobs, or school insignias to define us, then we are still lacking in self-esteem. This type of behavior broadcasts the fact that we aren't comfortable just being ourselves and that outside conditions create our identity. Ask yourself today how you'd feel if an external—such as your job—was taken from you without warning. Would you feel naked and without purpose? If so, this is a warning flag to start nurturing what's beneath the costume you wear. If you devote time to developing your interests, your spiritual conditions, and your character, you won't ever need to feel the fear of losing your identity.

AFFIRMATION FOR THE DAY: I am a human being, not a human do-ing.

In every man a child is hidden that wants to play.
                              —FRIEDRICH WILHELM NIETZSCHE

A very good friend of mine went into treatment for alcoholism several years ago. When he left he was middle-aged, a respected pillar of the business community and the father of several grown children. He was also a very uptight, no-nonsense, boring person.

When my friend returned home six weeks later, he was still middle-aged, respected and a father; he was not, however, boring and uptight. When I asked what was responsible for his changed demeanor, he laughed and attributed it to volleyball, which his counselors had made him and the other patients play every day during treatment. Although he had initially resisted this activity as "stupid" and "a waste of time," my friend found that volleyball had gradually made him feel happy, and even childlike, for the first time in forty years. To his great surprise, he said, it felt good.

We all need to get in touch with our inner child as we recover, because by doing so we will recapture some of the joy and spontaneity that is missing from our daily life. Whether the game is volleyball, cards or horseshoes, dropping our maturity and joining in the fun with others will reawaken the young and playful side that we probably have denied and ignored for far too many years.

AFFIRMATION FOR THE DAY: When I am playful and spontaneous, I cannot be self-absorbed and arrogant.

What we call the beginning is often the end and to make our end is to make a beginning. The end is where we start from.

—T. S. ELIOT

All the truly significant times in my life that have marked the start of something new have been the ending of something else. When I decided to commit myself to recovering from bulimia, it marked the demise of close to a decade of insane, self-centered behavior. When I had my first child it was the start of learning how to unselfishly care for someone who was dependent on me for getting most of his needs met. And when I decided to enter the eating disorder field it was the beginning of a completely different professional life.

It's normal to feel scared when we start something new. The old is familiar and comfortable, even if it's something that causes us pain, and giving it up can be terrifying. The unknown is often better and more satisfying, but stepping into it takes courage.

Instead of mourning the endings, celebrate the beginnings in your life today. Look at them as opportunities for growth and excitement, not as scary excursions over which you have no control. Starting afresh with a job, a relationship or a meal plan is often what's needed to jolt us out of a rut, change our thinking and renew our excitement with life.

AFFIRMATION FOR THE DAY: When I am being nostalgic, I am not anticipating the future.

Worry is a form of fear, and all forms of fear produce fatigue.

—BERTRAND RUSSELL

How many times have we worried incessantly about something that might happen to us, only to discover much later that all of our fears were unjustified? That everything worked out fine and all of the energy we spent obsessing about some unknown event could have been better used elsewhere?

As compulsive eaters we are old friends with worry. We have often worried about our next meal, our last meal and what we would look like tomorrow. We obsessed about what others would think of us wearing a certain outfit and we were sure they would talk about our size, weight and character deficiencies when we were out of earshot.

When we live in the future, especially one as gloomy as we are wont to imagine, enjoying the present is impossible. Today stop yourself if you are slipping into this mode and ask yourself if you are avoiding something that needs attention now, and if you can really afford to spend time worrying about something you can't even control. Work instead to improve your trust in your Higher Power's plan for you and acceptance of whatever happens. You'll be delighted to find wellsprings of energy and optimism within that have just been waiting for you to unleash them.

AFFIRMATION FOR THE DAY: Worrying about the future robs me of today's joy.

True intimacy with another human being can only be experienced when you have found true peace within yourself.

—ANGELA L. WOZNIAK

Many compulsive eaters nurse more than one addiction, and one of the most common ones is an addiction to sex. For some this behavior will emerge as a replacement for food and for others it is a condition that has coexisted with compulsive eating for many years.

There are many reasons why we might be attracted to compulsive sex. It could be a history of rape or incest. It could be internal confusion that attraction always must lead to intimacy. For others it is an insatiable need to conquer and to rack up as many "victims" as possible.

It's important for us to remember that feeling good about ourselves doesn't mean submitting to random sexual advances so that we will feel attractive or needed. While the initial feelings may be pleasurable—like the start of a rip-roaring food binge—the end result is usually the same sense of despair, emptiness and abandonment.

As compulsive eaters we need to be mindful of this tendency to have multiple addictions. We must also be honest about the fact that replacing food with excessive coffee, cigarettes, alcohol, drugs, sex or shopping will eventually erase any progress or positive feelings we have about our abstinence from bingeing, and that awareness and early detection of cross-addiction is our best weapon against multiple dependencies.

AFFIRMATION FOR THE DAY: When I seek love and intimacy from people who cannot give it, I am not affirming my self-worth within.

Little strokes fell great oaks.

—BENJAMIN FRANKLIN

Researchers have found that many of the hassles and irritations of daily life—stubbing your toe, missing the bus or finding the toothpaste cap unscrewed—can have a cumulative effect that is more physically and emotionally damaging than major stressors such as divorce, losing a job and death. They say that as minor irritations pile up there is a rise in depression, fatigue, poor job performance and sickness.

We compulsive eaters have a particularly hard time dealing with little problems because we tend to react quickly and blow situations out of proportion. Food has often been our solace at these times because we figure that as long as life isn't going our way we might as well give in to temptation. Tomorrow, we say, we'll be good. Thus we reactivate the self-destructive cycle of bingeing which leaves us feeling trapped, angry and even more disturbed than we did when the little thing upset us in the first place.

Try these proven techniques the next time a small problem leads you to want to break your abstinence: Make a "hassles" list in order of severity, deliberately find the positive side of your irritations and then make an honest effort to change your reactions. If you can reprogram your behavior and find less self-destructive ways to vent your frustrations, you'll be invulnerable to the nicks and cuts we all experience daily.

AFFIRMATION FOR THE DAY: I will not make a mountain out of a molehill today.

You may have a fresh start any moment you choose, for this thing that we call "failure" is not the falling down, but the staying down.

—MARY PICKFORD

I have often read about the difficulties of stopping smoking. Although it is considered a hard addiction to break, the people who stand the best chance of triumphing over the allure of nicotine are those who fail several times yet who don't give up trying to quit.

Nicotine addiction is very similar to compulsive eating. Unless we are remarkable exceptions we will fall down occasionally in our recovery. For some of us it will mean all-out relapses where we binge for days, months or years. For some of us it will be a relapse in our behavior and a return to the negativity that once dominated our lives.

Whatever our slip or setback, it is important that we not stay down. We need to bounce back to our feet, analyze our mistakes and determine not to fall into the same trap again in the future. We must remember that our failures are our best teachers, and that every time we start afresh we are that much closer to success.

AFFIRMATION FOR THE DAY: When I get back up again after falling, I overcome defeat.

Hearts are opened from the inside.

—ANONYMOUS

Occasional sadness is an inevitable part of being human. Situations will arise in our lives when we feel isolated, friendless and miserable. At times there is a specific reason for our feelings—the death of a loved one, a move to a new city or a sudden reversal of fortune—but sometimes there is no apparent reason. We just feel blah and don't know why.

As compulsive eaters our tendency is to run to food when we feel sad because it has been a comforting ally and friend in the past. Despite temporary feelings of fulfillment, however, food has always turned on us afterwards and left us feeling guilty and more unhappy. The feelings we have needed to express have now been stuffed deeper inside us where they will continue to fester.

We need to resist attempts to isolate and eat when we're feeling down. Instead of putting walls up around ourselves, we have to take the scary step of opening our hearts to others and sharing our secret fears and vulnerabilities. When we do this we give others the opportunity to connect with us on an important, not superficial, level and we pave the way for real friendship and healing.

AFFIRMATION FOR THE DAY: If I lock up my heart and throw away the key, I will always feel alone. Today I will open my heart to someone new.

Man is born free, and everywhere he is in chains.
                              —JEAN-JACQUES ROUSSEAU

When we are born we are like a clean slate. We have no fears, no addictions and no anger. As we grow older, though, we start to shackle ourselves with negative emotions and behaviors such as intolerance, compulsive eating and worry. Where we had once been spontaneous, trusting and happy we are now enslaved, by choice, to unhealthy prejudices and beliefs.

A similar situation arises among people who wear "golden handcuffs." These men and women work in high-paying, high-stress positions that they don't enjoy but that provide a standard of living that is hard to give up. Instead of readjusting their lives to require fewer possessions, they continue to add expensive debts that chain them to an unsatisfying way of life.

All of us feel shackled at times by attitudes or situations we don't think we have any control over. But often that's not true. Part of recovery means not seeing ourselves any longer as victims who are tied to behaviors and people who aren't beneficial to our health. Remember today that we all have decisions we make that we need to take responsibility for, and that some of these choices can free us from the chains that we have voluntarily bound around us.

AFFIRMATION FOR THE DAY: When I feel imprisoned, I am usually the one holding the key that can liberate me.

Now is the accepted time.

—II Corinthians 6:2

One week I was asked at the last minute to fill in for a speaker at a conference on a topic that was unfamiliar to me. Seeing this as an opportunity to improve my skills and learn something new, I accepted. Almost immediately, however, panic set in and I spent days obsessing about how awful I would be, how little I had to share with others and how dumb I had been to agree to substitute.

The conference came and went, and despite my certainty that everyone would walk out during my presentation, I received excellent reviews. This prompted me to examine the way I had prepared for the speech and whether I could behave differently the next time something similar happened. As I looked back at the week, I realized that I had expended so much energy "awfulizing" the situation and pondering on the negative what-ifs that I had completely ignored my own birthday, skipped a party for a friend, and given short shrift to the needs of my family. In essence, I had lost an entire week of my life by living in the future—not in the now.

Do you do this too? Do important events come and go that you can't enjoy because you are fixated on something that might happen tomorrow or next week? If so, return to the present right now. Look around and observe what is happening to you at this moment. Whatever it is, experience and enjoy it fully because we can't return tomorrow to relive what we ignore today.

AFFIRMATION FOR THE DAY: Today I will savor every moment instead of living either in the past or the future.

*There is in every true woman's heart a spark of heavenly
fire, which lies dormant in the broad daylight of prosperity; but which kindles up, and beams and blazes in
the dark hour of adversity.*

—WASHINGTON IRVING

I live near one of our state's largest dairy farms and
the hardy Hereford cattle have taught me much about
how to weather storms. Unlike other breeds of cattle
that are often felled by ice storms and nature's violence,
the Herefords usually stand side by side, heads down,
during storms, patiently waiting for the bad weather to
subside. Because they protect their vulnerable areas
and stand fast, they often survive storms that intimidate
or destroy other breeds.

What do we do in times of adversity? Do we put
our heads down and hold our ground, patiently waiting
for a break in the weather? Or do we isolate ourselves
and roam unprotected, allowing the storms to carry us
wherever the winds blow?

When we face adversity in our lives we need to
remember the lessons that nature teaches us. If we can
band together with others, and remain steadfast and
trusting in our ultimate well-being while waiting for the
hard times to dissipate, we will emerge from our stormy
periods with greater reserves of strength and confidence
than good times and prosperity can ever teach us.

AFFIRMATION FOR THE DAY: Today I will stand
my ground no matter how furious the weather around
me rages.

Of all the things you wear, your expression is the most important.

—JANET LANE

When you greet people during the day, what do you think they look at first? Your shoes? The expert tailoring of your clothes? Your hair? Wrong. Most people look at your face before they look at anything else and instantly make a decision about whether they like you or not, whether they want to spend time with you, and what you're like. And their decision is usually based on your expression.

Too many of us forget the importance of our attitude. We spend a lot of money trying to create the right impression by wearing expensive clothes, having facials, and dieting, but then we ruin our work by being angry, impatient and rude. We can be the most attractive and well-educated people in the world but we'll put others off if we're constantly pouting or looking like we've just lost our best friend.

Ask some friends today how you come across to people because you may be surprised to hear what they have to say. Your expression and body language might be saying "I don't like you" when you aren't even aware of it. Concentrate on radiating acceptance and love and be conscious of how you are presenting yourself at all times. If you worry more about your expression and attitude and less about the outside trappings, you'll be making a wise investment of time and energy.

AFFIRMATION FOR THE DAY: Today I will wear a happy expression.

It's never too late to have a happy childhood.
—TOM ROBBINS

Many compulsive eaters come from dysfunctional families where chaos frequently reigned because of the alcoholism or compulsive eating of a parent, or where sexual abuse occurred. An aura of unpredictability is common in homes like these which causes many to turn to food for the missing love and nurturance.

It's critical to work through the damage inflicted by these sorts of families, either in a support group or with a trained therapist, but it's also important at some point to leave the past behind with all of its negative messages and experiences. If a thoughtless parent told us at one point that we were unattractive, couldn't dance well or were stupid, we don't need to make these statements our reality as adults. We can erase these hurtful tapes if we so choose.

If you feel that your childhood was damaging and difficult, form a loving circle of friends who will "reparent" you and support you in the process of unlearning negative messages. Even if our own parents couldn't love us consistently and unconditionally, we need to know that other people can. Learning to dance with joyful abandon and becoming assertive and confident are skills we can foster as easily now as when we were growing up.

AFFIRMATION FOR THE DAY: My past does not have to define who I am today.

The language of truth is unadorned and always simple.

—MARCELLINUS AMMIANUS

During my years of bulimia I don't think I was really capable of telling the truth. Because I was so dishonest about my disease and its severity, it was impossible for me to be completely honest about anything, especially my feelings. I have vivid recollections of embroidering the truth to make it more exciting, and my lies were always elaborate and told with gusto.

In recovery I have learned the importance of being honest with myself and others. I have also learned that people who tell the truth usually do so succinctly and in few words because there is no need to cover up or pretend about anything. Honest people will meet your eyes unwaveringly, speak clearly and unhesitatingly, and not offer excuses for what they say. There is a "ring" to the truth that is unmistakable to others.

Ask yourself today if you are being truthful with yourself and others. Do you find yourself making excuses for your behavior and playing with facts to pull up your ego? If so, resolve to start changing this unbecoming tendency by eliminating the frills in your speech and remembering that honesty requires few words.

AFFIRMATION FOR THE DAY: Truth is always succinct.

We must always change, renew, rejuvenate ourselves;
otherwise we harden.

—JOHANN WOLFGANG VON GOETHE

A lot of compulsive eaters resist change. Although
we aren't always content in our little ruts, we will
frequently avoid making even the smallest changes
because we are afraid of the unknown. Staying stuck for
us is safer than experiencing the risks and rewards of
trying new things.

What are some of the old tapes playing in your
head that are keeping you from rejuvenating and moving ahead with your life? If you came from a family
where nothing you did was praised, you may be subconsciously sabotaging any efforts to improve yourself
because you are fulfilling Mom and Dad's prophecies
that you'll never amount to much. Or perhaps you
constantly find yourself in crisis situations where others
can rescue you and foster immature needs to be dependent.

These types of behaviors are dangerous to recovery
because if we aren't continually challenging our negative
beliefs we can't change or grow. Today be aware of areas
where you may be stuck and need to shake up your
faulty assumptions. Also keep in mind that just as our
body continually renews its cells, we must constantly be
renewing our goals, attitudes and commitment to recovery or we will remain stuck right where we are.

AFFIRMATION FOR THE DAY: Today I will remember that change feels awkward, but that it is
necessary to recover.

Blessed is the man who expects nothing, for he shall never be disappointed.

—ALEXANDER POPE

Perfectionism is a common trait of people who struggle with eating disorders. In fact, for many of us it was an overly high expectation of how we should look and behave that drove us to binge, starve, exercise compulsively and purge. Our waists were never small enough, our thighs were never slender enough and our cheekbones were never prominent enough to satisfy us.

To recover we need to lower our expectations, especially of ourselves. If we are recovering bulimics, we may have swollen salivary glands, puffy abdomens and periodic cravings to purge for some time, and if we are recovering anorexics it may take months before we aren't terrified of losing control over eating. Positive, lasting change requires time and patience, as well as an elimination of the "I want to be well right now" attitude.

In addition to being easier on ourselves, we need to be easier on family and friends. Just because we are trying to change doesn't mean they will too—at least not according to our timetable. Remember today that having exorbitant expectations for ourselves and others doesn't bring satisfaction, only disappointment, anger and frustration.

AFFIRMATION FOR THE DAY: When I confine my expectations to knowing that my Higher Power has a perfect plan for me, I can't be disappointed.

I measure success by how well I sleep on a given night.

—Rod McKuen

For many of us nights are the scariest, hardest part of the day. As we prepare ourselves for sleep we usually review our day, and if we have done wrong or hurt someone else, we feel a twinge of guilt. If we are carrying around a resentment, we feel angry and out of sorts. And if we have ignored a pressing problem that needs attention, we'll toss and turn all night.

One day I was listening to a radio talk show and the topic was "Guilty Consciences." A variety of people called up to confess to different things that they had done for which they had never been caught. Their crimes ranged from income tax evasion to gossiping. What I found most interesting was that all of the guilty people admitted that they had not slept well since they had done whatever was bothering them. Many were taking prescription drugs and drinking heavily to induce enough sleepiness so that they could get through the night.

When we are working a strong program of recovery and we make amends for our past and present errors, we don't need to take anything to help us sleep. As you prepare for bed tonight, ask yourself if your conscience is clear and if you made every effort to live an honest, moral life today. If not, resolve to make amends tomorrow and to behave differently. Restful, restorative sleep will always be your reward.

AFFIRMATION FOR THE DAY: When I am at peace with myself, I sleep well.

To pray is to work, to work is to pray.
— ANCIENT MOTTO OF THE BENEDICTINE ORDER

I once heard a story about a man who stopped in an airport to have his shoes shined on his way to catch a flight. Because he had a few hours before his plane departed, he didn't mind that the older man working on his feet took an inordinately long time to do his job. The businessman was also fascinated by the obvious pleasure the shoeshine man took in meticulously polishing each shoe. As he worked, he hummed happily and wore a broad grin.

Finally, overcome with curiosity and admiration, the businessman asked him how he could be so happy doing work that barely made any money and that was often thankless.

"I'm happy because this work is my gift to the Lord," the shoeshine man responded proudly. "I may not be the richest man in the world, but that doesn't matter to God. What He cares about is the joy I feel while I am going about my business."

Isn't this an important lesson for us to remember when we don't feel that what we're doing is important enough or good enough to matter to the God of our understanding? Resolve to go through today with cheerfulness, optimism and energy, and remind yourself that you don't have to be the president of a company to make a difference in the world. If you can bring joy to everything you do, you can contribute more to your surroundings and the well-being of others than you may have thought possible.

AFFIRMATION FOR THE DAY: Everything I do matters to my Higher Power.

*Be strong and of a good courage; be not afraid,
neither be thou dismayed: for the Lord thy God is
with thee whithersoever thou goest.*

—JOSHUA 1:9

One of my favorite stories is that of a man who,
finding himself in heaven, reviewed his life with God.
What he saw was two sets of footprints in the sand,
walking side by side, but at times of deep crisis in the
man's life there was only one set of footprints.

"Why," the man reproached God, "did you abandon me when the going was really tough?" God's
gentle reply was "Those, my son, were the times
when I carried you."

Although it's hard to believe that we have our
Higher Power by our side supporting us when life is
difficult, this is precisely the time when our faith is
most important. Even if our belief in the love of a
Higher Power is only a tiny shred of hope, this can
often be enough to sustain us and give us the required
courage to get through the day.

If you are feeling alone and buried in your
problems today, think about this story and consider
the possibility that your Higher Power is carrying you
right now. For it's when you have faith during your
darkest moments that you're given the strength and
support you need to face all your challenges.

AFFIRMATION FOR THE DAY: If I believe that I
am never alone, I can't feel lonely or hopeless.

The virtue of all achievement . . . is victory over one-self. Those who know this victory can never know defeat.

—A. J. CRONIN

The author of the above statement tells a story about how he once won the biggest battle of his life—the battle with self-doubt. In his younger years he decided to pursue the dream of publishing a book so he feverishly began to write, hundreds of pages. Soon, however, he was overcome with fear and self-doubt and decided to throw his work away and forget his dream of becoming an author.

That same day, he went for a walk in the country where he encountered a farmer who was trying to build a pasture where both his father and grandfather had already failed. The farmer's perseverance and determination to succeed in spite of the odds so impressed the other man that he rushed home, pulled his papers from the trash and started to rewrite. The book was eventually published in eleven languages and became an international best-seller.

When we are tempted to give up on something because the little voice inside us tells us that we're not good enough, consider the story of this author. If we can remain committed to new endeavors that challenge us and force us to take risks, we'll develop the confidence to see all our projects through as well as conquer our greatest enemy to growth and happiness—self-doubt.

AFFIRMATION FOR THE DAY: When I believe in myself, I always succeed.

Nothing is there more friendly to a man than a friend in need.

—PLAUTUS

One of the surest ways to beat depression, get beyond your woes, and strengthen your recovery is to reach out and help someone who needs a bit of encouragement or compassion. This can be done through a phone call, a friendly letter, or volunteering at an organization that helps those less fortunate than yourself, like a soup kitchen.

It's impossible to be self-pitying or down when volunteering. One woman who lost her daughter to leukemia found that the only antidote to her depression was to throw herself into work at a homeless shelter and with abandoned babies who had contracted the AIDS virus. She later said the experience had helped her put her own grief into perspective and allowed her to appreciate the other aspects of her life.

If you have never volunteered before, decide today that you will commit some time regularly to a cause you feel passionate about. It can be teaching illiterate adults to read, working in politics, building houses for the homeless or helping another compulsive eater. You'll soon find that although you may appear to be doing the bulk of the giving, the gifts you will receive yourself are priceless.

AFFIRMATION FOR THE DAY: I help myself most when I help others.

Be still, and know that I am God.

—PSALMS 46:10

One morning after a sleepless night worrying about a variety of obligations that faced me, I went for a walk in an effort to calm down. As the miles went by, I found the soothing phrase above going through my head again and again. By the end of the hour I felt strangely peaceful. I knew, deep down, that everything was going to work out fine.

I later realized that I had been practicing a form of meditation. Being a perfectionist, I had always thought that meditation meant sitting cross-legged, eyes closed, and repeating an unintelligible word for an hour or so. Because I get restless easily, this form of meditation had always eluded me. My walk showed me, however, that peace and stillness of mind could come with rhythmic motion and the repetition of a soothing phrase.

If you aren't yet meditating because you don't know the right way to do it, try today to find an alternative method. It may take the form of walking your dog, riding on a stationary bike or driving in a silent car. Whatever it is, don't judge yourself. We all have different ways we connect and commune with our Higher Power, and the only "wrong" thing we can do is fail to try at all.

AFFIRMATION FOR THE DAY: There are many ways to reach my Higher Power, and I must find what works best for me.

*We should be careful to get out of an experience only the
wisdom that is in it—and stop there; lest we be like the
cat that sits down on a hot stove lid. She will never sit
down on a hot stove lid again—and that is well; but also
she will never sit down on a cold one any more.*

—MARK TWAIN

Have you heard the saying: "Don't throw the baby
out with the bathwater?" It's an appropriate phrase for
learning how to live in recovery.

When you find yourself bingeing at a certain
restaurant, do you avoid that restaurant forever or do
you order a different dish next time? If you have a
disagreement with a friend, do you decide to end the
friendship or do you work through the problem? And if
you attend a meeting of a self-help group that doesn't
appeal to you, do you decide that the whole organization is worthless or do you try a different meeting?

We compulsive eaters need to be less extreme in
our judgments about situations that upset us. I was once
quick to leap to conclusions that weren't consistent with
my experiences. For example, if someone hurt me I
would conclude that I couldn't trust anyone, and I
would immediately isolate myself. This type of irrational, black-and-white behavior hurts only us.

Remember today that maturity in recovery involves making decisions that don't limit us in any way.
Be careful to extract some wisdom from every experience you have and then be thankful that you have been
given the opportunity to learn a lesson that will help you
in the future.

AFFIRMATION FOR THE DAY: My best teachers
are the hot stoves of life.

I am not a gold coin—not everyone is going to love me.
—ANONYMOUS

I was talking to a friend one day when another person's name came up. I said I hadn't heard from the woman despite repeated attempts to reach her. My friend responded by laughing and saying, "Give it up—she doesn't like you."

Immediately I felt a rush of anger, self-pity and confusion. What had I done to deserve this person's dislike? I had always been friendly and courteous to her, and had even gone out of my way on several occasions to help her. As I searched my memory I couldn't even think of a time when we had exchanged a cross word.

As a result of this experience and others, I've learned that I don't always have to know why other people don't like me. I used to think that everyone had to admire me or there was something wrong with me. My self-esteem rose or fell based on other people's opinions.

Remind yourself today that you are just a human being with faults and quirks that some are bound to find grating and disagreeable. Accept that just as you aren't comfortable with everyone you meet, others aren't always going to enjoy you, either. Our goal in recovery is not to be universally liked because that's unrealistic; our responsibility is to love ourselves enough so that outside approval is unnecessary.

AFFIRMATION FOR THE DAY: When I love myself unconditionally, I don't draw my self-esteem from the opinions of others.

There are two things to aim at in life: first, to get what you want, and after that, to enjoy it. Only the wisest of mankind achieve the second.

—LOGAN PEARSALL SMITH

Someone once told me, "Be careful what you pray for because you might get it." I scoffed when I first heard this because I was sure that if I prayed for something specific, then it had to be something I needed and deserved. How wrong I was.

In early recovery I prayed for a variety of things— all material—that I did indeed get, but that contained hidden pitfalls. In hindsight I realized that I had not let my Higher Power guide my life; I had imposed my ideas about what would be best for me without stopping to think about whether they'd be beneficial for me and those around me in the long run. It reminded me of the many Hollywood stars who admit that they have spent much of their lives wishing for fame, only to discover that once they "made it" they lost their privacy, security and close personal friendships.

Take time today to reflect on the things you have worked and prayed for, and whether or not you have enjoyed them once they came your way. If you are the type of person who only enjoys the chase, not the capture, then you are setting yourself up to be forever greedy, grasping and unfulfilled. Just for today, make an honest effort to be among "the wisest of mankind" who truly enjoy the fruits of their labor and experience contentment and genuine gratitude for the many blessings, large and small, that we all have in our lives.

AFFIRMATION FOR THE DAY: Knowing what I want and appreciating what I have are gifts of my recovery.

With knowing comes responsibility;
With responsibility comes choice;
With choice comes the future.

—ANONYMOUS

Once we know that we are compulsive eaters who have a disease, we have a responsibility to address it. We not only are obligated to change and create a better life for ourselves, but we also have the responsibility to change for the sake of others because it isn't fair to inflict our moodiness, anger and preoccupation with food on them, too.

Some people avoid taking responsibility for their compulsive eating through a variety of ruses. For example, they will look at a bulimic who is vomiting blood and say self-righteously, "I'm not that bad!" Or they will find someone heavier than they are and say, "I'm not that fat!" This attitude prevents us from being honest with ourselves and allows our denial to block our recovery efforts.

Is there something you are not accepting in your life because you don't want to take responsibility for it? Instead of being frightened that you will be unable to handle the choices that come with acknowledging and accepting the truth, take this opportunity to make a change in your life. Whether it is your compulsive eating or another situation you are avoiding dealing with, summon up your honesty and courage today to start the process of creating a better and different tomorrow.

AFFIRMATION FOR THE DAY: The gift of knowledge not only clears away my confusion, but also allows me to choose the direction of my path.

The real miracle is not to walk either on water or in thin air, but to walk on earth.

—THICH NHAT HANH

Throughout history and into the present, people have flocked to places all over the world where miracles are said to have occurred. Thousands of men and women make arduous and expensive pilgrimages to these sites hoping that they, too, will have their lives transformed by some wondrous occurrence. Many others wait expectantly at home for their own miracles, unable to enjoy life until something fantastic—like winning the lottery—happens to them.

This type of fanciful thinking keeps people from appreciating the mundane "miracles" that occur during each day of their lives. Many of us forget that it is a miracle to have a healthy child, to make a good friend or to experience a beautiful sunrise. When we stop and realize that the word's definition is anything that causes us to "marvel" or "wonder," we can see that many large and small happenings in our lives can be viewed as *bona fide* miracles.

Try not to live in a state of suspended animation today waiting for water to turn to wine or for the dead to be resurrected. Look around you and notice the miracles that you have in your life and give thanks for them. When you are able to appreciate the wonders that are already present, you won't need to live in or hope for a fantasy world any longer.

AFFIRMATION FOR THE DAY: If I am living a balanced and abstinent life today, that is a miracle.

The natural healing force within each one of us is the greatest force in getting well.

—HIPPOCRATES

I think it's interesting to note that the ancient meaning of the word "heal" comes from the same root as the words "whole" and "holiness." It makes sense that when we are healing from our wounds we are also becoming more whole and holy—i.e., getting back in touch with the God within us that we ignored in favor of compulsive eating.

In China, physicians used to be fired or not paid if their patients got sick. The belief was that the natural condition of the body is one of wellness, and that sickness is an aberration caused by improper thoughts, diet or actions. Through acupuncture and other gentle healing methods, the Chinese would stimulate the body's own system to help restore the patient to health.

As we continue our recovery we must remember to draw upon our own healing forces to help guide us back to health and spiritual wholeness. Through affirmations, prayer and meditation we have the ability to unleash powerful energies that can help correct the "mistake" of some illnesses and assist in restoring us to our natural condition of well-being, optimism and serenity.

AFFIRMATION FOR THE DAY: My own internal wisdom is one of my greatest assets in recovery.

The secret of being miserable is to have the leisure to bother about whether you are happy or not.
—GEORGE BERNARD SHAW

One morning I woke up miserable, angry and frustrated. Life just wasn't going my way and I knew it was going to be a long, sad twenty-four hours. Because I had no pressing engagements or work to do, the day got worse as it dragged on because every passing moment gave me more opportunity to brood.

The next morning I woke up with the same set of problems, but a different daily agenda. I had errands to run, letters to write and other important matters to tend to, and I was in a much more upbeat mood at the end of the day. The lesson I learned was that my misery was in direct proportion to how busy I was; when I did nothing it grew into a monster, and when I kept myself occupied it was manageable.

Don't let your unhappiness swallow up your day. If you are feeling depressed and out of sorts today, nip your emotions in the bud before they have a chance to overtake your entire outlook. Get busy, watch a movie or immerse yourself in someone else's problems. If you can redirect your energy away from your negativity and into another area, you'll discover how differently you'll view your problems and how much happier you'll be at the end of the day.

AFFIRMATION FOR THE DAY: When I give myself leisure to brood, my depression and problems grow by the hour.

We cannot swing up a rope that is attached only to our own belt.

—WILLIAM ERNEST HOCKING

One night as I carried my sleeping son to bed I was struck by how relaxed and free of tension his little body was. He had fallen asleep while I was holding him, utterly trusting of my strength and love for him. He knew that no harm would come to him while in my arms.

Don't we all desire this feeling of utter trust at times, and a sense that someone else will always love us and take care of us no matter what? Too often we'll look for this protection in relationships where we hope someone else will supply us with what we need. Instead of developing our own inner resources we focus on others—our spouses or parents, for example—and try to make them all-wise and all-powerful, which inevitably leads to disappointment.

As adults, the only way we are going to have the same peaceful trust of sleeping babies is if we have a strong relationship with a Higher Power. For it is only when we have faith that there is always a pair of powerful arms encircling us, giving us the necessary strength and courage to carry on when our own efforts fail, that we won't make the mistake of depending on others to help us feel loved and secure.

AFFIRMATION FOR THE DAY: When I can trust in the strength of a loving Higher Power, I am relaxed, confident and peaceful.

It is not the man who has too little, but the man who craves more that is poor.

—LUCIUS ANNAEUS SENECA

Being content with ourselves and our lives is one of the most difficult tasks facing a compulsive eater. Jealousy toward those around us for their slim bodies, happy families and self-confidence has consistently been a problem for us. No matter how much we have had in the past, whether it was emotional or physical blessings, we have rarely been satisfied.

Feelings of envy are usually tied in with low self-esteem. We don't value what we have or who we are, so consequently everyone else appears to have something we want. Often our jealousy will manifest itself in shopping sprees during which we accumulate scores of items we don't need but that we think will confer upon us the desired traits of beauty, power, success and self-confidence.

Take stock of your own situation today. If you're always wishing for something material that you feel will make you happy, focus instead on what's lacking inside. Work on enhancing your spirituality and resist cluttering your life with more unnecessary possessions. If you can discipline yourself to be grateful for every large and small blessing you receive, you'll discover what true prosperity is all about.

AFFIRMATION FOR THE DAY: If I say "I want" more than "I have," my gratitude needs work.

Whatever happens at all happens as it should; you will find this true, if you watch narrowly.
—MARCUS AURELIUS ANTONINUS

One day I spoke with a woman who had endured a difficult divorce compounded by her children's decision to leave her and live with their father. She told me how she had felt overwhelmed with fear about being a single, middle-aged, overweight woman with no skills, and how angry she had been at God for having put her in such a difficult position.

After months of crying and eating, she finally realized that she was only hurting herself with her self-destructiveness. Consequently she enrolled in some local classes, started to lose weight and began spending more time on her appearance. Within five years she was the successful proprietor of her own business, her children had come back to live with her, and she was at a comfortable weight. Now she is grateful for the disruption and hurt the divorce brought her and the changes it engendered, but candidly admits that she never would have believed that it would benefit her in the long run.

When I am totally baffled as to why I am going through a rough period, I think about what my friend went through and how much better off she is now. Remind yourself today that as hard as it may be to fathom, every dark time in our lives will bring us to a position of greater strength and wisdom if we can trust the process of change and wait for the reasons to present themselves in the future.

AFFIRMATION FOR THE DAY: Today I will remember that my Higher Power has a plan for me that I won't always understand.

Look out how you use proud words.
When you let proud words go, it is not
  easy to call them back.
They wear long boots, hard boots.
—CARL SANDBURG

One day someone called to ask if I would consider speaking at a gathering in another state. The woman then asked if I could send my resume and list of honors so that the full committee organizing the affair could approve my appearance. Feeling a bit challenged, I boasted about my background and assured her that I could do an excellent job.

When I hung up the phone, I felt sick. Instead of letting others decide my merits themselves, I had had to go and puff myself up so that others would think I was wonderful. It hit me like a truck that my humility, or lack thereof, sorely needed attention.

There is nothing quite so distasteful as someone carrying on about themselves, desperate to draw attention to their accomplishments because they fear others won't notice them. Try not to be guilty of bragging today. If you deserve acclaim you will receive it, and not always in ways you expect. When admiration, support or attention come from people whom you don't have to prompt, you'll always find that it sounds sweeter and carries more weight than anything you could possibly say about yourself.

AFFIRMATION FOR THE DAY: Today I won't toot my own horn.

An optimist expects his dreams to come true; a pessimist expects his nightmares to.
                                        —LAURENCE J. PETER

As compulsive eaters we are often guilty of pessimism. We find excuses to fail, we expect the worst to happen and we put a damper on other people's enthusiasm. I heard my share of pessimists when my first child demonstrated an angelic temperament: "Wait till your next one comes!" they all happily warned me.

I was once a terrible pessimist. If I got a good grade in school, I was certain that the teacher had made a mistake. Every time I boarded an airplane, I "knew" deep in my gut it would crash. And when I got pregnant, I spent nine months worrying about birth deformities, the pain of labor and what my body would look like afterwards.

I eventually stopped looking for the dark side of life, mostly because it depressed me so. I had also often found that much of what I feared never even came to pass. Switching to a more optimistic frame of mind wasn't that easy, though, because pessimism had long been a way of hedging my bets. If things didn't work out as I had hoped, I was able to pretend that it didn't matter because I hadn't expected it to anyway.

Try to be an optimist today, even if it means setting yourself up to feel disappointed if life doesn't go your way. You may also be surprised to find that if you can greet each day with joy and expectancy, you are more likely to have the positive outcomes you desire.

AFFIRMATION FOR THE DAY: When I am being pessimistic, I am living a life of fear.

Selfishness is the greatest curse of the human race.
—WILLIAM EWART GLADSTONE

When I first started to recover from my eating disorder, a number of people told me that I had to put my recovery at the top of my list of priorities if I were to make a clean break with the past. Although this sounded rather selfish to me, others explained that what was really selfish was to continue eating compulsively because by doing so I would never become the wife, daughter, friend or mother I wanted to be.

We need to understand the difference between being selfish with our disease and selfish with our recovery. When I think back over my bulimic years I remember countless incidences of dictating the restaurant my family and friends had to attend, demanding special diet foods, holding people up with my lateness, and saying cruel things to assuage my sense of inferiority. That was selfish in a negative way.

Selfishness in recovery means only one thing: making sure our needs get met so that our abstinence and serenity remain intact. We don't have to run roughshod over people to do this; we can simply be more assertive when we are being pushed around, shamed by others or encouraged to veer from our paths.

When you set your priorities today, remember to think "First things first." Your "first thing" should always be your recovery because from that will flow all of the other blessings and joys of being alive.

AFFIRMATION FOR THE DAY: It is not selfish to make my recovery my top priority.

The great man is he who does not lose his child's-heart.

—MENCIUS

What do you do for fun? Someone asked me that question once and I looked at her with a blank, uncomprehending stare. I didn't know about fun because fun wasn't a part of my thinking. I thought I was a mature, serious adult, or at least I hoped I was. Adults didn't have fun; they had important responsibilities.

My obsession with seriousness dates back to my childhood when I wanted to be grown-up so badly that I tried to be mature at all costs. Free time was filled with schoolwork and activities that would get me into the "right" college. I never joined friends who went on fun trips or outings because I didn't see the long-term value in participating. It never occurred to me that it was odd that I related best to people several decades older than me and that the company of my peers bored me.

In recovery we need to recapture the wonderment and joyful anticipation of children, because without it our journey will be difficult and unhappy. Can you allow yourself to be silly and carefree, or do you think that's embarrassing and beneath you? Is your idea of fun working hard and making money? Take time to be a child today and don't worry how others perceive you. When you can touch and identify with the youngster inside who sees life in an exciting, fresh way, you'll be given a new pair of eyes that will allow you to see the world with unlimited joy.

AFFIRMATION FOR THE DAY: Today I will look at life through the eyes of a child.

Even when walking in a party of no more than three I can always be certain of learning from those I am with. There will be good qualities that I can select for imitation and bad ones that will teach me what requires correction in myself.

—CONFUCIUS

A woman called me once to say that she had stopped attending her favorite Overeaters Anonymous meeting because of a certain man there who was intent on converting everyone to his way of thinking. When called on he would often preach loud and long despite the obvious frustration and boredom of those around him. The woman said that she and others like herself were deserting the meeting in droves despite its convenient time and location.

I pointed out that she was the only one who was being hurt by her actions. By not going to meetings she was jeopardizing her recovery and depriving herself of the input of everyone else who was in attendance. Besides, I said, she could always learn how *not* to act by observing this disagreeable person.

When we are thrust into similarly unpleasant situations, instead of trying to escape from them we should see what we can learn. The next time you are in a group of people, look around at your companions. Often you'll find someone who has qualities you'd like to emulate and someone who grates on you. If you can remember that life is like a classroom where we are all teachers and students to one another, every situation you're in will enrich and enlighten you in valuable ways.

AFFIRMATION FOR THE DAY: Every person I meet can teach me something about myself.

Oh, a trouble's a ton, or a trouble's an ounce,
Or a trouble is what you make it,
And it isn't the fact that you're hurt that counts,
But only how you take it.
              —EDMUND VANCE COOKE

I have a very low pain threshold. I usually scream or faint when I have shots, and I'll put off even routine visits to the dentist for fear of the drill. I also tend to have a low threshold for emotional slights and I've been known to brood for hours about things that wouldn't bother someone else.

To aid my recovery from compulsive eating I've had to learn how to disregard some of my mental pain, or at least view it in a different light. If someone doesn't return my phone call, I can't automatically assume that they don't like me; perhaps they haven't even gotten my message yet. Or if I'm at a party and the hostess barely acknowledges me, it doesn't mean I'm not important to her; she just may feel the need to help other nervous people feel comfortable.

How we accept these kinds of slights and misunderstandings says a great deal about our maturity. Being able to minimize our own importance and put ourselves in other people's shoes is a difficult but crucial skill we must learn. Remember today not to blow situations out of proportion or be quick to see hurts where none may be intended. If you can be generous and give others the benefit of the doubt, you'll bestow upon yourself peace of mind.

AFFIRMATION FOR THE DAY: When I make my troubles weigh a ton, I always get crushed.

The mind . . . can make a Heav'n of Hell, a Hell of Heav'n.

—JOHN MILTON

Many of us feel like we have lived in a hell on earth. Our compulsive eating has driven us to do things that shame us, anger us and worry others. Frequently when we look back at our behavior while bingeing, we feel like a monster has been responsible for many of the things we've done.

Compulsive eating is indeed a hell on earth, but we have the tools to create a heaven right now for ourselves, too. By making amends for past actions, learning to love ourselves and others, and continuing to evaluate our actions daily, we can renew ourselves—essentially, be "born again."

No one can make you stay in a prison of your mind without your permission. Resolve today to make a fresh start, and ignore any negative self-talk that you are too old or too "bad" to have a rewarding and happy life. Every day, every moment, is an opportunity to renew ourselves and do things differently, and if we are ready to accept it, the kingdom of heaven can be ours right now.

AFFIRMATION FOR THE DAY: Today and every day I have the ability to choose whether I want to live in heaven or hell.

Reputation is what you're supposed to be. Character is what you are.

—ANONYMOUS

As compulsive eaters we generally fall into two categories—those who overestimate our charms and are blind to our faults, and those who cannot state a single positive attribute we possess. In conjunction with being unable to accurately assess ourselves, we often don't know how others view us.

If we are to be in recovery, we must strip away the self-deception that keeps us from seeing ourselves as we really are. It took a few brave friends to let me know that despite my efforts to be friendly and loving, I was generally perceived as cold, judgmental and a know-it-all. This painful awareness finally spurred me to look at and change many of my mannerisms and attitudes.

Write down today what you believe are your chief characteristics, then ask some trusted friends if they see you that way. If there is a great disparity between the two views, work on ways to make your character and reputation come together in harmony. Ask yourself if you put up barriers to friendship because you don't trust people, or if the anger that frightens others is related to an old, unaddressed issue that you're afraid to deal with. Once you can take this difficult and painful step, you'll be closer to allowing others to see your true, beautiful essence and you won't need to put on masks and pretenses any longer.

AFFIRMATION FOR THE DAY: When my reputation doesn't match my character, I need to change the messages I send to others.

Comparisons are odious.

—JOHN FORTESCUE

We tend to be rather hard on ourselves and wish that we were better-looking, thinner, shapelier, richer, funnier and smarter than we are. We usually hold ourselves up against others and find ourselves lacking, which leads to envy, anger and depression.

One sure way to stay stuck in our disease is to compare our progress—or anything else—with that of other people. I used to stare enviously at pictures of models wishing I had their bodies, and worship people who I thought had wonderful, exciting lives. What I inevitably found was that the people I put on a pedestal came tumbling down at some point, resulting in broken friendships and disillusionment.

To recover we need to remember that we all progress at different rates. To compare our weight loss, abstinence or meal plan with another's can only set us back. By the same token, to covet someone else's life is dangerous, for not only do we not know what difficulties they have to deal with, but we remain blind to the many gifts and blessings we already possess ourselves.

AFFIRMATION FOR THE DAY: Envy prevents me from seeing myself clearly and lovingly.

Forgiveness offers everything I want.

—A Course in Miracles

We all want to be free, happy and unencumbered by the past. But many of us have lived with a chip on our shoulder and anger in our hearts for so long that we've forgotten what it's like not to feel aggravated whenever we don't get our way, or when someone does something to annoy us. We know we want peace of mind but we don't know how to achieve it.

What usually holds us back from this type of serenity is the absence of forgiveness. When we are brooding over past slights and injustices, we aren't allowing ourselves to fully experience either the giving or receiving of love. I find that when I am incapable of forgiving another person, the feeling inside me is acid, all-consuming and painful. I become obsessed with justifying my behavior, and I often fail to notice that I'm destroying myself in the process.

We need to recognize that withholding love and acceptance from just one person can severely erode the quality of love we extend to ourselves and others, because then our loving has become conditional. Imagine yourself forgiving someone today and think about how good it will feel to experience harmony with this person. Remember also that it takes a strong and secure person to make the first move in healing a break, but that the peace of mind you will feel as a result will quickly outweigh the fear you have in taking this scary step.

AFFIRMATION FOR THE DAY: Today I'll remember that forgiveness is a gift I can choose to give myself and others.

Let your tears come. Let them water your soul.
—EILEEN MAYHEW

When I was growing up I tried hard not to cry when I was sick, wounded or frustrated. I thought that being in perfect control of my emotions was admirable, but my repression of my true feelings started to take strange forms as I got older. For example, during sad movies I giggled and in light-hearted moments I was almost always the only person not laughing.

Being in recovery means being in touch with our emotions. One of the strongest ones we experience, too, is grief—grief about past actions, grief about missed opportunities and grief about things we have never properly mourned. If we try to stop our tears when these feelings surface, we will be damming up valuable emotions that can help heal us and that need to be expressed.

It is not a sign of weakness to cry; in fact, to be able to express sadness without fear is a sign of courage. Remember today that tears are a necessary part of working through the past and accepting the present, and that when you are finished—like the calm after a storm—you will always feel more peaceful, clearheaded and unburdened.

AFFIRMATION FOR THE DAY: Today I will accept and express my emotions appropriately.

It's amazing how fast doors open to us when we dare to take control of a situation.

—Catherine Ponder

Several years ago my husband and I started a business and we hired some experienced people to help us. As time went on I found myself avoiding difficult and unfamiliar tasks because I felt unsure of my abilities and afraid of failure. When someone unexpectedly left the company and all of her duties fell into my lap, I panicked.

Then an amazing thing happened. Not knowing what else to do, I called a lot of friends who had knowledge in the various areas I now controlled. I admitted my ignorance and asked them for help. Everyone was generous with their time and resources, and before long I was comfortable with my new tasks.

The same lesson holds true with our recovery. Once we decide that we are going to make it and that we're going to ask for help in getting the job done, doors fly open to us. We find that a lot of people are willing to share their expertise without thought of recompense and that they genuinely want to see us succeed. Remind yourself today that although it takes courage to seize control of a situation, when you finally take a deep breath and bite the bullet, doors will fly open to help you.

AFFIRMATION FOR THE DAY: When I accept a new responsibility or attempt something unfamiliar to me, the help I need will be readily available if I ask for it.

Challenge is the correct way to view an inconvenience, and inconvenience is the incorrect way to view a challenge.

—ZEN BUDDHIST SAYING

What do you do when you find yourself inconvenienced or challenged in some way? If you are like 60 to 90 percent of Americans, you get "stressed out" and then visit the family doctor for complaints ranging from muscle spasms and insomnia, to depression and ulcers.

Many researchers now believe that these conditions can be alleviated by strengthening our immune system through positive thinking. Although a lot of people will become ill as a result of stress, there is a group that won't: the "stress hardy."

When people in this group were asked how they would react to being fired or losing all their money, they invariably responded that they would find a silver lining in the challenge, look for a way to rebuild and, most important, would view the experience as an inevitable stepping-stone to something better.

Try today to be one of the "stress hardy." Don't allow your challenges to overwhelm and depress you. Fight back instead with hope, positivity and resourcefulness. When you can look at everything that happens to you as a ticket to greater fulfillment and success, your health will be an accurate reflection of your outlook.

AFFIRMATION FOR THE DAY: My challenges are all stepping-stones to a better way of life.

You just have to learn not to care about the dust-mice under the beds.

—MARGARET MEAD

I have a friend who is a compulsive neatnik. She can't go to bed at night until her house is impeccably spotless. This means that she is frequently up past midnight doing laundry, mopping floors and rearranging her cabinets and drawers. It's no wonder that she enjoys little and is usually exhausted.

Perfectionism is not only impossible, it is boring. When we find ourselves trying to make everything "just so" we need to stop and think about the Japanese. They believe that having things in perfect order is fatal to the imagination and kills individual experience. For example, when laying out their gardens they place the plants asymmetrically so that the uneven areas stimulate the viewer to complete the picture in his own mind.

For compulsive eaters who often strive for perfect bodies and perfect lives, this is an example worth heeding. Ease up on yourself today and learn to appreciate the uneven features and asymmetry of your life. Loving yourself unconditionally, whether you are perfect or not, may leave you with a few dust-mice under the bed, but it will also help free you to live with more serenity and self-acceptance.

AFFIRMATION FOR THE DAY: I don't have to dress impeccably, have a spotless house or look like a model to love myself.

Nothing is stronger than habit.

—OVID

When I was bulimic I often found myself binge-ing whenever I was depressed, confused or alone. I also found that certain people, situations and stores evoked uncomfortable feelings that I could not describe or cope with, but that bingeing and purging temporarily relieved.

When I began to recover I realized that just like the ex-smoker needs to learn that a cigarette doesn't always go with a cup of coffee, I needed to reprogram my habits. Being home alone didn't mean I had to raid the refrigerator. Facing writer's block didn't mean eating a gallon of ice cream. And walking through a shopping mall didn't mean eating four lunches at different fast-food places.

Learning new habits isn't easy but it *can* be done. All it takes is time and the willingness to feel uncomfortable for a short period—usually a minimum of three weeks. Make a commitment today to begin reprogramming an undesirable behavior. Write about it in your journal and then share your decision to change with another person. Remind yourself often that you can only deal with your discomfort one day at a time and that the first day of a new behavior is always the most challenging.

AFFIRMATION FOR THE DAY: I can choose to break any habit I have.

I think I can, I think I can . . .
—WATTY PIPER, IN *THE LITTLE ENGINE THAT COULD*

Negative, self-defeating attitudes and behaviors are a sure way to sabotage recovery. If we subconsciously believe that we will never achieve abstinence, joy or personal satisfaction despite all of our best efforts, we won't.

The mind is a very powerful tool. Some researchers believe that once a person truly thinks he will achieve a certain goal, he will. Basketball players who mentally see themselves shooting perfect baskets often play better than those who don't practice this mental imagery. Top athletes and other professionals now often travel with their own relaxation experts who help them visualize success in their chosen fields because of the dramatic results.

We don't necessarily need our own relaxation experts to benefit from these techniques. When we hear negative talk in our heads like "I have no willpower," "I'm a big failure," "I'm ugly" or "I'll never be successful at anything," we can immediately counter with positive affirmations like "I'm beautiful," "I can be successful at anything I set my mind to" and "I'm a good friend to others." Just like The Little Engine That Could who talked himself into going up and over a difficult hill by repeating "I think I can," so too can we tell ourselves "I think I can" whenever we are facing our own big hills.

AFFIRMATION FOR THE DAY: When I believe I can, I can.

Nothing so needs reforming as other people's habits.
—MARK TWAIN

We compulsive eaters are familiar with denial about our problems with bingeing, but one of our biggest difficulties lies with our denial about our own behavior. Although we are usually able to acknowledge dysfunctional eating patterns, we are slower to recognize and address the ways that we sabotage our recovery through judgmentalism of others.

If we find ourselves constantly criticizing others for their faults, we can take this as a sign that we have similar problems of our own to work through. I once found myself getting angry at people when they were rude and arrogant. I also found fault with people who were thoughtless and concerned only with themselves. Finally I admitted that my anger stemmed from the fact that those were some of the qualities I disliked about myself and that I was really the one who needed reforming, not them.

Do you find yourself constantly taking inventory of others' character defects? Are you short-tempered because you feel no one can live up to your expectations? If so, you need to examine yourself carefully today for the problems you see in others because the chances are high that you embody them instead. If you probe your behavior honestly and persistently and then take steps to change what you don't like, you might be surprised to find that your irritation and obsession with the faults of others is eliminated.

AFFIRMATION FOR THE DAY: Today I will focus on improving myself, not anyone else.

Never bend your head, always hold it high. Look the world straight in the face.

—HELEN KELLER

One night as I sat at a meeting for recovering compulsive eaters, I heard a bulimic who was entering her fifth year of abstaining from bingeing and purging say that one of the biggest benefits of recovery was that she was now able to look people in the eye.

When I was bulimic I rarely looked people in the eye, either. How could I when I was too depressed about the way I looked to go to parties, or I was constantly lying to cover up for missing food and bizarre behavior? I knew it was true that the eyes were the windows of the soul, and I thought that if anyone looked at mine they'd see how hollow I was inside.

Holding our heads up without fear is one of the biggest payoffs of recovery. Instead of staring at the ground and avoiding people's looks, we learn that facing ourselves means we are now able to face others. Looking in the mirror also isn't the tortured experience it once was because we are learning the art of self-love and acceptance.

Remember also today that we must also look life in the eye. Don't let your bills pile up, phone calls go unreturned and obligations go unmet because of some irrational fears. Usually you'll find that nothing is ever as bad as you think it is, and that recovery gives you plenty of inner resources to deal with whatever is before you.

AFFIRMATION FOR THE DAY: When I am always bending my head down, the scenery never changes.

Miracles are propitious accidents, the natural causes of which are too complicated to be readily understood.

—GEORGE SANTAYANA

So many of us look outside of ourselves to find examples of our Higher Power's presence in life. We tend to think miracles are dramatic events when deaf people learn to hear, someone is rescued from certain death or when a severely retarded person is a gifted musician.

I revised my definition of miracles one night after hearing one woman's story of recovery from compulsive eating. Despite years of sexual abuse, failed marriages and multiple traumas, she had managed to lose two hundred pounds and keep them off for several years. She said proudly to the group, "I'm a miracle!"

I realize now that I'm a miracle, too. I'm not perfect but I'm binge-free, honest and more fun to be around than I once was. I'm also a good mother, wife and friend. These statements amaze me when I think about how many years were filled with unhappiness, poor relationships and little energy for anyone but myself.

Do you think you're a miracle? You are if you're in recovery, trying to improve yourself and working to have a closer relationship with your Higher Power. Take time today to celebrate your accomplishments and recognize how far you have come. Don't look to others to see examples of divine intervention when you are a living, breathing example yourself.

AFFIRMATION FOR THE DAY: I am a miracle!

Where there is patience and humility, there is neither anger nor vexation.

—St. Francis of Assisi

When was the last time you stood impatiently in a checkout line, making snide comments about the ineptness of the clerk? Or honked loudly at an older person in front of you because you felt he was driving too slowly?

As compulsive eaters we are familiar with impatience. Anyone who stood in the way of a binge was subjected to our impatience or anger. We dealt harshly with waiters or waitresses who got our orders wrong or delivered meals slowly. We drove like maniacs as we gobbled binge foods or headed for a binge spot. We recklessly endangered ourselves and others as we pursued our god—food.

Impatience needs constant attention because it can crop up with the slightest provocation. Instead of getting annoyed, try telling yourself that the supermarket checkout clerk is slow because she's trying to make ends meet by working two jobs and that the older person who is driving slowly is stiff with arthritic pains and is struggling to live an independent life.

Take the time today to put yourself in others' shoes and see life through their eyes. If you work daily on developing patience, humility and tolerance for others, your anger and self-pity won't serve as a barrier to your recovery any longer.

AFFIRMATION FOR THE DAY: When I am angry, cynical and impatient, I am thinking only of myself.

A vision without a task is but a dream, a task without a vision is drudgery, a vision and a task is the hope of the world.
— FROM A CHURCH IN SUSSEX, ENGLAND, c. 1730

Do you know where you are going? Do you have a plan for your life? Or do you rarely think about your future and goals but let outside forces shape your destiny instead?

Some of us have dreams about what we'd like to accomplish but we never take steps to realize those dreams. And then some of us have no dreams; we go through the daily motions monotonously, then wonder why we feel like being alive is more of a chore than a joy. But those of us who have a plan, and a blueprint for carrying out that plan, are the ones who can inspire others and bring a fresh perspective to old ways of doing things.

If you are unclear about where you are going with your life, take several minutes today to try to visualize what it is you'd like to accomplish during the next week, month or year, and then do something that will bring you closer to that goal. If losing weight is your dream, have an abstinent meal plan today. If you want to change jobs, update your resume. And if you want a harmonious relationship with your family, reach out to them with love. Thinking about the changes you want to make is important, but don't forget the important step of backing up your ideas with positive action.

AFFIRMATION FOR THE DAY: Today I'll have a vision and a task.

This too shall pass.

—ANONYMOUS

There have been many moments in my recovery process that have been filled with despair and pain. Initially I thought that not being bulimic meant my life would be effortless and that I would never be depressed again. I was certainly in for a rude awakening when I first found this wasn't so.

When we put down the food, we are confronted with the reality of life, which isn't always a bed of roses. Whereas before our setbacks were cushioned with food or the deliberate lack of it, now we don't have that crutch anymore. Perhaps for the first time we feel the searing sadness of being fired, losing a loved one, or finding out that someone we thought was a friend really wasn't. Unaccustomed to the depth of our emotions, our first reaction is usually to run and hide.

Experiences like these call for the strength of inner resources, as well as the recognition that hurts don't last forever, as bad as they might seem at the moment. The next time you feel unloved, abandoned or slighted, ignore the little voice inside that tells you that your plight is worse or more painful than anyone else's. Remember also, that although many things may come to pass, they almost never come to stay.

AFFIRMATION FOR THE DAY: Today I will remember that hard times never last forever.

To be loved, be lovable.

—Ovid

Compulsive eaters are known to crave love, and when they do not get it, tend to turn to food and other addictive substances and behaviors to satisfy that longing. There is never enough to sate the compulsive eater, however; what would be sufficient for another person is unacceptable to one who does not know moderation.

I fell into the "You don't love me enough" trap frequently before I started to recover. If my parents, siblings, friends or business colleagues didn't appear to approve of me or something I had done, I would sink into anger, self-pity and food. I would also look for a way to gain their affection, often sacrificing my own needs in the process.

I have since learned that we can't make others love us, but that we stand a better chance of gaining their affection when we are lovable first. Being endearing probably won't come easily to us initially because we were often quite selfish and annoying while compulsively eating. But if we are patient as we start to shift our preoccupation from ourselves to others, we'll find that not only will we gain their affection and trust but that achieving outside approval ultimately becomes less important than how much love we feel for ourselves.

AFFIRMATION FOR THE DAY: When I crave approval and love from others, I know I need to work on loving myself instead.

It is the individual who is not interested in his fellow men who has the greatest difficulty in life and provides the greatest injury to others. It is from among such individuals that all human failures spring.

—ALFRED ADLER

I once read a story about the man who invented the transistor radio. He was scheduled to receive an award one day, and on the way to the ceremony he stopped at a fast-food restaurant. There he was astonished to see a family of four sitting around a table, each member silently listening to his or her radio with a pair of earphones. He drove away depressed, wondering if his invention had been a benefit to mankind after all.

Unfortunately, civilization has moved to a place where we so prize independence that too many people look out only for themselves. We are often so isolated and self-seeking that we've even forgotten how to connect with others.

Remember today that lacking interest in your fellow man is sure to leave you feeling lonely and unhappy in the long run. If you don't know how to start caring, begin by asking someone how they are and then really listen to the answer. Keep the conversation focused on their interests, not yours. Although this may not seem to be a significant act of love, you'll be surprised to discover that some of our smallest gestures of thoughtfulness carry the greatest weight.

AFFIRMATION FOR THE DAY: I nourish myself when I interact with others in a caring way.

First keep the peace within yourself, then you can also bring peace to others.

—THOMAS À KEMPIS

Many of us who begin to recover and experience the blessings of a moderate, well-adjusted life are filled with the desire to show others how to do the same. Although this urge is well-intentioned, it has many pitfalls we need to be aware of before we set out on our crusade.

When I first became active in a self-help group for compulsive eaters I achieved physical recovery: I lost weight and began to take pride in my appearance. Others noticed and complimented me, leading me to feel I was "fixed." Mistakenly I had bought into the notion that "thin is well."

Thin is definitely not always well and in hindsight I can see that I had little of value at that time to share with others. It was only after I had the courage to address difficult self-esteem issues and improve my spiritual condition that I was able to assist anyone else. My peacefulness was finally permanent.

Make sure today that you already have what you'd like to give others. Heed the old saying: "Those that can't, teach; those that can, do." Do instead of teach and you'll find how much more you can give to yourself and others.

AFFIRMATION FOR THE DAY: I don't have to push recovery on others; if I radiate health and vitality, my message is loud and clear.

Pain is short, and joy is eternal.
— JOHANN CHRISTOPH FRIEDRICH VON SCHILLER

Change is hard for compulsive people. Even little things like using a different brand of cereal or altering our hairstyle can cause discomfort. We are not necessarily known as people who roll well with the punches.

When we are faced with a change we must make, however, such as getting rid of a personality trait that makes us or others unhappy, the initial transformation period is not easy. In fact, it's often quite painful. We are uncertain about our new feelings, we don't know how to react properly, and part of us is resistant because we fear we are making a change only to conform to someone else's wishes.

What we have to remember is that whenever we undertake a metamorphosis, particularly one that is worthwhile, our initial reaction will be discomfort. We need support at times like these from people who have walked the same path so that we can know that our efforts will eventually bear fruit.

Allow yourself today to feel anxiety over a change you are trying to make in your life. Know deep within yourself that you are doing the right thing and remain committed to your journey of recovery. If you can sit with painful emotions and not run from them during your transformation, you'll develop the wisdom and strength to tackle other difficulties that face you.

AFFIRMATION FOR THE DAY: When I am experiencing pain, I am often changing for the better.

If you only knock long enough and loud enough at the gate, you are sure to wake up somebody.
— HENRY WADSWORTH LONGFELLOW

When I was younger and a competitive swimmer, I often heard the slogan "When the going gets tough, the tough get going." Our coaches emphasized the need to push our aching bodies harder and harder because that was how champions separated themselves from second-place finishers.

Although I don't compete anymore, I try to remember the lessons I learned as an athlete when life hits rough patches. It's easy to give up, concede defeat and shelve dreams when our plans are thwarted. It's immeasurably harder to regroup, keep going, learn painful lessons and stay motivated during these times. Again and again I've seen, both in sports and in life, that it's the persistent people who won't take no for an answer who eventually are able to make their dreams come true.

To recover from compulsive eating we have to have the stamina to keep "knocking at the gate" when slips or relapses occur. No one's abstinence is guaranteed to be easy or perfect. But if we continue on our paths, avoid getting sidetracked by disappointments and setbacks, and remember to be persistent, we'll be sure to "wake up somebody" and get where it is we want to go.

AFFIRMATION FOR THE DAY: Today I won't give up.

Let the words of my mouth, and the meditation of my heart, be acceptable in thy sight, O Lord, my strength, and my redeemer.

—Psalms 19:14

I believe that the words we speak and the thoughts we think have a great deal of power over what happens to us. Frequently I've seen people use phrases and exhibit attitudes that are self-defeating, negative and depressing. They are the ones who are intent on putting a gloomy spin on everything; they're always "poor," "tired" and something is "killing" them. Then they wonder why their situations never improve and why they never feel better!

We need to be careful about what we give power to in our thoughts and words. When we visualize bad things happening or voice a fear that they might, we are unconsciously bringing them one step closer to manifestation. By the same token, when we say that we feel good and that our lives are abundant, we start the ball rolling that will bring this about.

Scrutinize your words and thoughts carefully today. If you have a temporary cash flow problem, don't visualize yourself as destitute and tell everyone you are "broke"; see yourself overcoming your financial challenges with determination and creativity. And don't give in to feelings of depression and worthlessness; tell others you are "doing well" and then be that way. The more we use the powerful tools of our minds and our words in a positive way, the greater will be the dividends we reap.

AFFIRMATION FOR THE DAY: Today the words of my mouth and the meditation of my heart will be optimistic and joyful.

It's all right to hold a conversation, but you should let go of it now and then.

—RICHARD ARMOUR

I have a friend who is extremely generous with me. She remembers all of my birthdays with expensive gifts, takes me to glittery gatherings and sends me funny cards from time to time. The problem with our relationship is that she is incapable of giving me what I need most—her attention.

Several times I have called her to ask for assistance with a problem, only to find myself unable to get a word in edgewise. When I finally do get a chance to speak I'll hear her working on her computer in the background, and her responses to my questions will betray her lack of attention and interest.

Through my experiences with this friend I've learned that when someone needs assistance, it doesn't mean sending a potted plant, a book, or even a funny card. It means listening, either on the phone or in person, which is infinitely harder than calling the florist or opening your wallet. Learning the art of listening takes time and effort, but the payoff is a rich treasure of friends.

AFFIRMATION FOR THE DAY: Today I will give my full attention to others.

Learning to love yourself is the greatest love of all.
—MICHAEL MASSER AND LINDA CREED

Many addictive people grew up in families where there were great expectations for physical accomplishment yet little acceptance or appreciation for one's true feelings or real self. As a result we often were hungry for love and approval, which translated into compulsive eating, people-pleasing, low self-esteem and neediness.

Unfortunately, as many of us have discovered, none of these behaviors are capable of satisfying our inner needs. For example, all of the food in the world cannot teach an insecure person to nurture himself, nor can trying to make everyone else happy raise our self-esteem.

Learning to love ourselves begins with the admission that we are not perfect, but that we will strive to improve ourselves one day at a time. We need to stop trying to measure up to others' expectations for us and remember that our most important audience is our Higher Power, who is far less judgmental than we are of ourselves.

Look in the mirror today and say, "I love you." If you feel sad, inadequate and resistant as you do this, do it again. Get into the practice of thinking kind, gentle thoughts about yourself and of sending yourself positive messages. If you can begin to honestly appreciate yourself for your uniqueness, then you'll be seeing yourself just as your Higher Power does.

AFFIRMATION FOR THE DAY: I love myself because I am who I am.

> *As a white candle*
> *In a holy place*
> *So is the beauty*
> *Of an aged face.*
>
> —JOSEPH CAMPBELL

As compulsive eaters we have often been impatient to get things done and heard only what we wanted to hear. This has frequently led us to ignore some of the older people in our lives because they weren't quick enough to keep up with us, were prone to forget things, or their sage wisdom didn't flatter us.

In some countries the elderly are the most revered people in society. They are sought out for their opinions, and families will live in cramped quarters so that the older ones can have more space and attention. In other countries, however, older people are not treated as well. Frequently they will be shuffled off to nursing homes where their families rarely visit or go out of their way to let them know they care about them.

As part of your recovery today, go out of your way to make an older person feel good. Hold the door for the elderly woman behind you, smile at a withered, lonely face, and call up your grandparents just to say "hello" if you are lucky enough still to have them in your life. When we can learn to be tolerant, kind, and patient with those who challenge our ability to give it, we will find that we are better able to be that way with those who need it most: ourselves.

AFFIRMATION FOR THE DAY: Today I will be compassionate and patient with an older person.

It's astonishing in this world how things don't turn out at all the way you expect them to!

—AGATHA CHRISTIE

I went to a career symposium once where several very successful people talked about how they had risen to the top of their respective professions. One by one they detailed chance encounters, lucky breaks, strange coincidences and other unplanned occurrences that had resulted in their successes. The common theme was: Don't try to plan your life because you never know what will happen.

I have also found this to be true. When I was growing up I thought I knew what I wanted to be, and then when I graduated from college I had completely different ideas. Now I'm engaged in work that I couldn't have predicted even a few short years ago. So much for planning my future!

Trying to arrange our lives in five- and ten-year blocks is a waste of time that we shouldn't even consider. Allow today to be unscripted and don't ignore unusual doors that might open to you. When you can stretch the boundaries of what you believe is possible in your life, you'll find a wealth of opportunities and new experiences awaiting you at every turn.

AFFIRMATION FOR THE DAY: Today I'll expect the unexpected.

Chances are that right now you are standing in the middle of your own acre of diamonds.

—EARL NIGHTENGALE

One morning I found myself cross and frustrated with the way my day was going. My car wasn't running properly, I needed new clothes, it had been three years since my last vacation and my baby was shrieking for attention.

As I felt self-pity washing over me, a little voice inside reprimanded me for my attitude. I found myself thinking about all the people who ride buses because they can't afford a car, about poor men and women who rarely receive new clothes, about families whose work on farms demands constant attention and supervision day in and day out for years, and about couples who would do anything to have a healthy baby. It struck me that I was, indeed, standing in the midst of my own acre of diamonds, and I didn't even know it.

Are you moping because nothing seems to be going according to your desires right now? Is it possible that you are standing in your own acre of diamonds and you don't know it?

AFFIRMATION FOR THE DAY: My happiness and satisfaction often depend on my perceptions.

Follow me, and I will make you fishers of men.
—MATTHEW 4:19

One day I was idly flipping through a magazine when I saw a letter a woman had written to the editor. "If Jesus came back to earth today," she asked, "what would He say to us?"

The editor, a religious scholar, had a thought-provoking answer. "I think He'd take us into a quiet place and ask us what we had done in response to His command to 'follow me.'"

I felt chastened when I read this exchange because I knew that if I were asked the same question, I'd have to hang my head and make excuses for why I still had trouble forgiving people, practicing unconditional love and turning the other cheek when people slapped me. Although I knew intellectually what I should do, and was quite capable of telling others what the moral approach to any situation was, I wasn't always able to translate my beliefs into action.

If someone you admired—Gandhi, Martin Luther King, or another important historical leader—were to take you aside today and ask if you had really tried to live up to the principles they had espoused during their lives, what would you say? Would you shuffle your feet, hang your head, and make excuses? If so, can you take the opportunity today to be truer to what it is you believe in?

AFFIRMATION FOR THE DAY: Having moral beliefs and putting them into practice are two different things.

Laughter is the infallible sign of the presence of God.
                                    —TEILHARD DE CHARDIN

One morning I set out on my daily walk hoping that the fresh air would clear the cobwebs and confusion from my head. As I walked along I became increasingly dejected, kicking pebbles angrily, mentally fighting with a variety of people I felt had wronged me.

As I worked myself into a state of depression and loneliness, I got madder and madder at my Higher Power for deserting me. I found myself thinking, "If there really is some kind of God, He'd better get down here right now because I don't believe in Him anymore." At that point I looked around for the first time during my walk and saw my little black Labrador, Ajax, trotting alongside me with a Frisbee in his mouth. I had been so preoccupied I hadn't even noticed his hopeful face and eagerness to play.

I burst out laughing as I looked at him, and immediately felt the dark cloud over my head evaporating. Although a man with a long beard hadn't materialized in the bushes, I realized that my Higher Power had sent Ajax to restore my good humor and faith in His presence. If you are searching for proof today of the existence of a power greater than yourself, look for Him in the lighter moments of your day, because wherever there is laughter and joy, there is your Higher Power.

AFFIRMATION FOR THE DAY: My spirituality is reinforced when I am lighthearted.

The cost of giving is receiving.

—A COURSE IN MIRACLES

Have you ever noticed that whatever you put out into the universe, be it friendship, rudeness or just a telephone call, you tend to get back?

Once I heard a woman complaining that she had no friends. No one invited her to parties, her children rarely called her and most salespeople were short with her. After listening to her complaints for a while, another person asked her how often she invited people to parties, called her children or was rude to others. Her uneasy silence answered the question.

Whenever I feel a lack in my life, it's probably a sign that I am not exhibiting that same quality or attitude myself. For example, if I feel like my friends have deserted me, I know that I probably haven't been a good friend to them. Likewise, when I'm feeling a dearth of love and unconditional acceptance in my life, a quick check of my own behavior usually reveals isolation and rejection of others.

Try analyzing what is missing from your life. Is it happiness, friendship or respect? Whatever it is, put that same quality out into the universe today. If it's kindness you want, be kind to others. Phone calls? Call someone. You'll find that if you practice giving diligently what is valuable to you, you'll always receive what you desire most.

AFFIRMATION FOR THE DAY: When I can't give, I can't receive.

Always I've found resisting temptation easier than yielding—it's more practical and requires no initiative.
—ALICE B. TOKLAS

We are all tempted at times in our lives by various "bad" things—foods that spell trouble for us, speeding, extramarital sex or taking something we want that isn't ours. It's a rare person who has not succumbed to temptation at one time or another; I cringe when I think of things I've done for fleeting pleasure that have brought pain to myself and others.

There usually comes a time, however, when we have to resist temptation. We can't do everything we want, regardless of whether it brings us enjoyment or not. Foods we know we shouldn't eat will bring hours or days of guilt and self-recrimination, and so will stealing and extramarital sex. Part of recovery involves realizing that we will hurt ourselves, and possibly others, if we continually give in to the hedonistic side we all possess.

When we do give in to temptation, we mustn't allow ourselves to wallow in it forever. Right the wrong that has been committed, learn a painful lesson and move on. If you need to make amends to yourself or another person, do so, and if you frequently find yourself in tempting situations, change your actions so that that won't happen so often. Resign yourself to the fact that temptation is a part of life and that just because it's there doesn't mean our participation is inevitable.

AFFIRMATION FOR THE DAY: It is as easy for me to say no when I am tempted as it is to say yes.

Prayer should be the key of the day and the lock of the night.

—OLD PROVERB

    I used to feel guilty about the quality and amount of time I spent in prayer. I thought that truly religious and spiritual people were the ones who dressed nicely on Sundays and knelt in prayer before flickering candles, not people like me who had private daily conversations with my Higher Power, usually in my sweatpants.

    But while reading the Bible one day, I stumbled across a passage in Matthew where Jesus told his followers not to pray loudly on the street, but privately where no one would see them. Apparently even two thousand years ago it was recognized that you didn't need to put on a show to feel a connection with, and warmth from, the God of your understanding.

    If we can find a time during the day, preferably when we wake up or before we go to sleep, to give thanks and ask for assistance from our Higher Power, we will find ourselves more peaceful, secure and invigorated. If we don't feel that our prayers are perfect enough or long enough, remember that even one of our century's most spiritual people, Mother Teresa of Calcutta, has said that what is most important to God is not that we actually pray all the time, but that we intend to.

AFFIRMATION FOR THE DAY: The prayers our Higher Power hears don't need to be perfect or public.

If you feel as if your life is a seesaw, perhaps you are depending on another person for your ups and downs.
                                                    —ANONYMOUS

As compulsive eaters many of us find ourselves carrying our addictiveness into relationships. Instead of feeling good about ourselves because of who we are, we often measure our self-worth by how others treat us. We become dependent on others' reactions to, and feelings about, us.

I heard a woman say at a meeting once that she had decided to stop picking up "strays." Strays, she explained, were people she felt she could mother, teach and love. The problem with these men and women, however, was that although she spent a lot of time and effort loving them and helping them feel good about themselves, they never returned those same affections to her. Her conclusion: "I can't keep loving people who can't return my affection just to try to feel good about myself."

Where do you get your positive strokes? From work? Friends? Family? Does your self-esteem rise or fall depending on the size of your paycheck? How often do you look in the mirror and think to yourself, "You're a terrific person!"? Remember today that our emotional health is steady only when we truly love ourselves, and that the price of being unable to do this is that we'll always allow others to dictate our position.

AFFIRMATION FOR THE DAY: If I am living on a seesaw I will be down as often as I am up.

Trust everybody but cut the cards.
—FINLEY PETER DONNE

Someone I know who thought she was being generous and kind made a big mistake that has caused her a lot of grief. Thinking that she was doing God's bidding, she gave her next-door neighbor a $500 loan to help him through what he said was a difficult period. As time dragged on she realized that the money had mostly gone to buy beer and other party items, and that he had no intention of ever paying the money back.

The young woman was trying to get through college on a tight budget so $500 was a lot of money to her. As the dimensions of her misjudgment became apparent, she despairingly complained, "I thought that helping people in need was God's will! How could this have happened?"

Being spiritual and generous doesn't mean being naive. Our Higher Power does want us to help others, but only if it is within our means and prudent to do so. We shouldn't send rent money to television ministries or devote time to others that we don't have for our own well-being. Remember today to have good judgment in everything you do and to avoid acting in an impetuous or rash way. Our goal in recovery is to give as much of ourselves to help others as possible, but also to ensure that we have enough for our own happiness and security first.

AFFIRMATION FOR THE DAY: My Higher Power gave me good judgment and common sense so that I could take care of myself.

There can be no defense like elaborate courtesy.
—EDWARD VERRALL LUCAS

All of us have unlovable people in our lives. These are the souls who try our patience with incessant demands, lack of gratitude and surly behavior. They seem to delight in provoking us and watching our tempers flare.

You have two choices when faced with people like this: You can respond in kind with nastiness or you can act sweet, courteous and loving. It's very easy to behave the first way, especially because it's hard to understand why disagreeable people shouldn't get a taste of their own medicine. But this type of response guarantees that the chain of unpleasantness will be perpetuated and that more people are going to be affected. You, in fact, will be the biggest loser when you choose this option.

It's far better to try a little "elaborate courtesy" when an unlovable person darkens your day. Try to smile when they frown at you. If they are rude, be understanding. People who are unpleasant are usually the ones who most need our love, and if we can learn to extend it when we don't want to, we'll have learned one of the secrets of giving unconditional love.

AFFIRMATION FOR THE DAY: I grow comfortable with people who agree with me, but I grow with people who disagree with me.

Say you are well and all is well with you
And God will hear your words and make them true.
— JAMES RUSSELL LOWELL

One night I was watching a report about the devastation a major hurricane had brought to an American city. Thousands of people had been left homeless and penniless by the storm, and endless lines snaked throughout the city in which people waited in the rain for such necessities as ice, drinking water and food.

There was a wide range of emotion exhibited to reporters as to what the future held for those most affected by the hurricane. The majority of the people interviewed were defeated, despairing and unable to imagine that life would ever improve for them. There were others, however, who chose to be cheerful in spite of their losses. One woman who had lost her house and all her possessions smiled broadly when asked how she was coping, and replied, "I think God took my house because he plans to give me a better one!"

We all have the power to choose optimism over pessimism if we want. Pessimism will feed on itself and keep us and those around us downcast, while optimism will open our eyes to possibilities that we might not see when we're despairing. Today remember that Abe Lincoln once said that men are about as happy as they make their minds up to be, and resolve that you, too, are going to choose the half-full, not half-empty, glass.

AFFIRMATION FOR THE DAY: Today I will focus on the plusses in my life, not the negatives.

Between the time a gift comes to us and the time we pass it along, we suffer gratitude.

—LEWIS HYDE

Every now and then I get so far off the gratitude track that I need another person to knock some sense into me. One day this happened while I was speaking with a friend about some of the business problems I was facing. As I detailed lawsuits, creditors and other problems, I casually mentioned that I couldn't imagine turning to bingeing, purging or starving anymore as a way of escaping my difficulties, as big as they were.

"Stop!" she cried. "Did you hear what you just said? Do you realize how far you've come? I remember when you used to call me because bingeing was the biggest problem you had!"

My friend's outburst was what I needed that day to remind me of how grateful I was for my new life of recovery. As much as I had once prayed for relief from my food abuse, I had already lost my sense of gratitude and replaced it with other worries. It struck me that I had much to be thankful for, but that my appreciation was missing.

Ask yourself today if you have something in your life that you had once ardently prayed for and gotten, but that you now take for granted. One way to restore your thankfulness for your recovery and other blessings in your life is to pass them along to someone else. You may have forgotten how difficult it was to attain what you now have, and seeing your life through another's eyes may be the perspective you need to be grateful once more.

AFFIRMATION FOR THE DAY: Today I will have an attitude of gratitude.

The battle, sir, is not to the strong alone; it is to the vigilant.

—PATRICK HENRY

When we have a disease like compulsive eating, we have to remember that slips and relapses are often a part of any problem that is compulsive and chronic. To pretend that missteps don't or won't occur is to set yourself up for failure. Recovery involves being vigilant about the signs that could trip us up.

One of my friends was certain that she was abstinent, but she kept gaining weight. When I ate at a restaurant with her one day I discovered why. Telling herself that vegetables were acceptable, she made multiple trips to the salad bar for heaps of food—and it wasn't just lettuce. What she had forgotten was that quantity, not just quality, is an important factor in recovery.

It wasn't long after our lunch that my friend was in full-blown relapse. She had stopped being honest and had started to tell herself cunning stories—like cake is the same as bread. Check yourself today for self-deception and be mindful of the slippery ways your disease can reactivate. We can't win the battle of recovery unless we remember that strength and vigilance go hand in hand.

AFFIRMATION FOR THE DAY: No matter how long I have been in recovery I need to remain watchful of my compulsive nature.

In all things of nature there is something of the marvelous.

—ARISTOTLE

I am fortunate to live in a region of valleys, hills and wide-open spaces. I have often found that when I am confused or depressed, a long meandering drive through the country is all I need to solve a problem or clear my head. Somehow my concerns become trivial and my mood lightens when I see fields dotted with spring flowers, acres of trees changing color and purple haze shrouding the mountaintops.

The healing power of nature has long been acknowledged by health-care professionals. It's hard not to feel a oneness with the universe, or awe at whatever force created the perfection of flowers, when we take the time to appreciate the world around us. I know many people who return from hikes in the mountains speaking of their spontaneous spiritual experiences while gazing at the horizon or resting in the shade of a tree.

Take the time today to celebrate the beauty, majesty and mystery of nature. If you can't escape to the country, work in a garden instead. Surround yourself with the life and vitality of the world, and give thanks that when you are in recovery you have genuine appreciation for what was invisible while you were eating compulsively.

AFFIRMATION FOR THE DAY: Today I will let nature heal me.

*It's a capital mistake to theorize before one has data.
Insensibly, one begins to twist fact to suit theories
instead of theories to suit facts.*
                              —SIR ARTHUR CONAN DOYLE

One of the ways we sabotage our own success
and happiness is by making rash, impulsive decisions
before we have all the necessary input. We are apt to
take hunches and feelings as hard data instead of
gathering all the information we need to make a
decision, and we usually find ourselves twisting whatever facts we have to suit our own theories.

Too often this is because we come from a lack of
trust, and we're sure that others are out to get us.
Unanswered letters mean that someone is angry with
us, not that they might be out of town. We're also
quick to judge others' motives even when we only
have half of a story to work with. We find ourselves
creating elaborate conspiracy theories where no mal-
ice exists, and we make ourselves and others miserable in the process.

We must remember that it's impossible to make
wise choices if our data is incomplete or faulty.
Instead of acting impetuously today, be sure to check
your facts thoroughly, and make wise decisions based
on them, not just your impressions. In this way your
behavior will become more mature and responsible,
and you'll learn to act rather than react to the world
around you.

AFFIRMATION FOR THE DAY: Today I will not
jump to any conclusions.

Constant togetherness is fine—but only for Siamese twins.

—VICTORIA BILLINGS

I have a friend who, after eight years of apparent wedded bliss, suddenly learned that her husband wanted a divorce. She had thought they were ideal companions because they never made a move without consulting each other and they had voluntarily shunned personal friends because they seemed to get everything they needed from each other.

What my friend ultimately learned was that her husband had begun to chafe at their constant togetherness. He felt neither one of them had an identity any longer and, instead of trying to work the problem out, had just opted for a clean break.

Many of us are guilty of being in this sort of strangling relationship. We look for someone whom we think will "complete" us and make us happy, and then we stick close to them, not realizing that we possess all of the necessary qualities to be happy ourselves. We need to remember that good partnerships have a healthy amount of give and take, and that no one person can ever make us feel whole unless we feel that wholeness within ourselves.

AFFIRMATION FOR THE DAY: Today I will remember that good relationships have a balance between togetherness and being apart.

When God is doing something wonderful He begins with a difficulty. But when He is going to do something very wonderful He begins with an impossibility.

—Anonymous

How many times have we been discouraged at the immensity of a task facing us, whether it was becoming a parent, losing weight or performing some feat that we thought was totally beyond our abilities? Feeling overwhelmed is a common occurrence, especially when we are starting from a place of low self-esteem and we are unable to recognize or praise ourselves for past achievements.

We may still think that complete recovery is impossible. When we examine our shortcomings, the amends we must make and the obstacles facing us, we might conclude that our salvation is a lost cause and that happiness is reserved for others. We might also be contemplating starting our own business or taking a similar risk, but think that the odds against us are so immense that success is but a dream.

Today remember that with a Higher Power by your side, nothing is impossible. Instead of being overwhelmed by what's facing you, break it down into manageable steps and tackle them one at a time. Don't be discouraged if your dream seems to be completely out of your reach because with faith, persistence and a refusal to label anything "impossible," you can accomplish whatever you set your mind to.

AFFIRMATION FOR THE DAY: When I am feeling most overwhelmed, I have my greatest adventures ahead of me.

*Be patient towards all that is unsolved in your heart and
learn to love the questions themselves, like locked rooms
and like books that are written in a very foreign tongue.
Do not seek the answers, which cannot be given you
because you would not be able to live them.*

                —RAINER MARIA RILKE

So many of us want to have the answers to questions that perplex us, and to know the outcomes to
thorny situations before they are resolved. It isn't
enough to let life unfold before us; we want to produce
the solutions we think are most desirable. Not only that,
but we want them now and we don't want to wait.

When we are overly controlling like this we lessen
our chances of complete recovery, partly because we
sap all the joy and anticipation from our lives. Learning
to be flexible and roll with the punches is essential if we
are to remain abstinent and serene when our meals are
delayed, we miss airplanes, people forget to run errands
for us and unforeseen crises arise at home.

Every morning I try to imagine myself prying my
fingers off my life and handing everything over to my
Higher Power. I find when I can do this successfully I
am calm and trusting, even in the face of unsettling
news. Today try not to open every box and solve every
riddle in your mind. Relax, let your Higher Power run
the show, and trust that answers will appear when you
are ready to live them.

AFFIRMATION FOR THE DAY: When I am at ease
I can enjoy the unsolved mysteries of my life.

Humor is a prelude to faith and laughter is the beginning of prayer.

—REINHOLD NIEBUHR

Think of someone whose company you truly enjoy—someone who you will go out of your way to spend time with. Chances are you are thinking of someone who makes you laugh, who can poke fun at themselves, and who doesn't take life or themselves too seriously.

Compulsive eaters too often are humorless, or else are actors and actresses who constantly try to be the life of the party to mask the pain they feel inside. Spontaneous, genuine laughter does not come easily to such people.

I have found during my years of recovery that the men and women with the greatest amounts of self-esteem and spirituality are those with the best sense of humor. They don't exhibit jealousy or resentment so they don't need to find their fun at others' expense. While they may take their recovery seriously, they are refreshing and fun to be around because they don't take themselves seriously.

Gloominess is not just an unpleasant characteristic, it is a signal that we are not in touch with our Higher Power. When we are in good spirits we are saying, "I'm okay and I'm going to be taken care of. There is nothing so awful that my Higher Power won't help me through it." Be carefree and laugh often today because when you can find the humor in life, you are giving genuine thanks for the privilege of recovery.

AFFIRMATION FOR THE DAY: My faith is strengthened by my laughter.

She had trouble defining herself independently of her husband, tried to talk to him about it, but he said nonsense, he had no trouble defining her at all.
—CYNTHIA PROPPER SETON

One friend of mine who is a compulsive eater and a naturally ebullient person had a difficult childhood during which she was not only sexually abused, but was constantly told to be quiet, sit still and not rock the boat. As she grew older she took out her frustrations with food and piled on enough weight to be considered critically obese by the time she was in her forties.

When she entered treatment for compulsive eating, and later for being an adult child of an alcoholic, she learned to express her love, creativity and joy. As she unlocked her personality and began to allow her true inclinations to show, the weight, anger and fear that had dogged her for years began to disappear.

When we make the mistake of trying to conform to others' expectations of what we should be and how we ought to behave, we will pay a stiff price. High blood pressure, compulsive behavior and fits of anger are all likely when we deny who we really are.

If you feel you are still trying to play a role that doesn't fit you, spend some quiet time today getting in touch with the squelched child within. Allow yourself to express whatever emotions you have hidden away. When you discover your individuality and then have the courage to let it show, you will have freed yourself from one of the most restraining bonds of compulsive eating.

AFFIRMATION FOR THE DAY: When I define myself by others' expectations, I never have the opportunity to really know myself.

I can't. God can. I think I'll let Him.

—ANONYMOUS

For many compulsive eaters the word "surrender" conjures up images of losing and of not being up to the challenge of something. For perfectionists who like to win, the idea of surrendering our obsession with food to a Higher Power is anathema to our way of life. We've lost the battle with our bingeing so many times that being asked to surrender to something we can't even see or touch means losing again.

But to truly triumph in the battle against our disease of compulsive eating, we need to start by surrendering to a superior force—which many call God—so that we can begin taking responsibility for our actions. To surrender doesn't mean to lose; it means we have finally gained the humility to admit we haven't done a very good job of running our lives and that we could use a helping hand.

People come to their point of surrender with compulsive eating in different ways. Some are caught shoplifting food and are finally faced with the horror of their food addiction. Many bulimics are shocked to find their children imitating Mommy in the bathroom with their fingers down their throat. Others finally reach a clothing size that is frightening and unacceptable.

However you have reached the moment of admitting that your food problem is out of your control and you need help, remember that the line to your Higher Power is always open, and is as close as a heartfelt prayer away.

AFFIRMATION FOR THE DAY: My Higher Power is always there for me when I have the humility to ask for help.

Everything that goes around in my head doesn't have to come out of my mouth.

—ANONYMOUS

There are people—and I used to be one of them—who think that they should always give you the benefit of their wisdom, whether it hurts your feelings or not. Their philosophy is that they have to tell you exactly what is on their mind or else they are not being completely honest.

Someone close to me usually sees fit to comment on my appearance, my weight, my friends and my beliefs. If he thinks I look tired, he tells me; if I cook something that tastes bad, he'll point it out; if there's anything negative to say about anything, he says it. Not surprisingly, I avoid him.

Being honest doesn't have to mean hurting people's feelings. And even if the person is in your family it still doesn't give you the excuse to be brutally honest with them. The next time you are tempted to criticize a brother, mother or other relative, ask yourself if you would say the same thing to a friend. If you wouldn't, don't say it.

Sometimes silence is golden, even if you think your words are brilliant and important. Instead of always blurting out what's on your mind, try to remain quiet and observant more often. We need to remember that weighing and measuring our words is just as important as weighing and measuring our food, and that we can't neglect either activity if we are to recover from compulsive eating.

AFFIRMATION FOR THE DAY: Today I won't give everyone the benefit of my thoughts.

In order to see God, a man must first cleanse and empty himself, and stand outside of himself.
—ST. GREGORY PALAMAS

When I was new to recovery I didn't understand the concept of needing to go back and make amends to people I had harmed in order to be free of my eating disorder. In some cases my amends involved repayment of a great deal of money; all of them involved developing an attitude of humility and repentance.

Since I have now made most of my big amends, I have come to understand the importance of this step. As long as I carried around guilt, shame and remorse for past wrongs, I was unable to feel good about myself or develop trust in a Higher Power. Many religious traditions have recognized the importance of this type of spiritual cleansing. It is well-known that the act of confession and the righting of old wrongs have the ability to give people hope and peace where there was despair and confusion, and that acceptance of our flaws leads us to the belief that our Higher Power accepts us, too.

If there is an amend you have been putting off because you are frightened or unsure about how to proceed, take action today to put your mind at rest. Approach your task with courage and energy and don't worry about how anyone else will react, for it's only when you cleanse your soul of its stains that you are given the gift of clear vision.

AFFIRMATION FOR THE DAY: Today I will stand outside myself and assess what needs changing.

The only limits I have are those I place on myself.
—CREDO FOR OUTWARD BOUND'S WILDERNESS
ADVENTURES

There is a story in the Bible about Jesus healing a man who had been unable to walk for thirty-eight years. His excuse for still being incapacitated after all that time was that the conditions had never been right for him to be healed. Jesus' response to his plight was "Rise, take up your pallet and walk," at which point the man did.

One of the main lessons of this story is that the lame man was suffering from the limitations of what he thought he could do. Instead of searching for ways to make himself whole and healthy, he had looked for reasons why it would never happen.

We are often guilty of setting the same limitations on ourselves. We find ways to avoid new situations because we are afraid we won't succeed. We decide we will never be at the right weight because we'll be too hungry to maintain it. Or we abandon hopes for exciting future employment because we don't think we're capable enough.

What are the limits you have placed on yourself? Do they have any basis in fact or are they creations of your own imagination? Are you preventing yourself from accepting a challenging situation because of a festering childhood comment about your abilities? Acknowledge the existence today of any self-defeating thoughts you have and work to eliminate them because once they're gone, you're free to succeed.

AFFIRMATION FOR THE DAY: I will not be my own worst enemy today.

The worst bankrupt is the person who has lost enthusiasm.

—H. W. ARNOLD

We all know that we should be enthusiastic and joyful if we are to keep negative thoughts and conditions at bay. But some of us don't know how to do this, and we may not even want to because it's easier to act discouraged and needy, and to allow others to comfort and care for us.

Enthusiasm comes from the Greek word *entheos,* meaning "full of god." When we are filled with God we radiate hope, love and happiness. We see conditions in our lives in a positive light and we are able to communicate our enthusiasm to others.

Being enthusiastic takes work but pays handsome dividends. Often it requires a daily "charge up" period during which we fill our minds with nothing but positive thoughts. I know one personally and professionally successful man who lies in bed every morning and won't get up until he has told himself every good thing he can think of. Other friends listen to motivational tapes in their cars on the way to work.

What is the right way for you to instill enthusiasm in yourself? Whether it is through affirmations, spending time with a person who believes in you or having a quiet devotional period in the morning, make sure you do something along these lines every day. If you can keep your zest for life alive, even during hard times, you'll never lose the spark that fills you with God.

AFFIRMATION FOR THE DAY: When I have lost my enthusiasm, I have lost touch with my spiritual side.

We need only to lift our head to see somebody always within reach of our hands whose sparkle will meet our eye.

—CLAUDE M. STEINER

Sometimes when we feel that we have no friends, no Higher Power and no hope, it is because we are too stubborn to look for them. We have become so accustomed to relying only on ourselves and so immersed in self-pity, that we have forgotten that support and guidance are closer than we think.

Not long ago I heard about a middle-aged woman who died of a heart attack. Her husband had been convicted of fraud and sent to jail, and she had retreated from life in shame, refusing to acknowledge the friends who reached out to comfort and love her. Her only source of pleasure was food and she became extremely obese, which contributed to her death. A friend of hers sadly observed the hundreds of people at the funeral and lamented that had the woman cared to look, scores of people would have been there to help her.

Are you feeling sorry for yourself today, imagining that no one cares about you? Are you helping to create this situation by hiding or arguing with anyone who tries to help you? If so, take off your armor today and raise your head. Your friends and Higher Power are right there, always ready to assist if you'll let them.

AFFIRMATION FOR THE DAY: Help is never far away.

Least said, soonest mended.

—CERVANTES

In the past I was known for my smart mouth and my ability to quickly put down something or someone that threatened me or my fragile self-esteem. When I was bulimic, all it took was a lingerie ad featuring a perfect-looking model, or hearing about someone's good fortune to unleash my sharp and jealous tongue.

I thought my put-downs were clever; others did not. Some turned away in disgust and others gently told me that my behavior was unbecoming. I didn't realize the extent of the damage, though, until I began to recover and made a list of people I had belittled. The lengthy and difficult process of making amends to many of them impressed upon me the importance of learning to keep my mouth shut and minimize the negativity I was capable of creating.

Now I try to remember "least said, soonest mended" when I am tempted to express my displeasure or uncharitable opinions. I know that to stay in recovery I can't let caustic comments linger without an amend, and I'd rather not have to undergo that humbling process so often. Remind yourself today of the time and energy you will have to spend cleaning up after yourself if you let your hurts and resentments get the better of you. If you can learn to hold your tongue you may even be surprised by how much better people suddenly like you.

AFFIRMATION FOR THE DAY: When I am quick to anger and condemn, I hurt myself more than anyone else.

The meeting of two personalities is like the contact of two chemical substances: if there is any reaction, both are transformed.

—CARL GUSTAV JUNG

A well-known healer, Dr. Gerald Jampolsky, started an organization in 1975 called The Center for Attitudinal Healing that has helped bring inner peace to thousands. One of the principles of this organization is "We are students and teachers to each other."

At one time I didn't understand this concept. The only real learning, I thought, came from schooling and books, and certainly I wasn't a teacher of anything! But as I have progressed further into recovery, I have seen how accurate Dr. Jampolsky's idea is. Whenever I interact with someone, positively or negatively, we both come away affected. Either I absorb a lesson about how I don't want to behave and I scrutinize myself to see if I am guilty of the same attitude, or I enjoy someone's company so much that a bit of their personality and outlook rubs off on me.

If we aren't aware of the benefits of our daily interpersonal dealings we can miss some of our greatest learning experiences. Our Higher Power often sends us people who challenge us in different ways to take a look at ourselves, and we need to remind ourselves today that whether we have a positive reaction or not, we can always let the experience be a beneficial one.

AFFIRMATION FOR THE DAY: Today I will be both a willing pupil and ready teacher.

*What is the source of our first suffering? It is in the fact
that we hesitated to speak. It was born in the moments
when we accumulated silent things within us.*
                                        —GASTON BACHELARD

An acquaintance of mine once told me about a
young woman she knew who had recently entered an
eating disorder treatment center. The woman had experienced years of physical and mental abuse, first in
her family and later in her marriage, and she had never
spoken up for herself. Instead she had bottled up all of
her rage, fear, sadness and frustration within and used
bingeing as her escape valve.

When she finally began to express her feelings in a
supportive group therapy atmosphere, it seemed like a
dam had broken. Unlocked, her mind started to spill
out countless scenes of neglect and violence that she had
never processed internally. As a result she stopped
sleeping and eventually was transferred to a hospital
where she was treated for psychosis. The sudden on-
slaught of unspoken feelings had so immobilized her
that she needed medical stabilization to proceed.

Although this is an extreme case, we all need to
heed the lesson of this story. Pain and suffering only
intensify when we keep them inside. Breaking the
silence and daring to air our feelings with others will
help heal us and bring balance and perspective into our
lives. If you feel negative emotions today, don't store
them up; let them out in a supportive atmosphere. The
peace and self-acceptance that accompany this type of
catharsis is among the most powerful tools we have to
transform ourselves.

AFFIRMATION FOR THE DAY: When I lock my
hurts inside, I poison myself.

There is a time for many words, and there is also time for sleep.

—HOMER

I once sponsored a young lady who was recovering from many years of bulimia. Her path to wholeness was a joy to behold. In a rather short period of time her abstinence became solid, her mood and appearance changed dramatically for the better, and she got engaged.

Then the cracks started to appear. Her work performance declined. Slips with her meals became frequent. Her moods swung crazily and her engagement was broken. What had happened?

After a lot of soul-searching she realized that in her zeal to recover she had neglected to schedule "down time" for herself. Virtually every night she attended a meeting for compulsive eaters, recovering alcoholics, children of alcoholics, or sex addicts.

This frenetic pace of recovery is a common pitfall for compulsive eaters. We feel we must be doing something at all times or we aren't productive or worthwhile people. Today allow yourself some unscheduled time during which you will just "be." Don't try to learn something, help someone else or be a super-achiever. Just as muscles need rest between workouts to get stronger, so does our recovery.

AFFIRMATION FOR THE DAY: Overscheduling myself is a red flag that I am avoiding something.

*You don't have to look any farther for a helping hand
than the end of your arm.*

—Anonymous

One afternoon a friend called to tell me that she
had taken a huge step: She had purchased the house she
had been renting for a number of years. Friends had
encouraged her for a long time to stop throwing thousands of dollars away on something she didn't own but
she hadn't listened.

Then one day she had looked in the mirror and
realized that she wasn't getting any younger. Her
two daughters were growing up quickly and as a
single mother she needed to gain some security for
their future. She decided to learn what she needed to
do to buy the house but quickly became overwhelmed
and frightened. She had always assumed that
someone—especially a man—would take care of her,
and when she finally acknowledged that she was responsible for her own future, she had panicked.

Ultimately my friend gathered her courage, taught
herself the basics of finance and bought the house. But
not only did she gain a house, she developed a healthy
respect for what she could accomplish when she attempted to do things herself.

Are we waiting for someone to save us? Do we
think that we aren't capable of doing something only
because we haven't tried it before? Are we ignoring the
helping hand at the end of our own arm?

AFFIRMATION FOR THE DAY: Today I will help
myself instead of waiting for someone else to help me.

Live life in day-tight compartments.

—DALE CARNEGIE

One day I went to an anniversary celebration at a self-help meeting for recovering alcoholics where a man was marking his forty-second year of sobriety. Many of the people who attended went to hear his stories about his friendship with the co-founder of the movement; others simply wanted to know how he had managed to not take a drink for so many years.

This older man's message about how he had stayed sober was simple: Despite going through numerous calamities, bad days and disappointments, he had asked his Higher Power every morning for the willingness not to take a drink for just that day. He hadn't resolved never to drink again each morning, because that type of all-or-nothing attitude had gotten him into trouble in the past, he said. Instead, when he only asked for help with the next twenty-four hours he was given the ability to string together days, then weeks, then months, then years of unbroken sobriety.

We compulsive eaters need to do the same thing. Rather than making harsh resolutions about never bingeing, purging or dieting again, we must ask for help in just sticking with our meal plan on a daily basis. Although resolving not to do something for the rest of our lives is scary and hard to contemplate, we must remember that there is nothing we can't accomplish during the next twenty-four hours if we have the necessary commitment, courage and faith.

AFFIRMATION FOR THE DAY: When I focus only on what I can do today, there is much I can accomplish.

Promises that you make to yourself are often like the Japanese plum tree—they bear no fruit.
                                                    —FRANCIS MARION

One day I received a call from a woman who had been struggling with compulsive eating for years. She had been in and out of self-help groups, in and out of therapy, and in and out of hospitals. She wanted to know why she wasn't making much headway with her recovery and why, despite all her efforts, she felt the binge monster nipping at her heels every hour of every day.

As we explored her feelings, I learned that in her self-help groups she had never had a sponsor—"I never found the right one," she complained. Therapists were all "wrong" in one way or the other. And in the hospital programs she candidly said she'd conned the doctors and staff members by telling them what she thought they wanted to hear, not how she really felt.

I soon saw that this woman had never truly loosened the grip on her compulsive eating and allowed anyone else to help her. Promising herself that she would do better next time never brought success. Although she thought she was able to dupe others, she was pulling the biggest con job on herself.

Recovery means admitting humility and asking for help from others. Making deals only with ourselves and promising ourselves that tomorrow will be different is guaranteed to keep us mired in self-destructiveness and unavailable for the help that's always available to us.

AFFIRMATION FOR THE DAY: Today I will rely on others rather than depending only on myself.

Lead me to the rock that is higher than I.
—PSALMS 61:2

I have a friend who always spends her weekends rock-climbing and hiking. Once she has mastered a certain course she moves on to a more challenging one and she never stops in her quest to be better, stronger and higher.

We have to emulate this quality in our recovery from compulsive eating. No matter how far we have come or how strong our relationship is with our Higher Power, we can always improve our positions. If we can see ourselves as pioneers on a mountain who are always reaching for another rock, we won't fall into the trap of getting to a certain altitude and then resting contentedly forever. When we become this complacent it's a sign that we are stagnating and not growing any longer.

As you climb your own mountain of recovery today, imagine that your ultimate goals are at the top and that your achievements on the way are the rocks you will be relying on to help you get there. Choose the right rocks—the ones that are solidly grounded and that won't dislodge to hurt anyone else. If the goals you set for yourself are moral, beneficial to others, and not greedy or self-seeking, your ascent will be pleasant, steady and safe.

AFFIRMATION FOR THE DAY: When I try to climb mountains on loose gravel, not firm rocks, I am apt to take a fall.

The value of a sentiment is the amount of sacrifice you are prepared to make for it.

—JOHN GALSWORTHY

A lot of us profess to care about certain things— our country, our parents or our abstinence—but when push comes to shove, we aren't willing to sacrifice anything for them. We are, in short, all talk and no action.

Do you say you love your parents but only call on holidays or to ask for money? Do you hang your country's flag outside your house yet are always too busy to vote? Do you say you really want to abstain from compulsive eating yet won't stop eating your binge foods or follow the advice of a caring sponsor?

Rather than just giving lip service to ideals today, make sure that you back up your sentiments with action. Don't shy away from supporting something because it requires effort; extend yourself for what you believe in. Whether your state of commitment is to your abstinence, a loving relationship or your Higher Power, the more you are prepared to sacrifice for it, the more valuable it will be to you.

AFFIRMATION FOR THE DAY: I often have to fight hardest to preserve what's dearest to me.

Anything forced into manifestation through personal will is always "ill got" and has "ever bad success."
—FLORENCE SCOVEL SHINN

In the English language there is just one word for the concept of time, therefore it has many meanings. In the Greek language, however, the words *chronos* and *kairos* both mean time, yet in different contexts. *Chronos* means clock time, as in minutes, hours, and days. *Kairos*, on the other hand, refers to God's time, or when events happen for the right reason at the right moment.

When I was bulimic there was only one time for me and that was "Caroline's Time." I hated waiting and when I wanted something I wanted it right then. The concept of allowing events to occur in God's time was alien to me because I didn't want to acknowledge that I might not have total control over my own future.

Now I am more relaxed about timing. If I want something to occur and it doesn't, I am usually able to tell myself that if it ever does come to pass it will happen when it should, and that if it doesn't, something better awaits me.

Remind yourself today that everything happens when it is supposed to. It's not your job to understand why things occur when they do; you only have to learn to fit yourself into life as it presents itself. If you can turn the reins over to your Higher Power, relax and enjoy the ride of life, you'll find that a perfect plan for you unfolds and that the less you tamper with its timing, the greater will be your satisfaction and rewards.

AFFIRMATION FOR THE DAY: There is a proper time and place for everything that I may not yet comprehend.

[We] came to believe that a Power Greater than ourselves could restore us to sanity.
—STEP TWO OF OVEREATERS ANONYMOUS

The idea that any of us could be insane is rather frightening. I certainly don't think I'm insane; after all, I graduated from college with honors and have always excelled in my academic pursuits.

Yet insanity is a word that defined my behavior for years around food. I lied for it, stole it, ate superhuman quantities of it when I wasn't even hungry, and let it dictate my emotions. I can't think of a single person for whom I would do similar things, so isn't it rather insane that an inanimate object like food could have had so much power over me?

Once we admit that food has made us crazy, we also need to acknowledge that a Higher Power can assist us with a return to sanity. This is the part that most compulsive eaters balk at, especially because they believe that any loving Higher Power would not have let them become so miserable in the first place. But we also must remember that we all have the free will to do whatever we choose, and when we opt to make ourselves miserable, there isn't much that can stop us. It is only when we choose recovery, do the necessary footwork, and ask for help from our Higher Power that we are infused with the strength and vision we need to return to sanity.

AFFIRMATION FOR THE DAY: I must remember today that there is a power greater than my own.

There are two ways of spreading light: to be
The candle or the mirror that reflects it.
—EDITH WHARTON

If we have strong recovery or a way of life that brings us happiness and fulfillment, it's only natural to want to share that with others. But we also must keep in mind that how we choose to spread our joy can ruin our message if we're not careful.

One way to ensure that we turn others off is by preaching self-righteously at them. Telling someone that they ought to do something is a quick way to lose their interest, particularly if we aren't perfect ourselves. Another way to annoy people is to badger them with newspaper clippings or books that contain your message; they will wind up unread in the trash.

The two best methods of influencing others are to be a "candle" or the "mirror" that reflects the candle. Not many people are candles; this honor is reserved for the truly inspirational men and women who come up with the original words, theories and ways of life that positively affect others.

If you can't be a candle, you can be a mirror of the values others have defined. Neither candles nor mirrors force their ways of life on others—they just attract converts because of the examples they set. Resolve today to be a quiet, shining beacon of whatever values you hold dear and you'll find that the light you spread is always pure and never glaring.

AFFIRMATION FOR THE DAY: I will let my inner flame of beauty shine today.

The things which are impossible with men are possible with God.

—LUKE 18:27

Recovering from any addiction or compulsive behavior requires a change in attitude. For us to transform ourselves from compulsive eaters into happy, healthy humans who don't abuse food means accepting the fact that our past failures at total recovery are meaningless. If we believe we can and will recover, we will.

Perhaps we tried to lose weight once before by making lists of forbidden foods and calorie restrictions that were all but impossible to adhere to. Or we tried to stop bingeing and purging by keeping our refrigerators at home empty, only to find ourselves desperately heading out to a fast-food place in the middle of the night.

Imposing our will on the situation, or telling ourselves that we "should" be better, will always result in failure, hopelessness and isolation. We need to remember that petitioning a Higher Power for assistance is what distinguishes ongoing recovery from just another diet. If we ask for help and expect to receive it—much like turning on a light switch and knowing there will be light—we'll find that the source of our strength is unlimited.

AFFIRMATION FOR THE DAY: My Higher Power gives me the strength and enthusiasm to do whatever I desire.

The best plan is to profit from the folly of others.
—PLINY THE ELDER

It used to be thought that to begin recovery from an eating disorder, or any other crippling addiction, one had to hit a real low—that is, become so miserable that there was no alternative but to change.

Now we know that this does not have to be the case. It isn't necessary to lose all your self-respect, emotional balance and happiness to admit defeat. As more people have begun to reveal details about their own battles with eating disorders, others who have not yet lost everything can benefit from their experiences and stop their own self-destructive behavior before it reaches a critical stage.

The best places to learn about what types of behavior to avoid are self-help groups where people who have similar addictions can share experiences, strength and recovery. It was in this type of gathering that I learned how to deal with difficult situations like wedding receptions, all-you-can-eat restaurants and the cravings of pregnancy. I saved myself a lot of heartache by listening closely and allowing others to guide me.

Remind yourself today that you do not have to be a pioneer of recovery. With so much help and knowledge now available about eating disorders, we would be wise to arm ourselves with education and the experience of those who have gone before us so that we can lessen our chances of relapse and improve our odds of freedom from food addiction.

AFFIRMATION FOR THE DAY: Just as I can learn from my own mistakes, I can benefit from hearing about those others have made.

Those who succeed are those who look for the circumstances they want, and, if they can't find them, make them.

—GEORGE BERNARD SHAW

One friend of mine decided that although he lived comfortably he wanted to become very wealthy. Others laughed at him as he went about achieving his goal, but he stuck to his belief that he would hit it big if he worked hard enough. His first few attempts at money-making soured but his attitude remained upbeat and he told others that his big break was just around the corner.

Then my friend struck gold. Overhearing a conversation at a party, he asked about the problem being discussed. Sensing an opportunity he said that he might be able to help with the troublesome issue and then set about learning everything he could about the topic. Before too long he had formed a company, assembled an expert staff and become a multimillionaire, just as he had said he would. His secret to success was simple: He had seized an opportunity and created favorable circumstances for himself instead of just waiting for them to happen.

This story illustrates the importance of creating our own luck. To be successful we must constantly be on the lookout for opportunities that we can turn to our advantage. And if we can't find them, we have to create them. Don't waste your time today waiting for good fortune to tap you on the shoulder. Like the early bird who gets the worm, be diligent, resourceful and go dig for what you want.

AFFIRMATION FOR THE DAY: Today I will make my own luck.

I want, by understanding myself, to understand others.
—KATHERINE MANSFIELD

When I think back on my years of compulsive eating, I have an image of living in a fog. I didn't give much thought to anything except the outer trappings of my life: my weight, my appearance, my status and my own comfort. I rarely engaged in introspection or self-analysis. I did not know myself, nor did I want to.

Because I didn't understand my own motivations, fears and desires, I couldn't understand anyone else's. I found myself frequently misinterpreting people's actions and being unable to connect with them beyond the superficial level of words. In addition, I kept everyone from penetrating my facade, so I remained closed off and isolated.

When food was stripped away from me I had no choice but to probe my psyche. I started to understand what motivated people to behave with greed, compassion, jealousy, self-hatred and love because I saw those behaviors in myself. The world no longer seemed like a big puzzling gathering where everyone spoke the same language except me.

If you still feel like you're different from other people, you're holding yourself back from intimacy. Take a risk by revealing part of yourself to someone today, and concentrate on what the similarities are between you. As you continue to practice connecting and identifying with others, the gift will be a new feeling of belongingness and increased self-awareness.

AFFIRMATION FOR THE DAY: Today I will not hold myself apart from others.

I have always known that at last I would take this road,
but yesterday I did not know that it would be today.
                                                    —NARIHIRA

As much as we would like to know what is going to
happen to us from day to day, it is impossible to plan our
lives accordingly. Usually when I have tried to predict
what would happen to me at every turn in the road—
whether it was tomorrow, next month or next year—my
efforts were wasted. Not once has my scenario been
implemented; somehow my Higher Power has always
seen fit to solve things in a different and better way.

One day I read a poem by an eighty-year-old
woman who summed up her life's regrets in a few
cogent lines. Looking back, she lamented, she wished
she had sat on the grass more and worried less about the
grass stains, laughed louder and more often, and been
more spontaneous. Instead of enjoying each day and
filling it with life, she had spent more time wondering
"What if?" instead of "Why not?"

Are you putting something off because you can do
it tomorrow, you're feeling timid, or you're comfortable
in a certain rut? Make it your goal to go to bed tonight
contented and fulfilled by today's activities. Challenge
yourself to hug the person you've been meaning to hug,
visit the museum that intrigues you and pursue the
sport that you've always wanted to try. If you practice
doing this on a daily basis, you'll never have any regrets
about your life.

AFFIRMATION FOR THE DAY: Today I will be
spontaneous, laugh loud and get some grass stains on
my pants.

Many receive advice, few profit by it.

—PUBLIUS SYRUS

When our recovery becomes solid and our progress is apparent to those around us, frequently we will be asked by those who are looking for guidance to help them with their recovery process. If we are in a self-help group such as Overeaters Anonymous, this relationship is known as "sponsoring."

For compulsive eaters, the position of being a sponsor can unleash unpleasant behaviors such as bossiness and grandiosity. Some of us jump at the chance to tell others what to do. We dictate what they should eat, what they should read and what meetings they should attend. We justify this behavior by saying that we were asked to be guides, therefore we have every right to offer advice, solicited or not.

If we behave this way it won't be long before everyone turns away from us, hurt and bored. The best sponsors or teachers are those who talk least and listen most. The next time someone calls you, stop before you offer any advice because there's a good chance they only want an ear, not your pearls of wisdom. Not only that, but it's remarkable how—when allowed to talk things out with a supportive, nonjudgmental friend—most people can find their own solutions inside themselves.

AFFIRMATION FOR THE DAY: When I can avoid preaching to others, I allow them to grow at their own pace.

*There are many reasons, then, to start the spiritual
journey—possibly as many different reasons as there
are people who undertake it. . . . We turn to the
teachings and practices of the great spiritual traditions
when the time is right, just as a flower blooms and rain
falls when the time is right.*
—"CHOP WOOD, CARRY WATER" BY RICK FIELDS, PEGGY
TAYLOR, REX WEYLER AND RICK INGRASCI

When we begin to recover, especially if we are in
a self-help recovery program, we learn that a relationship with a Higher Power is important in facilitating
recovery. Independent, stubborn souls that we are,
many of us resist this notion. We have been our own
Higher Powers for so long that the idea of trusting in a
force we can't see is laughable.

Finding a force you can call your Higher Power
and that you can pray to for guidance is an intensely
individual experience. Trying to duplicate someone
else's system is like trying to copy their meal plan; it
won't work. Because we are all created differently, it
stands to reason that we will all have our own interpre-
tations of what is spiritual. I firmly believe that if
something works for you and improves your life, then it
is right.

Don't worry at first if your Higher Power is an
abstract image or a beautiful force like nature. Just start
by accepting that something greater than you does exist,
and remember that just as you will grow, change and
mature in recovery, so will your relationship with, and
conception of, your Higher Power.

AFFIRMATION FOR THE DAY: Instead of forcing my
spiritual growth, I'll let it bloom when the time is right.

"Failure" should be a required course in every grammar school and high school curriculum.
—FRANK C. TRIBBE

If we had nothing but success all our lives and got everything we wanted, we'd never learn anything. Failure is what teaches us how to accept setbacks, what needs changing and how to be persistent.

Many successful people have failed repeatedly before becoming successful. One well-known author had her manuscript rejected by thirty-two publishing houses before she published it herself, and it became a runaway international best-seller. Former U.S. president Harry Truman declared bankruptcy before running for public office. And another well-known U.S. president, Abraham Lincoln, was defeated several times in local elections before he was chosen for our nation's highest office.

When we fail we have to make sure that we don't deny it, shift the blame to anyone else, excuse it or waste time wishing it hadn't happened. Take a look at some of your "failures" today and ask yourself what you learned from them. If you have changed a bad habit, formulated new goals or begun a healthier lifestyle, then you haven't failed, you've succeeded. Remind yourself not to look at setbacks as negatives, because without them we'd never have the opportunity to pause and see if we're going in the right direction.

AFFIRMATION FOR THE DAY: There are no failures—only slow successes.

Man should not try to avoid stress any more than he would shun food, love or exercise.

—HANS SELYE

I remember asking a friend of mind who had won numerous academic awards in high school despite a crowded schedule of study and extracurricular activities, how she had managed to thrive with all of the different pressures on her. She responded that she had always found that the busier she was, the better she performed in all areas of her life.

I've never forgotten that conversation because although it didn't make sense to me at the time, observation of similarly successful people over the years has proven her right. The go-getters of life all seem to live life to the fullest and push themselves to dream bigger and do more than many others think is feasible. Instead of shunning stress they actively seek it out and thrive on it. But they also make sure that they balance their busyness with relaxation and rewarding personal relationships so that they don't become one-dimensional people.

As much as I detest stress I try to ensure that there is enough in my life that I remain alert, active and growing. If there is too much, my emotions and actions start to deteriorate; but with too little I often fail to feel challenged or realize my potential. Remember today that stress is not always a negative condition to be avoided, but that if applied creatively to our lives, can galvanize us to become the best we possibly can.

AFFIRMATION FOR THE DAY: As a tube of toothpaste needs the right amount of pressure to produce results, so do I.

Perhaps someday it will be pleasant to remember even this.

—VIRGIL

There's nothing like a little time and distance from a trying situation to find the humor in it. Sometimes it takes a day, sometimes weeks, and sometimes years to look back and laugh at our misfortunes. The really well-adjusted people can even find humor in bedlam as it occurs.

This is not a skill that is easy to develop. Laughter requires faith that our lives will ultimately work out fine, and the basis for this faith is a belief that there is a Higher Power taking care of us who only has our best interests and well-being at heart.

This has been one of my most challenging lessons in recovery. When I'm in the midst of difficulty, I tend to feel I'm being punished and that no one cares about me. But this is precisely when I should have the most faith and remain calm and trusting. This, however, requires wisdom, perspective and serenity.

There is a passage in the Book of Matthew that states that everything in nature gets its needs met—i.e., the birds always gather enough food to survive and animals grow a protective winter coat—and that if they're always taken care of, why should we worry that we'll be abandoned? Try to remember this lesson, and even laugh, the next time you feel baffled and alone. If you can find the humor in the midst of your challenges, they'll never be as awful or overwhelming as they might initially seem.

AFFIRMATION FOR THE DAY: Laughter is always the best medicine for trying times.

To err is human, to forgive divine.

—ALEXANDER POPE

One of the most important things we compulsive eaters need to learn is forgiveness—of ourselves as well as of others. We also need to seek that same forgiveness from people for the pain we have caused them during our years of being compulsive eaters when our needs and wants overrode everyone else's.

Asking others to forgive us is a very humbling experience. It involves honestly stating our errors and hoping that the other party will understand why our minds and actions were so impaired in the past. We have to accept that some people will meet us halfway and others won't. When our olive branch is rebuffed, we must remember that we have done our best to right an old wrong and that the burden at that point is no longer ours to carry.

More important than making amends to others is that we begin by making amends to ourselves. This doesn't mean excusing past behavior or not taking responsibility for it. What it does mean, however, is accepting that we may not have always been the kind of people we wanted to be, but that given the circumstances at that time, we had done our very best even if it was flawed. Remind yourself today if remorse surfaces that any energy spent trying to undo the past is wasted, but that efforts poured into creating a different future will always reap rewarding dividends.

AFFIRMATION FOR THE DAY: When I am having trouble forgiving someone, I know that there is something I have not forgiven myself for yet.

There is no grief like the grief that does not speak.
—HENRY WADSWORTH LONGFELLOW

Many of us come into a recovery program harboring the feeling that we experienced childhood traumas, disappointments and losses that no one else could ever possibly understand. Some—especially those who have undergone sexual abuse—are so ashamed of their past that they have trouble admitting to themselves, let alone others, that they have been victimized.

One of the phrases to remember at times like these is that "we are only as sick as our secrets." To keep our feelings locked inside is tantamount to letting a sore fester and become infected. A healing force is unleashed within when we can discuss our fears and concerns with someone we trust, and what we frequently discover is that when we examine our concerns openly, they are never as crippling or as unsolvable as we once imagined.

Many studies support the theory that sharing and group therapy bolster the immune system, enabling us to successfully fight depression, illness and isolation. Allow yourself to open an unhealed wound today and share your pain with another person. Not only will you find yourself feeling relieved and unburdened, but you'll also probably discover that this action has carried you a long way toward healing your trauma and feeling the joy of wholeness again.

AFFIRMATION FOR THE DAY: When I let others into my heart, it mends more quickly.

What soon grows old? Gratitude.

—ARISTOTLE

One day a friend called me to ask how I was. Eager to dump on someone I angrily talked about ungrateful friends, my broken car, my fitful sleep, and various financial problems.

At the end of my tirade, almost as an afterthought, I said, "How are you?" My friend, who had developed multiple sclerosis in middle age, commented that she had fallen the previous night, fractured her ankle, and was completely confined to a wheelchair. Then she laughed and made a joke about how she missed playing golf, but all things considered was doing just fine.

When I hung up I felt chastened, knowing that I had the freedom to walk around a golf course all day if I wanted. Later that same day I saw a blind man at a mall, sitting close to a fountain so that he could hear its splashing and gurgling. His old, creased face radiated simple joy. Moments later a retarded man cleared the table next to me, happily whistling while he performed his menial chores.

When I have a lesson to learn I find that my teachers appear quickly, and all of these people were my teachers that day. They showed me the importance of gratitude, especially for the really important things in life like health, sight and mental well-being. We all need to remember to give thanks on a daily basis for what we have instead of focusing on what we lack. For if we cannot learn to express basic gratitude for the blessings around us we will never know contentment or peace.

AFFIRMATION FOR THE DAY: My good fortune multiplies when I am grateful.

"Fool!" said my muse to me, "Look in thy heart, and write!"

—SIR PHILIP SIDNEY

Sometimes our minds are cruel to us. Faced with a problem or challenging situation, we can analyze it to death and lose sleep thinking about the what-ifs. When this happens we feel we're caught in an endless loop that leads nowhere, and we remain fixated on certain facts and conditions that don't add up to satisfying solutions.

When we are experiencing this type of anguish and confusion, putting pen to paper can be the solution. Research has shown that people who spend some time every day writing about their thoughts are more emotionally stable and less depressed than those who don't. From personal experience I know that answers to seemingly unsolvable problems can appear after a few minutes of writing, and that a pro and con list about a decision that needs to be made is easier analyzed when it is written down in black and white.

If you don't already have a journal, make it a point today to buy an inexpensive notebook and find a secure place to keep it. Don't worry about perfection; allow yourself to write whatever comes to mind, whether it is punctuated correctly or not. If you can get yourself into the habit of being honest and self-searching during your daily writing sessions, you'll find that your stress and confusion levels will decrease and that you'll have greater wisdom and clarity in your life.

AFFIRMATION FOR THE DAY: Writing is an important tool that can help me with my recovery.

Think in terms of poverty and you will live in poverty.
—NAPOLEON HILL

One day I was talking to a friend who was telling me about how visualization had helped her create many favorable conditions in her life. I agreed with her about its importance, but said that I was having trouble visualizing and manifesting something that was very important to me.

"Are you seeing this thing you want happening to you in the future?" she asked. "Of course!" I replied. "Well, that's your problem," she said. "If you see what you want happening in the future, it will always happen in the future; it will never happen to you now." Although I was skeptical, I started trying to visualize my dreams happening to me at that very moment. To my surprise, I did find that conditions improved when my focus changed.

Do you always see your dreams manifesting in the future, not now? Could you be blocking your happiness because you don't feel ready for it or you don't think you deserve it at this time? If so, remind yourself today that our Higher Power wants us to be happy right now and at every moment, and that we don't have to always wait a long time to experience joy and abundance.

AFFIRMATION FOR THE DAY: When I visualize my good fortune in the distance, it will forever remain out of my reach.

Almost all absurdity of conduct arises from the imitation of those whom we cannot resemble.
—Jean-Paul Sartre

When I was younger I watched a movie about the six wives of Henry VIII. One of his wives was a feisty, earthy woman whose sexual indiscretions earned her the guillotine. Somehow her character captured my youthful fancy and I went about mimicking her words, pretending I was a member of the British royalty. Soon my parents pointed out how annoying and ridiculous I was, and, embarrassed, I became plain old me again.

When we try to be someone we're not, we are guaranteed to look absurd. Although we may not realize it, others will spot our falseness a mile away and make fun of us. I saw this happen once in a company I worked at where many people tried to emulate the president's mannerisms, speech and clothing, thinking it would earn them valuable brownie points. Others, however, only saw them as indecisive brownnosers.

It's fine for us to have role models in recovery but when we lose our own special qualities in the process of adopting theirs, we run the risk of continuing the same deception we practiced during our years of compulsive eating. Don't try to be anyone but yourself today. If you can behave naturally and not assume anyone else's mannerisms, attitudes or appearance, you may be surprised to discover that when you are genuine and truly like yourself, others will accept and like you, too.

AFFIRMATION FOR THE DAY: Other people's shoes never fit me comfortably.

It would all be so beautiful if people were just kind . . . what is more wise than to be kind? And what is more kind than to understand?

—THOMAS TRYON

I once heard a sermon about the commandment "Thou shalt not kill." The pastor said that he had observed that there were many ways to kill someone without using a knife or gun, such as through thoughtless, uncaring behavior. His example was the many lonely elderly in nursing homes who don't want fancy gifts and cards, only a feeling that they still matter to their family and friends.

I, too, have felt the sting of another's thoughtlessness and have found that it causes the deadliest blows to self-esteem and happiness. My own painful experiences have made me more aware of the damage I can incur with a sharp word or by simply ignoring someone's opinion. Although I may not be physically harming them, I know that this type of behavior has the ability to kill another's spirit.

If we want to obey the commandment to "not kill," we can start by visiting someone who's lonely instead of just sending a card. We can also give people our full attention and not dismiss their opinions. Be careful today not to inflict the invisible pain of thoughtless behavior because although it may not produce physical scars, the wounds can be deeper and more hurtful than any others.

AFFIRMATION FOR THE DAY: When I am rude, condescending and angry, I destroy the happiness and self-confidence in others.

Don't hurry, don't worry. You're only here for a short visit. So be sure to stop and smell the flowers.
—WALTER C. HAGEN

Too often we're in a hurry. We want to hurry up and be totally recovered. Hurry up and get through the day so we can go to bed. Hurry up and get to the end of the year so we can go on vacation.

When we are constantly focusing on the future, wishing that the present were over, we are completely missing out on life. Before we know it we have aged, our children have grown up and good times have come and gone without us even enjoying them. One of the liabilities of living this way is that the events we so eagerly anticipate rarely live up to the advance billing in our heads, so we feel cheated, angry and unfulfilled much of the time.

We must remember that life is a journey, not a destination. The joy and fulfillment we experience don't come from reaching our goals, they come from working to achieve them. Try thinking about this well-worn phrase the next time you ache to speed life up: "Yesterday is a cancelled check, tomorrow is a promissory note, and today is cash, which I need to spend."

AFFIRMATION FOR THE DAY: When I am wishing tomorrow were here I'm throwing away the many gifts of today.

A little thing comforts us because a little thing upsets us.

—BLAISE PASCAL

As compulsive eaters we tend to be hypersensitive and quick to see offense where none is meant. Sometimes even a little thing—like a sharp word or a missed appointment—can send us into a tailspin which is capable of ruining our day or our abstinence.

If we are to recover from our eating disorder we have to learn to roll with the punches and not allow small, insignificant events to throw us off balance. Instead of being extremists who see our days as either all good or all bad, we have to remember that no one's life is perfect, and that a little rain falls on everyone at some point. Rather than plunging into anger and depression at the first sign of trouble, we need to put the situation into perspective and learn whatever we can from it.

We also should keep in mind that just as little things can upset us, so can little things restore our equilibrium. Indulge a simple pleasure today if you're feeling out of sorts. Take a hot bath, call a friend long-distance or go to a movie by yourself. If you start bestowing little kindnesses upon yourself, you'll find that the daily annoyances and slights we all experience lose their power to derail our serenity.

AFFIRMATION FOR THE DAY: Part of my recovery means learning to respond to the normal inconveniences of life appropriately.

He that lies with the dogs, riseth with fleas.
—GEORGE HERBERT

One of the best ways we have to ensure that our abstinence is rocky and our recovery is slow is to surround ourselves with negative people. These are the ones who will laugh at your efforts to improve yourself, encourage you to binge and fill your head with negative thoughts and attitudes.

Negativity is contagious and can erode your self-esteem. If the people around you tell you you'll never be thin, you'll never amount to much and that you're a failure, chances are you'll fulfill those expectations. Because I had such a dreary outlook on life prior to recovery, I surrounded myself with other pessimistic, self-defeating people who did nothing to help me. Now, through my own choice, I have different friends—people who are positive and uplifting, who encourage me, and who feel good about themselves.

Examine your own situation today. If you are surrounded by people who don't assist your recovery, it's up to you to spend your time more wisely. You have the power to choose your friends, your environment and the messages you hear, so make sure that the input you are receiving is loving and supportive of your goals.

AFFIRMATION FOR THE DAY: When I surround myself with optimistic, forward-thinking people, I become that way, too.

If someone accused you of recovering, would they have enough evidence to convict you?

—Anonymous

If we are really living in recovery we should be able to pinpoint daily changes in our behavior and see where we have made some progress. These don't have to be dramatic upheavals; they can be simple changes such as not feeling victimized, forgiving an old resentment, or sharing a difficult sentiment at a self-help meeting or with a good friend.

So often we can fall into a rut and stop doing the work necessary to recovery. We feel we've lost enough weight, made enough amends and helped enough people that we can rest on our laurels. For recovering alcoholics this is called being on a "dry drunk," where you can be sober yet not in recovery. This condition is usually a precursor to relapse.

Every once in a while, "convict" yourself of recovering. Think about the previous day and identify the signs that prove you are making progress. We must keep in mind that our recovery is not a static condition and that daily changes, however minor, are what keep us from falling into dry drunk ruts.

AFFIRMATION FOR THE DAY: My recovery needs to include noticeable emotional and spiritual improvements, not just physical ones.

It's not whether you get knocked down. It's whether you get up again.

—VINCE LOMBARDI

Life is full of hard knocks. Although we'd like to think that things will go our way if we do right by others, mind our own business and are honest, it just doesn't always happen like that.

I used to wonder why handicapped children were born to wonderful parents, why good people died when their lives were just starting to improve, and why unscrupulous men and women often received the best promotions at work. I have also been angry when I haven't binged but the rest of my life hasn't been so charmed.

In recent years I've seen that no matter who we are, we will all be knocked down hard at one time or another, regardless of whether we're "good" or not. Being abstinent will help us cope with our difficulties but that alone does not exempt us from problems. What is most important to our growth is how we choose to deal with our setbacks. Do we run away? Switch addictions? Lie to get out of an uncomfortable spot? Or try even harder to reach our goal?

If you've been knocked off your feet today and are contemplating giving up, don't. Get back up on your horse and start riding again. If you are persistent and committed to trying to make something happen despite setbacks, you will not only earn the respect of others, but more important you will gain self-respect.

AFFIRMATION FOR THE DAY: It is entirely my choice to give up or press on when I am discouraged.

I think the enemy is here before us . . . I think the
enemy is simple selfishness and compulsive greed.
—THOMAS WOLFE

I know a variety of people who are extremely
selfish, but who would be very surprised if they thought
others saw them that way. Their major problem is their
disregard for others' feelings and a general thoughtlessness in behavior. I'll give you a few examples.

One person I know never sends birthday cards or
thank-you notes because he doesn't mind not receiving
them himself. He thinks that if it doesn't bother him, it
shouldn't bother anyone else. Another person never
responds to any invitations she receives, be they birthdays, weddings or parties. Her excuse is that she gets a
"mental block" when she has to RSVP. Yet another
person won't return phone calls because she says that "if
they are really important," the person will call back
again.

What these three people fail to see is that what may
be unimportant to them is not always unimportant to
others. Today examine your assumptions about your
behavior. Is there a chance you have hurt someone's
feelings by not acknowledging their gift to you? Have
you disrupted a hostess's party by not responding to her
invitation? Remember today that selfish, greedy behavior may take forms we are oblivious to, and that healthy
recovery involves being aware and considerate of the
feelings of other people.

AFFIRMATION FOR THE DAY: When I am thoughtless I inflict pain on others.

You have no idea what a poor opinion I have of myself, and how little I deserve it.

—WILLIAM GILBERT

One morning I read a column in a newspaper by a woman who wanted to know why people routinely disparaged themselves. She noted that she had slaved over a recent article, yet when a reader had called to compliment her she had downplayed its excellence, protesting that "it really was nothing."

"Why do I do this?" she wondered. "It was an excellent column, yet I can't even bring myself to admit it!"

I still have to watch my own behavior in this area. One day I was talking to someone and saying that I had little to offer anyone in the way of friendship, I was a bad mother, and my wifely skills were substandard. The look on my friend's face went from disbelief to amusement, and finally she said in bafflement, "Where did you get these ideas? Do you beat yourself up like this all the time?" Upon reflection, I found that I did.

In recovery we have a choice. We can choose to send ourselves positive messages of love and worthiness, and to absorb nice comments from others, or we can amplify what we believe is negative about ourselves and play those tapes in our heads again and again. What is your opinion of yourself? Is it accurate? Do you give yourself credit for what you do well? Or are you stuck in a mind-set that devalues every aspect yourself? Know today what messages you are sending yourself, subtly and otherwise, and remember that until you can appreciate yourself, no one else will, either.

AFFIRMATION FOR THE DAY: I don't deserve to have a low opinion of myself.

Sin is a queer thing. It isn't the breaking of divine com-
mandments. It is the breaking of one's own integrity.
                                        —D. H. Lawrence

I know of a man who thinks of himself as a fine person. He is present at church every Sunday, he is a recovering alcoholic who counsels others like himself, and he is a devoted father to his three young children. He even has a Bible prominently displayed in his office.

His problem is his lack of integrity. He routinely pads his expense account, fudges on his taxes and sees a young lady from his office on the sly. His colleagues don't trust him, his wife is suspicious, and many of the men and women who see him at Alcoholics Anonymous meetings shake their heads whenever he talks about his wonderful life, amazed at his ability to live so dishonestly and deceptively.

When we profess to have a moral code yet repeatedly violate it, even in small ways, we lose the respect of others and, eventually, all self-respect, too. Be honest with yourself today about the way you conduct your life. Are you against adultery, theft, and deceptiveness yet make small allowances for yourself here and there? If so, remind yourself today that sinning doesn't just take the form of killing, grand larceny and treason. Sometimes the most unforgivable sin you can commit is the breaking of your own integrity.

AFFIRMATION FOR THE DAY: Today I will remember that if I don't have my integrity, I have nothing.

When you're at the bottom there's nowhere to go but up.
—ANONYMOUS

I received a call one afternoon from a woman in a hospital. Only twenty-four, she was on her eighth hospitalization for bulimia. The physical tortures she had brought upon herself were frightening—among them a torn esophagus, brain-wave abnormalities, irregular heartbeat, osteoporosis, pancreatitis and a permanent black eye. What made me saddest, however, was her plaintive question: "When do you finally hit bottom?"

I hit mine after seven years of lies, misery, self-deception and weight swings. The woman who called me had lost far more physically and emotionally than I ever had, but still wasn't in enough pain to want recovery. Her call was a powerful reminder to me that everyone has a different moment when they throw in the towel and scream "Enough!" and that some people need to lose more than others before they are willing to change.

When we can stop being stubborn and admit that we're licked, we'll feel a sense of peace. Whether the struggle is with food, a professional problem or another person, there is relief in knowing that we've gone as low as we're willing to go, and that there's nowhere to go but up. If there is something you are holding on to today that you think you can resolve by yourself, try to relax and let go of the problem. Ask your Higher Power for help and feel the tension leave your body. When you can permit yourself to look for solutions and support from a power outside yourself, you've already started the journey upwards.

AFFIRMATION FOR THE DAY: When I acknowledge I have hit bottom, there is nowhere to go but up.

Be faithful to that which exists nowhere but in yourself—and thus make yourself indispensable.
                                                   —ANDRÉ GIDE

Some of us participate in a perpetual Halloween party where we are always wearing costumes and masks, trying to be someone we're not. But the celebration never ends for us; uncertain of who we are, what we want out of life and where we are going, we are forever trying on new personalities and mannerisms, never really finding a comfortable persona.

When I was bulimic and especially unsure of myself, I was constantly trying to be someone I wasn't. This effort was always doomed to failure because the real me kept popping out. I was also never consistent in being any one way because my impulsiveness and chronic dissatisfaction led me to behave different ways with different people.

To recover we need to spend time in prayer and reflection discovering who we are and what we want to be. Allow yourself to follow your urges today and ignore any childhood messages you may have internalized that don't sound right to you any longer. Discovering yourself and learning what motivates you takes work, time and commitment, but when you can accept yourself with confidence, you'll be able to throw out all the masks you have hidden behind for so long.

AFFIRMATION FOR THE DAY: I like myself enough not to have to pretend I am someone else any longer.

You can't appreciate home till you've left it, money till it's spent, your wife till she's joined a woman's club, nor Old Glory till you see it hanging on a broomstick on the shanty of a consul in a foreign town.

—O. HENRY

In a well-known advice column I often see letters from people who write to say how much they regret never having told their parents, spouse or children how much they love them, and that now they have lost that opportunity because of an untimely death. "Don't put off till tomorrow what you could do today," counsel these saddened men and women, "because tomorrow might not come."

I, too, have found that I don't fully appreciate something until it's gone. I didn't appreciate the intellectual stimulation of college until I had graduated, I spent so much time complaining about nausea when I was pregnant that I didn't enjoy the miracle of having a child grow inside me, and it took a close friend moving to another state for me to realize how much I valued her companionship.

If you've never made a gratitude list before, make one today. List everything in your life that you are grateful for. Include friends, situations and whatever you like about yourself. Ask yourself if the people on your list know how much you care for them; if not, tell them today. Sometimes this exercise is all it takes to change your outlook from depression to optimism, and to galvanize you to realize how much you have to be thankful for.

AFFIRMATION FOR THE DAY: I will be grateful today for my many blessings because tomorrow they might be gone.

God changes not what is in a people, until they change what is in themselves.

—THE KORAN

Sometimes recovery seems like a slow-moving train and we cannot sense how far we have come nor how much we have changed. But it is impossible to be in a self-help group such as Overeaters Anonymous for any period of time without having at least some outward change occur such as weight loss, a more frequent smile or a new wardrobe.

But the most important changes—such as a shift in outlook on life, a willingness to extend ourselves for others and a moderate attitude toward food—can only come with long, patient work. These are also the changes that we have trouble seeing ourselves, and that others often need to point out to us.

Remember today that whatever the change is that you are seeking to make in your life, your Higher Power is always there to assist you and make your work easier. The footwork is ours to complete, however, and we'll discover that once we have done what's necessary to challenge past behaviors and assumptions, the strength and encouragement to crystallize our new attitudes will be available to us.

AFFIRMATION FOR THE DAY: Prayer and honest efforts to change myself will not be successful unless they are done together.

No one returns with goodwill to the place which has done him a mischief.

—PHAEDRUS

Many people think that a good way to test their abstinence is to deliberately put themselves in situations where they will be tempted. For some this may mean taking a job as a cook or waitress in a restaurant, and for others it might involve going out to eat with a friend who was once a "binge buddy."

I tested myself in early recovery by defiantly continuing to collect recipes for rich desserts and by volunteering to bake them for work-related parties. I told myself that I "should" be able to do these things because recovery meant being able to be like everyone else around food. Sometimes I was able to withstand tasting and bingeing while cooking and sometimes not. I finally decided that spending time in the kitchen just wasn't worth the risk any longer, and that I would choose to invest my free time in less dangerous pursuits.

One of the best pieces of advice I was ever given was "If you don't want to slip, stay out of slippery places." So if entertaining usually results in eating all the leftovers, give them to your guests as they leave or go to restaurants instead. If reading the "Food" section of the newspaper makes you think binge thoughts, don't read it. And if you have a friend who pushes you to eat, find new friends. In short, try not to return today to a place that has done you mischief, because you may never emerge in one piece again.

AFFIRMATION FOR THE DAY: Today I'll avoid slippery places.

The world breaks everyone and afterward many are strong at the broken places.

—ERNEST HEMINGWAY

I used to be very embarrassed about my past as a bulimic. I avoided talking about the subject and when pressed to do so, only did reluctantly. It took me a long time to recognize that I had no reason to be ashamed, and that the qualities I had developed as a result of surviving and getting into recovery would stand me in good stead in many other areas of my life.

When pain breaks us it's often difficult to imagine ever mending or feeling strong again. But we always heal and, whether we are aware of it or not, are stronger because of the experience. For example, one friend of mine was constantly nauseous during early pregnancy and worried that she'd never eat normally again. However, when she started to feel better, she discovered that the morning sickness had given her a new flexibility around food which ended up being a bonus to her long-term recovery from compulsive eating.

Instead of moaning about the "breaks" in your life today, try to adopt an attitude of gratitude for the strength that you will receive from them. Don't worry if you can't immediately see what the benefits will be because it's not your job to be omniscient. Just trust that you won't feel broken forever, put one foot in front of the other, and allow the healing to take place in its own time.

AFFIRMATION FOR THE DAY: The person who has never been broken is the person who doesn't know his own strength.

There is a natural body, and there is a spiritual body.
—I CORINTHIANS 15:44

We all have an animating force within that defines us as individuals and that separates us from one another. We are not just machines of flesh, sinew and blood; we have special inner qualities that we need to recognize and nourish daily as devotedly as we tend to our physical bodies.

If we are careful to eat the right things and exercise diligently, yet we don't take the time or energy to rejuvenate our spirits, our recovery will only be half-complete. The most attractive, well-muscled person can be the most unhappy and unfulfilled if there is no faith, love or kindness within. The ancient Greeks didn't say "Sound mind, sound body" for nothing.

If you build time into your day to shop for your special foods and usually spend a few minutes exercising, then you should allot at least as much time and energy to your spiritual needs. A day without prayer, meditation and relaxation is a recipe for confusion and imbalance, and if left unaddressed for too long, will surely throw our physical recovery offtrack.

AFFIRMATION FOR THE DAY: Today I will remember that my recovery is threefold: physical, emotional and spiritual.

Intimacy is spelled H-O-N-E-S-T-Y.

—Anonymous

Many compulsive eaters often find themselves in unrewarding relationships. We date, live with and even marry people we think we get along with and understand, but who are, in fact, highly inappropriate for us. Frequently our companions are also addicts—workaholics or alcoholics, for example—and the unspoken agreement is "You don't bother me about my addiction and I won't bother you about yours."

True intimacy can't really grow in these types of relationships because there is so little honesty. Neither side is sufficiently in touch with their feelings to know what they need, and even if they do know, frequently won't express themselves for fear of driving the partner away.

A good relationship is one where honesty prevails and where both sides can discuss their feelings, fears, dreams and needs without worrying that they'll be rejected, laughed at or ignored. Intimacy is also a relationship that feels good and right—not one that we tell ourselves we "should" enjoy because it looks correct from outside appearances.

Ask yourself today if you are in a healthy relationship. If you aren't, be honest about the limitations it is placing on your growth, and then make a commitment to find a partner who supports and understands you. Don't sell yourself short; despite any subconscious beliefs you might have to the contrary, you deserve happiness and the right to have your needs met.

AFFIRMATION FOR THE DAY: True intimacy comes when my heart does the talking, not my head.

Criticism comes easier than craftsmanship.

—ZEUXIS

It is easy to put down another person with just a few disparaging remarks. Many compulsive eaters have sharp tongues that we have honed to a fine degree this way because it enables us to avoid facing our own shortcomings while masking our inadequacies.

It took a painful personal situation for me to realize the destructiveness of gossip and to examine my own tendency to pass along rumors. I was once the victim of baseless gossip and speculation because of an innocent association with a group of men. When I was stunned to learn what was being said and insinuated about me, I withdrew into a shell of hurt and anger. It wasn't until I decided to use the experience as a learning tool for myself that the wounds healed. As a result I am much more careful about giving credence to innuendos and half-truths, particularly if I sense that jealousy is involved.

When we are speaking about others today, we must remember the importance of our words. Don't be known as someone who relentlessly puts others down and promotes yourself. There is always something positive you can say about someone else without being a false flatterer, so find it and say it. Your words will live on long after you do, so make sure they are ones that you want people to remember you by.

AFFIRMATION FOR THE DAY: When I put people down, I am broadcasting the fact that I feel envious and insecure.

One can acquire everything in solitude—except character.

—STENDHAL

One friend of mine is fond of telling me that every difficult experience I undergo is "character-building." No matter what the situation is or how upset I am, she never indulges me with pity and soft words. Her favorite saying is "Out of the hottest fires come the strongest metals."

Unfortunately, she's right. Our maturity, our personalities and our attitudes are only tested and formed when we are in the thick of life, being challenged and pushed to the limits by others. Setbacks and sadnesses are what give us the opportunity to develop wisdom, tolerance and maturity, as well as to see what we need to work on. The person who has never fought for what she believes in, or taken a stand on a difficult issue, is someone who has not developed her character.

Solitude is important to our recovery because it is a renewing, healing time. But we must be careful not to take too much of it because it is only in the rough-and-tumble of life that we will acquire our passion and uniqueness. Make sure that today is balanced with appropriate amounts of reflection and action, and remember that too little or too much of either one can only leave us unbalanced, unhappy and unfulfilled.

AFFIRMATION FOR THE DAY: When I am spending too much time alone, I am missing out on life.

Happiness is beneficial for the body but it is grief that develops the powers of the mind.

—MARCEL PROUST

At one point in my life I was under tremendous pressure on a number of fronts, and I found myself unable to talk with friends for long stretches of time because I was so unhappy and preoccupied. I also didn't want anyone's opinions on what I was going through; I felt strongly that it was important for me to be introspective during this period.

Not long after I emerged from my hard time, I received a call from a friend who wanted to discuss some problems she was having. When she asked me for input, I was quite surprised to hear myself being reasonable, evenhanded and empathetic instead of judgmental and extreme, which had always been my tendency before. I suddenly realized that my long period of difficulty had molded and changed my outlook tremendously, and that I had benefited from my grief in ways I hadn't expected.

Remember today that happiness and pleasant conditions are important in the enjoyment of life but that it is grief and pain that will give you wisdom and character. Although it's never easy to appreciate the hard times we all encounter, try to recognize today the benefits your difficulties have brought you and give thanks accordingly.

AFFIRMATION FOR THE DAY: Hard times always bring unexpected rewards.

Love your neighbor, yet pull not down your hedge.
                                            —GEORGE HERBERT

I have learned a quick way to make enemies—don't put up a fence around your house. At one time I had two exuberant puppies at a farm in the country who delighted in bringing home other people's knick-knacks, garbage and food. Our neighbors, justifiably, became angrier and angrier, until finally we moved to a house with good fences where they couldn't escape and torment others.

Respecting people's boundaries, however, takes more forms than just a fence. For example, a friend of mine called one day to lament that a houseguest had extended her visit by weeks and was taking over the refrigerator, phone, car and every other facet of her life without asking for permission. Although my friend genuinely liked her houseguest, the violation of personal boundaries caused a rift in their relationship that has yet to be mended.

As needy compulsive eaters, we must fight our tendency to swallow up others in our efforts to feel appreciated and less lonely. Remember today that there are many healthy ways to develop closeness, intimacy and good friends, but that invading others' lives, privacy and boundaries in the process is a good way to make enemies.

AFFIRMATION FOR THE DAY: Today I will respect my own and others' boundaries.

Happy is he who bears a god within, and who obeys it.
The ideals of art, of science, are lighted by reflection
from the infinite.

—LOUIS PASTEUR

Some people think that having a "god within" means channeling the wisdom of extraterrestrial beings, or of two-thousand-year-old warriors who claim to be able to predict the fate of the world. They ignore the majesty of their own spirits, preferring to pay others to tell them how to live, what to do and where to put their energies.

Interestingly enough, "god within" is the ancient Greek definition of "enthusiasm." When I consider this, it makes sense that I feel closest to my Higher Power when I am filled with joy and a sense of purpose, because that is when I am most enthusiastic. Countless artists and other creative people have expressed the same sentiment; they say they feel transported into a spiritual realm when they are doing what they love. Their work, they say, is their gift to God.

Do you think that you have no sense of your own inner god? What about your bursts of joy or creativity? Aren't you ever enthusiastic about anything? Consider today the possibility that your god within is expressed in ways that you may never have thought about. Have the confidence to obey the spirit that brings you spontaneity and joy, and remember that the only prerequisite for hearing this "god" is having the willingness to listen.

AFFIRMATION FOR THE DAY: When I obey my god within, I can do no wrong.

True learning never restricts a search for truth wherever truth may be found, and true religion never closes the doors of truth's discoveries no matter where they lead.

—MARCUS BACH

As compulsive eaters we often run the risk of being rigid in our thinking and stubborn about new ways of doing things. Although our actions and behaviors may not make us happy, they are at least comfortable and predictable so we hesitate to change.

But to recover and grow, we must be open-minded and teachable. If we tell ourselves that certain people are just "wrong," or that a certain kind of religion or thinking is "wrong," we slam the door on potentially valuable learning experiences. We also set up an "us" versus "them" mentality that keeps us separated from others.

True learning comes in odd places. When I am least expecting to be taught something, I overhear a conversation or glance at an article that alters my perceptions. Children can also be excellent teachers because they are so guileless and untouched by the world that they will ask questions that startle us into a new awareness. Today remember to remain flexible and open-minded to the sources of your learning, for by so doing you will not only acquire much wisdom, but solutions to problems will frequently appear without an extended search.

AFFIRMATION FOR THE DAY: When I think that only certain people or situations can teach me something, I limit the dimensions of my education.

Don't go to the hardware store for milk.

—ANONYMOUS

One day a friend of mine called with a revelation. She said she had been depressed the previous week about various aspects of her personal and professional life and that she had called her mother for advice. Her mother, with whom she had had a difficult relationship for many years, had responded unsympathetically, leaving my friend angrier and more despairing than she had been before.

"The crazy thing is that I knew she would be that way before I even picked up the phone to call," my friend said, "but I called anyway.

She went on to say that at a support group meeting where she had relayed her frustrations, a woman had told her to "stop going to the hardware store for milk," meaning to stop trying to get something from someone who would never be able to give it.

As recovering compulsive eaters we need to make decisions about where we are going to get our greatest love and support. If our families are dysfunctional, we need to relinquish the idea of getting it from them, as much as we would like to. It's up to us to create a circle of honest and loving friends who will give us the feedback we need to continue growing, and that will enable us to stop looking to get our needs met in impossible places.

AFFIRMATION FOR THE DAY: When I continue to seek love where I've never gotten it before, I set myself up for disappointment.

Gratitude is not only the greatest of all virtues, it is the parent of all the others.

—CICERO

Right around this time of year Americans celebrate Thanksgiving, which we as compulsive eaters can use as an opportunity to be grateful for the multiple blessings in our lives instead of as a day to lose control at the dinner table.

When I was bulimic, Thanksgiving was an awful holiday because of my obsession with food. Gratitude and giving thanks were the farthest thing from my mind; I focused only on cooking, eating and compulsively exercising before and after the big meal in a frantic attempt to limit the caloric damage. I also usually found a way to ensure that I was the dishwasher, too, because then I could look helpful and kind while secretly eating everything left on the plates and in the pans.

This year remind yourself that Thanksgiving is not just a gustatory celebration; it is a time to be grateful and to share with others less fortunate than yourself. If you are in recovery, be grateful that Thanksgiving and the big meals don't have to mean bingeing and guilt anymore. If you have a number of material blessings in your life, share your good fortune with others through gifts of food, money or time. Remember, also, as you survey groaning tables of food on these sorts of holidays, that as mouth watering as everything looks, nothing tastes as good as abstinence.

AFFIRMATION FOR THE DAY: Holidays are an opportunity to experience gratitude, love and sharing, not just food.

We are worthwhile simply because we are, irrespective of any work we may produce.

—MARGARET R. STORTZ

I have a good friend who was once cross-addicted to work and to food. When she wasn't living and breathing her job, she was eating, and vice versa. Her self-esteem totally depended on her work output, how many new computer programs she mastered and how many new clients she could amass.

The extent of my friend's workaholism didn't become apparent to her until the company ran into difficult times and she had little to do. Although she invented work at first, she soon ran out of tasks and her self-esteem dropped because she wasn't getting any positive strokes. Soon, to fill the gap left by her job, she began to binge and her weight climbed dramatically.

It took this episode for my friend to see how much self-worth she derived from her work and how dangerously cross-addicted she was. The pain also forced her to evaluate where she received her self-worth from and what food really meant to her.

The lesson of this woman's experience is valuable for all of us: Do you feel worthwhile because of where you work, what your salary is or who you know? If so, remember that external validation—particularly from our jobs—never lasts forever, and that if self-worth comes from everything except your inner essence, there will always be a huge hole inside that you'll be tempted to stuff with food.

AFFIRMATION FOR THE DAY: When I believe that what I do is more important than who I am, my focus is still on my external appearance as opposed to my internal values.

*Children awaken your own sense of self when you see
them hurting, struggling, testing; when you watch their
eyes and listen to their hearts. Children are gifts, if we
accept them.*

—Kathleen Tierney Grilly

When I had my first child I found myself experiencing the most intense emotions of love, protective-
ness and wonder I had ever felt. As I watched him start
to grow and examine the world around him I felt a
longing to protect him from any pain, sorrow or disillusionment he might encounter. I even started to worry
about the inevitable separations that would come later
in his life, such as dating, college and marriage.

As protective as I felt, I knew that I had to learn to
let go if he was to become a happy, well-adjusted
person. Shielding him from pain or fighting his battles
for him would be a great disservice to him because those
would be the experiences that would shape his character and teach him his greatest lessons. I reminded
myself again and again that being a mother didn't mean
being a "smother."

I have to remember not to be too protective of my
own emotions as well. Whenever I feel myself running
from conflict and pain, I have to force myself to go back
and face it. My heart may pound, my breath may get
short and I might feel frightened, but—as with growing
children—it is only by facing our fears and testing our
limits that we gain confidence and maturity.

AFFIRMATION FOR THE DAY: When I try to shield
myself or anyone else from painful learning experiences,
growth can't occur.

Turn your typhoons into tailwinds.

—Norman Vincent Peale

I once read about a woman who wanted to start her own fudge-making company. She kept encountering a problem, though; her fudge always turned out soft and totally unsuitable for packaging. One day, surveying yet another pan of oozing chocolate, she hit upon the idea of selling it as sauce. Today her company has annual revenues of several million dollars and is renowned the world over as one of the best in the industry.

The moral of this story is that even typhoons can be turned into tailwinds if we are creative and resourceful. History is filled with stories of inventors who were trying to make one thing but stumbled on another, better, product in the process. For example, Charles Goodyear had no intention of creating rubber, and thereby becoming a millionaire, when he accidentally flung a handful of chemicals on a furnace and found that it became soft, resilient and very useful in a number of ways.

When I decided to stop treating my years of bulimia as a liability, I was able to redirect my personal energies to assist others. Today identify a typhoon in your life and make a decision to turn it into a tailwind. As soon as you can see silver linings where you may have only seen dark clouds before, you'll discover opportunities and good fortune in even the bleakest situations in your life.

AFFIRMATION FOR THE DAY: Making a silk purse from a sow's ear is a learned and valuable skill.

Peace is when time doesn't matter when it passes by.
—MARIA SCHELL

I once had an acquaintance who seemed incapable of experiencing any inner peace. In his early twenties he had decided to be a millionaire by the time he was thirty; if he didn't succeed, he thought, he'd be a failure. So as his thirtieth year approached, with no sign of the millions, his behavior became erratic. He dropped old friends, broke his engagement and started to have mood swings.

The passage of time for this man was like a loaded gun pointed at his head. Instead of just enjoying each passing year and doing the best he could in his work, he had set arbitrary and material goals that revolved around his age. Needless to say, he had no peace then and still doesn't today.

When you are jumpy and irritable and feel time isn't passing quickly enough to suit you, then you can't know the peace of having your days unfold naturally and without pressure. Remind yourself today that any goals you set for yourself need to mesh with your Higher Power's timing, and that if we just point ourselves in the right direction and turn the reins over to Him, everything will happen when it should.

AFFIRMATION FOR THE DAY: When I am serene and peaceful, time is my friend.

You should pray for a sound mind in a sound body.
—JUVENAL

Carl Jung once wrote to Bill Wilson, the co-founder of Alcoholics Anonymous, that he felt alcoholism was a quest for wholeness. His theory was that addicts were in a continual search to feel full, and that alcohol or any other substance that was abused was a poor substitute for the wholeness that spirituality could supply.

Many compulsive eaters in the early stages of recovery feel empty and don't know what to substitute for food. They turn to substances and behaviors that are just as addictive, such as shopping, exercising, sex, prescription and recreational drugs, and alcohol, thinking that as long as they aren't eating, they're okay. Before they know it, however, they have created a new compulsion that could be just as destructive as their food addiction, and that can tear down the foundations of recovery.

Studies have shown that recovering addicts who turn to a Higher Power and try to improve their lives remain abstinent longer than those who don't. Have you replaced food with an emphasis on spiritual growth, or has the hole been filled with a new compulsive behavior? If so, honestly address this problem today. Whether your new addiction is to gum, coffee, aerobics or shopping, if it is left unaddressed you may find yourself in greater denial and pain—not to mention relapse—than you were before.

AFFIRMATION FOR THE DAY: The most satisfying fullness comes from a sense that I am doing what my Higher Power wants me to do.

Don't let your heart depend on things
That ornament life in a fleeting way!
He who possesses, let him learn to lose,
He who is fortunate, let him learn pain.
—JOHANN CHRISTOPH FRIEDRICH VON SCHILLER

I have often heard the phrase "God giveth and He taketh away." This happens to everyone at one time or another; we celebrate a wondrous occurrence one day and mourn a death or loss the next. It's easy to be gracious, kind and generous during the times when we are given things. How we cope with our pain, however, is what ultimately defines our character.

In the past when we were hit with setbacks we turned to food, self-pity, isolating behavior and a lot of finger-pointing. In recovery we can't do that because our growth depends on not running from our pain. We also have a golden opportunity to learn from our losses what is truly important to us. Survivors of natural disasters, for example, usually don't worry about lost valuables if they have escaped alive.

Ask yourself today if you depend more on "ornaments" than on lasting treasures such as education, family harmony and inner peace to bring you happiness. Don't wait until items of true value are stripped from you to appreciate their worth, but, by the same token, learn and mature from your losses.

AFFIRMATION FOR THE DAY: Today I will value what is of lasting importance.

A turtle does the work of God slowly—but to get anywhere he must stick his neck out.

—ANONYMOUS

Everyone knows the story of the race between the turtle and the hare. Although the hare started out fast and was ahead most of the way, he eventually tired and lost the contest to the plodding, methodical turtle. The moral of the story is clearly that winners are frequently the less flashy, more meticulous people, but we should also take note of the fact that winners are also the ones who stick their necks out and take risks.

We compulsive eaters abhor sticking our necks out. We'd rather be safe than sorry. But it is to the risk-takers that the rewards come. As frightening as it is, we must risk rejection by being open and vulnerable if we are to gain lasting, loving friends. We also have to risk behaving and eating differently if we are to undo many of the destructive patterns we have fostered and hidden behind during years of compulsive eating.

There is a state lottery whose slogan is "You gotta play to win!" Remember today that to win the game of life and recovery, you've got to get out there and play. Make a promise to yourself to take a risk and do something you've been longing to do, but have been afraid to try. Like the turtle who sticks out his neck, emerge from your protective shell today and become one of the brave ones who wins races.

AFFIRMATION FOR THE DAY: When I conquer my fear of doing something new, I move ahead.

The worst deluded is the self-deluded.
—CHRISTIAN N. BOVEE

I know someone who amazes me and everyone else she knows with her capacity for self-delusion. If a man talks to her she is convinced that he is in love with her. If she gains weight she loudly insists that someone shrank her clothes. And even when she has setbacks that she should learn from, she convinces herself that she was right all along and that the outcome was a mistake.

Such self-deluded people live in a fantasy world. They reject helpful advice because they think they know everything, and they lie to themselves because the truth is so painful. These are the men and women who hop from job to job, too; at the first whiff of a problem they find an excuse to move on to another position, and even another state, because that's easier for them than staying put and working through the difficulties.

Is there something you are deluding yourself about? Are you telling yourself a certain story, but feel uneasy about it because deep down you know that the truth is different? Remember today that lasting recovery is built on a foundation of honest self-acceptance, and that the sooner you see yourself as you really are, the easier it will be to take whatever steps are necessary to ensure happiness.

AFFIRMATION FOR THE DAY: Today I won't kid myself.

Look to your health; and if you have it, praise God, and value it next to a good conscience; for health is the second blessing that we mortals are capable of; a blessing that money cannot buy.

—IZAAK WALTON

A friend of my parents' has always appeared to have the world by the tail. He was born into a wealthy family, was a handsome Olympic-caliber athlete in his prime, and everything he has touched in the business world has turned to gold. The international society columns usually pair him with gorgeous women and even his pursuit of hobbies has brought him acclaim.

Despite these surface trappings and wealth, though, this man cries himself to sleep every night. His only son is dying of an incurable disease and he now spends his days bathing his son, attending to his needs and comforting him. This man has learned after years of fame and affluence, he says, that money doesn't buy happiness, and that the only thing he wants now is to have his son's health restored.

As a result of hearing about this person's predicament, I now make a more conscious effort to remind myself that although I may not have everything I want, I do have my health back. While some of the side effects of seven years of bulimia are irreversible, a great number of them have improved because of my steady recovery and emphasis on living in a healthier way. Remind yourself today that recovery doesn't have to cost us anything but that when it restores our health to us, we've been given have a precious gift that money can't buy.

AFFIRMATION FOR THE DAY: Today I will give thanks for my health.

I have learned silence from the talkative, toleration from the intolerant, and kindness from the unkind.
—KAHLIL GIBRAN

My greatest lessons in the value of kindness, gentleness and love have been the result of having those same qualities withheld from me when I needed them most. Unfortunately it is this type of painful experience that often makes the biggest impression on us and is the greatest catalyst for changing our own behavior.

There was a time when I was totally dependent on others for help in untangling a sticky business situation. Although some people were supportive, others drew their feelings of superiority from treating me like a beggar and not even extending common courtesies like returning phone calls or being polite. A friend who commiserated with me wasn't surprised; he reminded me that many people won't visit sick friends in hospitals for fear of contracting the same illness, and that injured sports players who have to sit on the bench during the game are often shunned by their healthier teammates.

Do we turn on our friends when they need us the most? Are we only there in the good times because the bad times sap our energy and require effort on our part? Don't wait until you are the victim of others' cruelty before you learn to be a friend to someone in need. Extend yourself today to someone who needs support and love, and remember to do unto others at all times as you would have them do unto you.

AFFIRMATION FOR THE DAY: When kindness is withheld from me, instead of being hurt I can learn how important it is to extend it to others.

Experience is not what happens to a man. It is what a man does with what happens to him.

—ALDOUS HUXLEY

One day I was talking with a friend of mine whose life had been a series of tragedies and bad luck for over two years. She had somehow endured her husband leaving her, her children running away, being fired from her job and having both her parents die suddenly. Despite these problems she hadn't lost her dignity or her good humor.

I asked my friend how she had managed to retain her unshakable faith in God during this period. "I finally realized that there was a lesson to be learned from all of the turmoil," she replied. "Before any of this happened I was not a very compassionate person. As a result of what I've gone through, though, I've developed an enormous amount of empathy for other people who are having difficulties in their lives. I used to think they had brought their troubles on themselves, but now I see how that's not necessarily true."

Unfortunately, it sometimes takes a series of devastating events to get our attention and force us to notice some of our attitudes that need changing. Resolve to see your troubles today as opportunities to change, expand and improve yourself in some way. If you can allow yourself to develop experience as opposed to just having experiences, you'll be able to turn everything that happens to you to good advantage.

AFFIRMATION FOR THE DAY: How I respond to events in my life is more important than the events themselves.

*How many cares one loses when one decides not to be
something but to be someone.*

—Coco Chanel

We all know someone who is rarely the same
person twice because she is a slave to fashion trends.
If short hair is "in" she lops hers off. If pantsuits are
the rage, she covers herself up, even though pants
don't flatter her. And her makeup is an ever-changing
hue of iridescents, pale pinks and shocking reds. She
seems to always be searching for herself, but never
quite finding it.

Although I'm not obsessed with being cutting-
edge, I still have an annoying tendency to focus on
externals when there's something that needs attention
within. I call this my "fat and ugly" state of mind
because I'll suddenly become obsessed with having
the "perfect" haircut, the "right" makeup and the
"correct" clothes—even if they all seemed fine the
previous week! But I've gone through this cycle
enough times to know that fiddling with extraneous
superficial details won't help until I do "an inside job."

If your "fat and uglies" hit today, stop yourself
and ask what's really going on. Are you frightened of
something? Ashamed of your past? Feeling insecure
in a relationship? Once you know what you're really
trying to fix by changing your appearance, you can
stop trying to become something and instead be
someone.

AFFIRMATION FOR THE DAY: When I feel good
about my life, I feel good about myself.

Hate the sin and love the sinner.

—Mahatma Gandhi

As compulsive eaters most of us entered recovery with a long list of resentments. We had carried around grudges against others—for real or imagined slights—for so many years that we had forgotten what it felt like not to be angry. No one was exempt from our fury; friends, family members and co-workers had all offended us at one time or another and we had refused to forgive them.

These resentments were once good excuses to binge. When we didn't get invited to a certain party, we attacked the leftovers in the refrigerator. When our sister made a snide comment, we used it as an excuse to bake a cake and then eat the entire thing. And when we overheard a co-worker gossiping about us, we stopped at a convenience store on the way home to buy a dozen candy bars.

What we learn in recovery is that resentment, and certainly bingeing in frustration, only hurts us. We can detest something that happens to us without transferring that same hatred onto the person who may have unknowingly participated in our hurt. None of us are without sin, and all of us have needed forgiveness and love for something we've done and regretted in the past. Why not free another from the bondage of your resentment today while liberating yourself in the process?

AFFIRMATION FOR THE DAY: Today I'll let a bygone be gone.

Men must be decided on what they will not do, and then they are able to act with vigor in what they ought to do.

—MENCIUS

All of us have days when we wake up, the sky is gray and life looks bleak. We have trouble coming up with good reasons why we should eat sensibly, exercise and take care of ourselves. A self-pitying part of us wants to be coddled and attended to.

We have a choice to make when we feel depressed and negative. We can give in to our feelings or we can fight them. If we decide to wallow in self-pity there's a good chance we'll wind up bingeing, which will deepen our sense of failure and worthlessness. Or we can take the more difficult step of cutting off the negative thoughts, diverting ourselves with another activity and surrounding ourselves with people who can help us return to a better frame of mind.

Research shows that just the mere act of smiling releases "feel good" chemicals into our bodies. We don't even have to genuinely be happy to experience this phenomenon! So if you're down and discouraged today, fake a grin and see what happens. You might be surprised by how quickly this simple act can turn around your day.

AFFIRMATION FOR THE DAY: There's always something positive I can think about.

A wrathful man stirreth up strife: but he that is slow to anger appeaseth strife.

—PROVERBS 15:18

One of the maxims I heard repeatedly when I began to recover from my eating disorder was that anger—even if it was justifiable—was better left to people who could handle it more wisely than I. Addicts such as myself, I was told, were not adept at righting wrongs and tended to do more damage than good when attempting to settle the score.

Initially I ignored this advice. There were all kinds of situations I thought I had every right to be upset about, and I didn't like the idea that I should sit idly by. My motto was always "Don't get mad, get even."

It wasn't long before I saw the folly of my ways and understood the wisdom of this advice. I found that my fleeting moments of triumphant vindication were always followed by hours and days of guilt, uneasiness and depression. As much as I longed to take back my vengeful words and actions, they were like spilled milk that couldn't be scooped back into the carton.

Today I try to be a peacemaker, not the hellion I once was. Although there are still times when I simmer and long to vent my feelings, I find that the less I focus on getting even and the more I try to understand if my anger has different roots, the sooner the situation is resolved to everyone's satisfaction without me doing more harm to myself or anyone else.

AFFIRMATION FOR THE DAY: When I express my anger inappropriately I create more strife than I started with.

One's own self is well hidden from one's own self; of all mines of treasure, one's own is the last to be dug up.
—FRIEDRICH WILHELM NIETZSCHE

Many addiction treatment centers employ a therapeutic technique that patients find painful, yet helpful. It is the "oral autobiography" which involves sharing the story of your life and your addiction with your peers. During this process many find that their pasts are not as shameful as they thought, and that others with the same wounds can assist greatly in recovery.

I once thought that the things I had said and done during my bulimic years were so dreadful that if anyone knew about them I would be a social outcast for life. All that changed the night I shared the story of my life with my support group. As I voiced the darker secrets of my life, I felt such unconditional love and acceptance that my feelings of shame and unworthiness dissolved.

We must remember that we're only as sick as our secrets. Instead of fearing rejection, take a risk today and reveal a dark part of yourself to someone you trust. If you're honest, you'll find painful wounds being healed.

AFFIRMATION FOR THE DAY: When I really know and accept myself, I have mined the greatest of treasures.

*I am not afraid of tomorrow, for I have seen yesterday
and I love today.*

—WILLIAM ALLEN WHITE

Soon the end-of-the-year parties will be starting
and you are probably beginning to get nervous. Most of
the food and drink that will be served is liable to be
heavy, rich and not normally a part of your meal plan.
Even though these gatherings may not be today or
tomorrow, you are becoming preoccupied with thoughts
of potential binges. You may worry that you aren't yet
good at saying "No, thank you" and walking away from
temptation.

Early in my recovery I went to a wake and found
that the host was insistent about everyone sampling his
wife's famous chocolate cake. Although I refused repeatedly, he finally forced a piece into my hands and
commented that I needed "fattening up." I responded
by discreetly flushing the cake down the toilet and
leaving, satisfied that I had preserved my abstinence.

We probably won't be faced with hosts like these at
all the parties we attend, but be prepared for them just
in case. Don't show up ravenous and make sure you
enlist support from others if needed. Remind yourself
that you want to feel good about yourself when you go
home at the end of the night, even if everyone else
seems to be eating and drinking to excess. Remember,
too, that as tempted as you may be, nothing tastes as
good as abstinence.

AFFIRMATION FOR THE DAY: If I can always
remember how good it feels to take care of myself,
temptation won't derail my recovery.

The deeper a path is etched, the more it is used. . . .
The more it's used, the deeper it is etched.
                                                —ANONYMOUS

There are a lot of things we are told we must do to achieve strong recovery. We know we should be moderate, honest, courteous, generous and humble, among other things. But the sad truth is that years of compulsive eating probably haven't forged these qualities. In fact, doing something as simple as telling the truth after being dishonest for so long feels as awkward as learning to ride a bicycle for the first time.

The nice thing about learning new behaviors, though, is that they become familiar habits if we practice them long enough. For example, I used to eat everything put in front of me, regardless of my hunger, until I started to deliberately leave part of my food uneaten. Although it initially felt like cutting off my right arm to walk away from good food, it has now become second nature to stop when I'm full.

The same is true of other habits we need to learn. The more honest you become, the more automatic it will seem. The more moderate your actions, the less excessive you will eventually be. Just remember as you try new behaviors today that although they may feel strange at first, the more you walk that path, the deeper it will be etched for you.

AFFIRMATION FOR THE DAY: If I do anything long enough and diligently enough, it will become an ingrained part of my behavior.

*Time cools, time clarifies; no mood can be maintained
quite unaltered through the course of hours.*
—Thomas Mann

We've probably all seen people on television discussing painful subjects such as the untimely death of a
child, the kidnapping of a family member or the end of
a marriage. Sometimes when I hear them describing
what has happened to them I'll think to myself, "Why
aren't they screaming and crying? How can they discuss
this subject so rationally?"

The answer, of course, is that time is the greatest of
all healers. No matter what happens to us and however
devastated we feel at the time, it is impossible to remain
weepy or angry forever. As hours, weeks and years pass,
our hurts *do* heal and we are able to look back with
understanding at what has befallen us. I know that
personally I have had times when I never thought I
would feel joy or anticipation again, only to discover that
sometimes all it takes is a day to regain my perspective
on life and feel harmony once more.

If you are feeling enraged or particularly saddened
today, remember that you aren't always going to feel this
way. Try also not to take any actions in this frame of
mind that might cause you more pain. If you can divert
yourself with a walk, a peaceful drive or an enjoyable
hobby, you will generally find that your emotions
dissipate, an upsetting situation is soon seen in a
different light, and you gain maturity that will stand you
in good stead the next time you feel overwhelmed.

AFFIRMATION FOR THE DAY: Bad moods and
anger never last forever.

I have a dream.

—Martin Luther King

Some of us never take the time to imagine what kind of life we'd like to lead. We plod along from day to day, never lifting our eyes from our immediate concerns. We assume that life just happens in a preset plan, so we never pause to pray, to dream or to take an active part in creating a dynamic future.

When we begin to recover from our compulsive eating we become aware of a lot of choices we have that we may not have noticed before. For example, we may have previously assumed that our present career was the one we were destined to have for the rest of our lives, or that the person we were dating was the person we had to marry. Now, happily, we feel freer to question our beliefs and to go after what we think will bring us the most enjoyment.

We were all born with the power of imagination for a reason. I have often heard it said that whatever we have the power to conceive, we have the power to achieve. Today work with your Higher Power to design your future visually, and remember to be bold as you fashion your dreams. Above all, keep in mind that unless you have a plan for yourself, you are destined to always follow someone else's path.

AFFIRMATION FOR THE DAY: When I take time to visualize my future, I take responsibility for myself.

When in doubt tell the truth.

—MARK TWAIN

When I was eating compulsively and purging, I told a lot of lies. The lies were to cover for missing food, missing money and blunders on my part. My distortions of reality extended outside my eating, too; I was unable to live honestly in any area of my life because I didn't know what the truth was any longer.

Although I had thought that my white lies weren't noticed, I found when I started to recover that there weren't a lot of people left who trusted me. They had heard my wild stories and excuses for so long that people had gradually stopped believing me.

When we recover we have to learn to tell the truth, especially about the little things. Because if we continue to do things like make illegal turns and exaggerate the truth, then we don't yet have the mind-set that will allow us to eat honestly, make amends and acknowledge our own character defects.

Make an effort to be completely honest in every situation today. It may surprise you how often you shade the truth when you aren't even thinking about it. Let yourself say "I don't know" occasionally and fight the urge to make reality more exciting than it is. Remember, too, that no matter what you might say or do to the contrary, the truth always comes out eventually.

AFFIRMATION FOR THE DAY: Honesty is always the best policy.

*Only the brave know how to forgive. . . . A coward
never forgave; it is not in his nature.*
                                    —LAURENCE STERNE

Many compulsive eaters come from dysfunctional
families where their parents were unable to validate
them, treat them as worthwhile individuals or provide
them the unconditional love every child needs to develop self-esteem. These types of parents have been
called "toxic parents" by some therapists.

People from such families sometimes find that
"forgiving and forgetting" what made them unhappy as
children is all they need to do to feel better about
themselves and their parents. Often, however, the
wounds are so deep that a face-to-face dialogue with the
parent is called for. This can empower the wounded
child to feel mature, responsible and able to finally live
in a healthy way. It also shatters the secrecy and denial
so common to dysfunctional homes.

One well-known self-help authority believes that
recovery from any self-destructive behavior cannot occur until a person totally forgives his or her parents.
Examine your attitude toward your parents today. Are
you truly at peace with them? Or is there something you
are not saying to them for fear of rocking the boat? If
they have passed on, can you share your repressed
anger with a trusted friend or counselor?

If these questions strike a chord in you, don't run
from the uncomfortable feelings you're sure to experience. Confront your buried emotions honestly and
you'll remove one of the biggest obstacles to lasting
recovery.

AFFIRMATION FOR THE DAY: Today I forgive
others as well as myself.

Order and simplification are the first steps toward the mastery of a subject.

—THOMAS MANN

Compulsive eaters can complicate almost anything. Even simple, straightforward tasks run the risk of turning into major productions because of our tendency to exaggerate and inflate everything around us. We love to take uncluttered meal plans and change the food around because simplicity doesn't appeal to us. In fact, we thrive on chaos.

To recover we need to eliminate the unnecessary food, people and possessions from our lives. Don't overload "To Do" lists with trivial tasks that don't really need to be done immediately or we're liable to polish doorknobs and clean windows when deadlines for important projects loom.

One way therapists help people simplify their lives is to have them imagine that they've been given six months to live. They then ask their patients what they'd do, who they'd choose to be with and what emotions they'd want to feel. Most people respond by saying that they'd love and forgive those around them, take good care of themselves and spend time doing what they love most. Most are surprised to realize how much energy they are currently wasting on unsatisfying tasks, emotions and people and they resolve to try to behave differently in the future.

Eliminate the extraneous today and give yourself an imaginary six months to do what matters most to you. The more you can simplify, the more mastery you'll feel over your life.

AFFIRMATION FOR THE DAY: My life is organized and prioritized today.

Evil deeds do not prosper; the slow man catches up with the swift.

—HOMER

There are times when it is tempting to take shortcuts in life or in recovery because we see someone else doing it and they appear to be prospering and living the good life. As we look at our own plodding pace and slow progress, we may be drawn to flashier ways of making money, looking attractive and behaving because there is a quick payoff.

One lesson I've learned again and again in recovery is that shortcuts, particularly ones that harm us or someone else, are never worth the immediate gains. For example, starvation diets that lead to rapid weight loss almost always result in a return to the original weight, with a few pounds added on. I've also seen people be dishonest in business dealings to earn money quickly, only to be found out later and lose their job, savings and self-respect.

Remind yourself today that if something sounds too good to be true, it probably is. Lasting, positive change always results from slow, painstaking effort. Make an effort to give up your desire for immediate gratification and you'll find that the things that take the most time to achieve always bring the greatest benefits and lasting satisfaction.

AFFIRMATION FOR THE DAY: Whatever I gain quickly is liable to disappear quickly.

He steers—we provide the locomotion.

—ANONYMOUS

I once heard about a man who lost a fortune in the commodities markets. He and his wife had just finished building their retirement home and were looking forward to enjoying their remaining years in comfort and relaxation. Once all their money was lost, however, the couple was forced to sell their new house and go back to work. "I thought God was going to take care of me," the man disconsolately told friends.

Well, yes and no. We are all taken care of by our Higher Power but we're expected to do the footwork for ourselves, too. For example, this couple had left all of their investment decisions up to their broker and hadn't overseen his work. They had simply been careless, naïve, and overly trusting that the broker would always be skillful in his trades.

What about our recovery from compulsive eating? Are we putting out a minimum of effort, thinking that our Higher Power is going to deliver us from trouble and give us unbroken abstinence? It just isn't that easy. As much support as we receive, we are still required to make the right decisions about food, work to eliminate our character defects and invest a great deal of energy into creating a new life for ourselves.

Keep in mind today that recovery is like a two-seat bicycle. If you can sit in the back and pedal diligently, you'll never have to worry about where your Higher Power takes you.

AFFIRMATION FOR THE DAY: Today I'll remember that recovery is a partnership.

If we try too hard to force others to live in our world, because we think it is the real world, we are doomed to disappointment.

—WILLIAM GLASSER, M.D.

As compulsive eaters we are often obsessed with taking control of other people's lives and telling them what we think they should do. This tendency is usually magnified by the fact that we frequently find ourselves in relationships with alcoholics and other addictive people who appear to need guidance, which we happily supply in the form of anger, manipulation and tears. Our efforts to change them usually fail, however, which leaves us with two choices: letting go with love or staying miserable, controlling and obsessed.

When we cannot allow someone to live their own life we harm them as well as ourselves. Although our concern may be well-founded, the toll our criticism and pushing takes is heavy: The addict rarely responds positively to our efforts, and we feel frustrated and misunderstood. Our nagging also prevents the person from taking responsibility for his or her behavior.

When we learn to just let go of other people and situations that we cannot control, we feel a sense of peace and freedom that we may never have experienced before. But it's not something we should do once; we need to practice relinquishing control every day over whatever so obsesses us. Today give yourself and others the gift of letting go. When you can eliminate the illusion that your world is the only one that is acceptable, you won't have to feel disappointed any longer.

AFFIRMATION FOR THE DAY: I will remember that what works in my life does not necessarily work for anyone else.

All things are to be examined and called into question.
—EDITH HAMILTON

When we accept things at face value we are doing ourselves a great disservice. We were all born with the ability to think, question and reason for ourselves, and to abdicate that responsibility can place us in great peril.

I have learned this lesson the hard way. A number of times I have taken someone's promise as a sure guarantee that something will happen, only to be bitterly disappointed later. Had I taken the time to investigate the person's previous dealings or character, I might have avoided anguish and heartache. Now I know that doing my homework before agreeing to something is not a sign that I don't trust someone, it simply indicates that I care enough about myself to be thorough.

Would you buy a home without inspecting it or trust your child with a baby-sitter you didn't have excellent references for? If not, remember that the little things, not just the big things, all need to be carefully evaluated before you accept them into your life or consciousness. Whether it is someone's advice on meal planning or a friend's comment on your appearance, remember to use your God-given powers of evaluation and discernment before you make their opinion your reality.

AFFIRMATION FOR THE DAY: Today I will not accept anything at face value.

When a person is concerned only with giving, there is no anxiety.

—GERALD G. JAMPOLSKY, M.D.

As compulsive eaters we have been chronic "takers." We took food, money and other material things with rarely a thought of compensation. When we could not get what we needed for our food fix, some of us resorted to shoplifting so that we could have the laxatives, syrup of ipecac, diuretics and binge foods that would satisfy the raging monster within.

In recovery we learn that giving, not taking, is what will restore much-needed balance to all areas of our lives. It often amazes us that the best prescription for our blues and anxieties is to forget about our concerns and just focus on giving smiles, love and friendship to others who need it. Almost as a side effect we find that our binge cravings are less intense or they disappear altogether.

One of the phrases I have often heard is "You can't keep what you don't give away." I take this to mean that if I want to stay in recovery I must continue to share my joy in abstinence from compulsive eating with others. Some wealthy people have even said that the more money they give away, the more they seem to make!

Be a giver today, particularly of the qualities you most value in yourself or that you would like to feel more deeply. As you find yourself being less of a taker, you'll discover that you are always blessed with what you need and that your capacity to give freely is multiplied.

AFFIRMATION FOR THE DAY: I benefit most when I am generous.

No one can build his security upon the nobleness of another person.

—WILLA CATHER

Guidance in negotiating the tricky curves of life and abstinence can come from several different sources. For some it takes the form of having a sponsor in a self-help group, for some it is a therapist, for some it is a religious leader and for some it is a trusted friend.

There are limits to the guidance we can receive from anyone, however. What is true for one person may not work for another, and the greatest mistake we can make is to let another person dictate how we should live. Equally dangerous is to place someone we admire on a pedestal because sooner or later they will topple, and if we haven't learned to make decisions for ourselves, this event will devastate our equilibrium and hurt our recovery.

I have discovered that there are many people from whom I can draw strength and wisdom as I recover. But I need to continually remind myself to shore up my own self-esteem so that I don't create gurus or idols who will inevitably let me down in one way or another. Try to remember today that building your joy and security on a friend, spouse or lover is like building on quicksand, and that it is only when your own inner foundations are solid that you can construct a stable home for yourself.

AFFIRMATION FOR THE DAY: Today I will remember the limitations of those whom I admire.

Giving is the same as receiving.
                              —GERALD G. JAMPOLSKY, M.D.

I used to look forward to Christmas for one reason only—because of all the gifts I would receive. The time I spent thinking about what I would give others and then shopping for them was minimal because I was too wrapped up in my own desires and anticipation to consider anyone else's needs.

With recovery has come a new appreciation for giving. I have found that genuine pleasure doesn't come from accumulating possessions, many of which I don't need anyway; it comes from making a concerted effort to think about someone else's happiness and then doing something to help bring it about. Although I once never would have believed that the act of giving could bring me so much joy, when I am thoughtful and my gifts have no strings attached, I receive more pleasure from the exchange than the person who receives the gift.

During the holiday season this year make sure your emphasis is not on giving hints about what you want; focus instead on finding out what you can give to others. Make your gifts personal and don't err in thinking that more expensive means better. You'll find that when you can give graciously and without any thought of recompense, you'll receive the most enjoyment of all.

AFFIRMATION FOR THE DAY: When my giving is from the heart, I am enriched.

The only deadly sin I know is cynicism.
—HENRY LEWIS STIMSON

Compulsive eaters tend to be people who see the glass as half-empty rather than half-full. We tend to be great cynics who assume that all politicians are crooks, all big businesses are greedy and everyone is out to get us somehow. We also are prone to point out the problems and pitfalls of any solution we're offered because we don't necessarily want to be happy.

Research shows that this type of negativity can be hazardous to your health, not just to your mental well-being. Investigators report that coronary heart disease is often connected to the emotions and behavior that accompany cynicism. For example, professionals who score high on scales of negativity, hostility, anger and aggressive behavior die much earlier than positive people who see life more beneficially.

If you find yourself being cynical and pessimistic today, try telling yourself that not everyone wants to hurt you. Make an effort to see other people differently and give them the benefit of the doubt. Try to understand why you feel compelled to be so defensive and angry, and then allow yourself to be more vulnerable and trusting, even if for just an hour. As you start to change the way you see the world you may be surprised to find that not only will your optimism blossom, but your physical health will improve as well.

AFFIRMATION FOR THE DAY: Today I will assume the best, not the worst.

The most elusive knowledge is self-knowledge.
—MIRRA KOMAROVSKY

I have a friend who has a few years of recovery from compulsive eating and codependency under her belt, but she acts as if she has twenty or more. She is fond of giving other people articles or books that she thinks will help them with their recovery, but she resists any similar assistance for herself.

At one point several people became concerned about her. She was obviously gaining weight and had returned to an emotionally abusive relationship. Gently these men and women confronted my friend, asking her if she needed help and whether she was aware of the dishonesty she was practicing. My friend became angry and defiant, citing the number of books she had read and workshops she had attended as proof that she was in recovery.

This situation pointed out to me quite eloquently the dangers of ignoring our own recovery in favor of that of others. When we start being more concerned about how our friends are doing than how we're doing, we run the risk of relapsing without even being aware of it. Remember today that self-knowledge is a precious commodity we need for recovery, and that although books, meetings and workshops can point us in the right direction, they aren't a guarantee that we have attained it.

AFFIRMATION FOR THE DAY: Understanding myself is one of the hardest, yet most important, goals of recovery.

One self-approving hour whole years outweighs.
—ALEXANDER POPE

There is a respected healer who believes that all addictions and self-destructive behaviors stem from a basic lack of love for oneself. In her work she has observed that when people truly love themselves and don't want to be unhappy, they cease doing whatever it is that is making them so miserable. She believes that when we are in total harmony, our lives are peaceful because of the way in which we choose to accept conditions and react to difficulties.

Some people argue that this is a simplistic attitude. But I have found in my own journey of recovery that whenever I can honestly accept a personal flaw and love myself in spite of it, another roadblock to my happiness has been removed. I am also vigilant about the chatter that periodically starts in my head that tells me I'm not good enough, pretty enough or smart enough, and I try to cut it off immediately.

Every morning when you wake up, make it a habit to look yourself squarely in the eye in the mirror and say, "I love you. What can I do to make you happy today?" If you can enlist your own support first thing each day, you won't need to look to others to feel good about yourself any longer.

AFFIRMATION FOR THE DAY: Today I will approve of myself, flaws and all.

God always pairs off like with like.

—Homer

When we were eating compulsively, purging and abusing our bodies in the pursuit of eternal slenderness, there's a good chance that we surrounded ourselves with people of the same mentality. The men and women we sought out for companionship were often just like ourselves, and it's unlikely that these friendships brought us much warmth or happiness.

When I first started to recover, someone warned me that I would feel like I was in the midst of a funeral. "You will find yourself outgrowing old relationships and attracting a different kind of person," she said. "It's okay to mourn the death of the old you, but remember to celebrate the birth of your new personality and new friends, too."

This was sage advice. As I steadily recovered my binge buddies disappeared. Although some were surprised and hurt by the changes in me, I knew that my recovery depended on surrounding myself with people who saw life differently, and who were kinder and more insightful than my former friends. The transition was difficult, but necessary.

Remember today that life is short and that the people we spend our precious time with are mirrors of us and our values. Given this premise, ask yourself if your circle of friends is compatible with the goals and values you have established for yourself.

AFFIRMATION FOR THE DAY: When I am thoughtful, joyous and spiritual, my friends are, too.

Throughout history, the most common, most debilitating human ailment has been cold feet.
—Reader's Digest

Do you know people who have big dreams about how they want their lives to be, yet are incapable of even taking the first step toward actualizing those dreams out of fear that they won't be successful?

I do. You often find these people in unsatisfying jobs, complaining bitterly to anyone who will listen that they hate what they do. However, they won't explore alternative jobs or career fields because they're afraid to act. These same sorts of people have a million excuses why they can't stop eating compulsively, go to self-help meetings or eat abstinently. If there isn't a guaranteed result to their actions they don't even want to try.

What are your dreams? Learning a new skill? Asking someone you admire on a date? Speaking up to ask for a raise? If fear and cold feet are holding you back then you are shortchanging yourself. Not taking action to begin reaching your goals means you're liable to spend the rest of your life wondering what would have happened if you had had the courage of your convictions.

AFFIRMATION FOR THE DAY: Today I will take a step toward realizing something I want.

It is idle to play the lyre for an ass.

—St. Jerome

Many compulsive eaters come from dysfunctional homes where loyalty to undeserving people is prized and where keeping the family secrets from outsiders is of paramount importance. Consequently, as adults we continue these patterns by spending time on people who don't care about us, defending their motives, and making excuses for their thoughtless behavior. Often we are the last ones to realize that they are disloyal to us and that our friendship has been abused or taken for granted.

I have a friend who considers another young lady her best friend despite having endured various indignities at her hands. My friend has been criticized in front of others, had her weight openly disparaged and even been blatantly lied to. When asked why she maintains the friendship she makes excuses for the other woman and says, "She doesn't mean any harm—that's just the way she is."

As part of our ongoing recovery we need to wake up and smell the coffee about friends and acquaintances who fit this description. To reclaim self-respect we have to stop playing the lyre for people who don't appreciate it and concentrate instead on those who can return our loyalty and affection, and support us in our healthy, recovering lives.

AFFIRMATION FOR THE DAY: Today I will not nurture friendships that are one-sided.

Reaction isn't action—that is, it isn't truly creative.
—ELIZABETH JANEWAY

As compulsive eaters many of us tend to be reactors to life instead of initiators of it. We wait for others to make the first move in anything before we decide to go along. We need our husbands' approval before speaking, our parents' approval before changing anything about ourselves and our friends' approval before we try something new.

I once saw a poster that summarizes this attitude. It showed a pack of lemmings scurrying toward a cliff and following the leader off the side. There was no initiative displayed; every one of the animals was simply reacting to what the one directly in front of it was doing. The thought that danger might be ahead obviously wasn't a factor.

Are you a lemming? Do you do whatever someone else does and rarely act independently? Do you seek approval for something prior to doing it, and then only act if others seem to think it's a good idea? If this describes your behavior, work today to separate yourself from the pack. Ask yourself what you would do in certain situations if you weren't reacting to another person or event. Being assertive and taking the risk of being a leader, not a follower, probably doesn't come easily to most of us but until you learn true independence you'll always be at the mercy of other people and situations outside yourself.

AFFIRMATION FOR THE DAY: To act, not react, I need to know who I am and where I hope to go.

Hatred is the coward's revenge for being intimidated.
—GEORGE BERNARD SHAW

One day a friend called to discuss some problems she was having with relationships, work and her self-esteem. As she talked, she used the word "hate" over and over. There were few people or things she didn't have active resentments against, and it was easy to see how paralyzed she had become with this negative emotion.

I asked her to tell me why she hated everything and everyone. As she detailed the situations that had upset her, it was easy to see that a number of people had intimidated her and consequently led her to feel dumb, worthless and humiliated. But instead of acknowledging that she needed to work on her own self-confidence, she projected her insecurities as hatred onto others which prevented her from taking the necessary steps to ensure different future outcomes.

Remember today that when you feel anger toward another person it's often because they have touched a place in you that needs to be examined. Hatred, in particular, often hides feelings of inferiority, worthlessness and victimization. Channel your energy today toward understanding yourself better instead of attacking back. Ask yourself if there's any truth to someone's criticism and if you can improve yourself in some way as a result. When you can work through a crippling emotion like hatred and turn it into self-awareness and change, you won't have to cower in anyone's shadow again.

AFFIRMATION FOR THE DAY: When I am angry, I am usually less furious than I am intimidated, envious and ashamed.

Wisdom is not bought.

—AFRICAN PROVERB

Compulsive eaters tend to be very intuitive and sensitive people. In fact, I've often heard it said that people with addictions are highly spiritual men and women who experience normal emotions so vividly and painfully, that they need to lose themselves in an addiction to a substance like food or alcohol so that they can periodically escape from the intensity of life.

Many compulsive eaters in early recovery feel a sudden connection with a Higher Power and begin to explore the netherworld of psychics, trance channelers, tarot card readers and astrologers to understand their growing intuition. Throwing all caution to the wind, they spend hundreds—even thousands—of dollars to find out if their auras are muddy, if their present situation is due to past life karma and what the future holds.

Some people in the psychic field have true gifts that defy easy explanation; others are charlatans who just want your money. In either case, the worst thing a vulnerable recovering person can do is turn over all judgment and power to someone else. If you begin to make major life decisions based on a psychic's advice, then you have forfeited your own powers of discernment and can only wind up disillusioned. Remember today not to be blinded by the light shone by others. If we stoke our own internal light, we'll always discover that our best guidance costs nothing and lies within.

AFFIRMATION FOR THE DAY: I will not turn my power over to anyone else today.

An investment in knowledge always pays the best interest.

—BENJAMIN FRANKLIN

Several years ago I attended a big conference where many leaders in the addictions field were speaking. Because of the rapid advances in this area it was important to hear the latest research and I particularly looked forward to listening to what a well-known authority had to say about a topic of interest to me.

Unfortunately the anticipated presentation was a disaster. Within fifteen minutes people were walking out of the seminar or shifting restlessly in their seats. The problem was simple: The man had arrogantly assumed he didn't need to prepare for his talk, and thus had ignored all of the newest discoveries and theories about the subject. His speech was a dull repetition of every other speech he had given during the last five years, and his lack of curiosity and scholarship showed.

Are we guilty of this same behavior? Do we fancy ourselves so smart that we don't stay current on various topics, and do we believe that others can't teach us anything? If so, take pains today to learn something new. Really focus on acquiring a piece of knowledge that requires concentration and effort. Not only will this investment of time and energy pay good interest, but it will keep us humble, vibrant and interesting.

AFFIRMATION FOR THE DAY: Today I will learn something new.

The only way to make a man trustworthy is to trust him; and the surest way to make him untrustworthy is to distrust him and show your distrust.
—HENRY LEWIS STIMSON

When I first told my husband I was bulimic he took it upon himself to be my policeman. Rather than allowing me to monitor my own behavior, he started to check the amounts of food in our house and to follow me around after meals to ensure that I didn't try to purge. Like a caged animal I started to look for escapes, and because he obviously didn't trust me, I found myself unable to trust myself either. Fortunately, we were both eventually able to change.

Many compulsive eaters tell similar stories of how they carried out their binges. One young woman told me that her parents were so keen on having her lose weight that they measured the length of butter sticks and never let her clean up after meals for fear that she'd eat while doing the dishes. Her response was to binge whenever they weren't around to get back at them.

Are we guilty of this same behavior? Do we stifle our children by keeping them on a tight leash for fear that they'll do something "bad"? At work are we incapable of delegating because we don't think anyone else can help us with our responsibilities? Do we join restrictive diet clubs because we don't trust ourselves to eat moderately without having to pay lots of money?

Try today to trust yourself and others. If you can take this risky step and leave the results up to your Higher Power, you'll discover a sense of freedom you may never have felt before.

AFFIRMATION FOR THE DAY: Recovery means learning to have faith in myself and others.

I have learned that success is to be measured not so much by the position that one has reached in life as by the obstacles which he has overcome while trying to succeed.

—BOOKER T. WASHINGTON

I once read about a poor family that had accomplished a remarkable feat: All eight children had graduated from college with honors. The parents had worked their fingers to the bone for years, moonlighting at odd jobs to scrape together tuition, and had raised their children with so much love and discipline that drugs and other problems had never entered the picture.

In the same newspaper I also read about a birthday party that a woman had thrown for her husband that was the epitome of excess and garish taste. The affair had cost at least one million dollars, and the money that paid for it came from the man's company, which essentially merged compatible organizations together and usually put thousands of men and women out of work in the process.

Who would you most like to emulate in these stories, and who do you think best defines success? Is it more successful to have enormous amounts of money, or to have priorities that include education, family togetherness and hard work? Remind yourself today that real success doesn't always come quickly and in ostentatious packages; it is more often achieved slowly and deliberately by some of the quietest, most self-effacing people we know.

AFFIRMATION FOR THE DAY: How far I've come is not as important as what I've done to get here.

I yam what I yam, and that's all I yam.

—POPEYE

As compulsive eaters we are often frightened to display our true personalities and opinions. Many of us harbor a fear that when other people find out what we're "really like" they'll want to have nothing to do with us. Consequently we're always apologizing for ourselves and trying to disguise our real thoughts and emotions.

When we live this way long enough we probably aren't certain what we stand for, either. During the years when my bulimia was most active I tried to stay on the sidelines of debates about all kinds of things. I had no opinions on politics, world events, local controversies and other hot topics. If I did manage to express myself and earn another person's disagreement, my tendency was to immediately backpedal and waffle on my position, trying to be accommodating.

When we are constantly engaged in people-pleasing behavior we aren't going to have any self-respect. We need to remember that everyone is unique and is entitled to different views, and that when we try to deny our thoughts and feelings so as not to differ with others, we run the risk of never knowing who we are or what's important to us.

Examine your people-pleasing tendencies today. If you are prone to apologize for your thoughts and hide them, make an effort not to. When we can learn to take responsibility for ourselves and not be ashamed or embarrassed, we'll be proud to say "I yam what I yam."

AFFIRMATION FOR THE DAY: My self-esteem increases when I am not afraid to express myself.

Compassion is the chief law of human existence.
                    —FËDOR MIKHAILOVITCH DOSTOEVSKI

One day I was talking to a man who had been through numerous valleys of depression and loss in his life. He had watched most of his family and relatives die in World War II, he had endured tremendous prejudice and discrimination because of his religion, and he had struggled mightily in his adopted country to become a successful businessman against many odds.

Normally I would have expected someone with this kind of life to be hardened, cynical and dour. This man, however, was one of the most compassionate and exuberant people I had ever encountered. When I asked him about his relentless good humor, he replied that his experiences had taught him to feel empathy for others and to enjoy the little pleasures in life—like being able to wake up every morning as a free man, not as a fugitive from repressive governments. He knew that he had had the choice to develop two entirely different personas based on his life, and had deliberately decided to focus on the positive rather than the negative.

Today look at the valleys in your own life and ask yourself what you've become as a result. If you've learned bitterness and cynicism, remind yourself that this is a choice you've made, not one that was forced upon you. If, however, you have chosen to become more compassionate and thankful for the good you have, then you have displayed the wisdom of maturity which will be of great assistance in your recovery.

AFFIRMATION FOR THE DAY: Today I will use my times of darkness as opportunities to develop compassion, strength and gratitude.

I know more about God than I can understand or say.
—ADA HARRIS

Early in my recovery I struggled to understand the notion of needing a Higher Power to aid me in my journey. Years of schooling had left me with an intellectual outlook that required everything to be quantified, proven and explained before I could accept it. For this reason, praying to an unseen force and believing it would take care of me was very challenging. But when a friend finally said to me in exasperation that it was arrogant to have to know and understand everything for it to exist, something clicked in my head, and faith and prayer became easier for me.

Are you fighting the concept of a Higher Power because it isn't concrete enough for you? Are you unable to trust your instincts because you can't rationally explain or control them? If so, loosen up today and try to follow your heart. Allow yourself to make decisions that "feel" right but that you can't necessarily support with facts. As you learn to turn inward for your truth you'll feel the guidance of your Higher Power growing, and with it will come feelings of self-assuredness and serenity.

AFFIRMATION FOR THE DAY: Many of the things that enrich my growth cannot be put into words or understood by others.

Without risk, you don't experience life.
—FREDERIQUE VAN DER WAL

One day a friend of mine called to say that she was about to make a radical change in her life. Over the protests and skepticism of family and friends, she had decided to leave her stable, well-paying job to join the Peace Corps in Africa for two years. She had always longed to do some form of public service work but had ignored her feelings and done precisely what her parents had wanted her to do all her life. Now, she said, it was time to honor her own urges and to take a risk.

My friend is just one of several people I know who defied convention to explore their inner urges and were positively transformed in the process. Since she returned from Africa she has changed dramatically and now does pro bono legal work for those less fortunate than herself. My friend is happy, fulfilled and constantly stimulated by her work, and is only sorry that she waited so long to follow her inner promptings.

Remember today that life is short and that to fully experience its richness and excitement we have to occasionally take risks. When was the last time you took a risk and did something that didn't meet with universal approval? Is there an urge you are stifling because it wouldn't fit your image? Give yourself permission to do the unexpected today and allow yourself to enjoy the uncertainty and anticipation that change brings. As you continue to take the risks that are necessary to your growth, you'll discover how rewarding and multifaceted your life can be.

AFFIRMATION FOR THE DAY: When I take a risk I always learn something valuable.

Thoughts are forces . . . they have form, quality, substance and power.

—RALPH WALDO TRINE

Shortly after I moved to a new area, I set out to find an airport I had never visited before. Armed with vague instructions, I started to drive but soon found myself lost. I had no confidence in my instincts so I followed the drivers who seemed to know where they were headed, hoping they were going to the airport, too. My strategy backfired, I wound up in a strange town, and I missed my plane.

I learned a good lesson from my experience. By mindlessly following the other cars, I had done what I sometimes do when I lack inner direction and self-confidence. If we don't know what we want or where we're going, we're always going to be following other people and ending up where we don't want to be, missing our calling in the process. Without a map of where we want to go, we have no choice but to get lost.

Remember today that your mind and your thoughts are two of your greatest assets in recovery. If you are able to visualize your dreams clearly, and also see what the route there looks like, you're not likely to get lost. Make sure you know where you're going today and follow the map with confidence and enthusiasm, even if you don't see anyone else on the road with you.

AFFIRMATION FOR THE DAY: When I follow my own sense of direction, not others', I will arrive at the right destination.

Author's Note

If you would like to correspond with Caroline Adams Miller, obtain more information about eating disorders and where to get help, or subscribe to The Foundation for Education about Eating Disorders (F.E.E.D.) bimonthly newsletter, *VITALITY!*, please write to:

Caroline Adams Miller
c/o Bantam Books
666 Fifth Avenue
New York, New York 10103

About the Author

A magna cum laude graduate of Harvard, CAROLINE ADAMS MILLER is the founder and president of the Foundation for Education about Eating Disorders and has worked to create residential eating disorder treatment centers for those suffering from eating disorders. She is the author of *My Name Is Caroline* and is a contributor to *The Eating Disorders Anthology* to be published in 1991. She is married and has a son.